Hugh Mortimer Cecil

Pseudo-Philosophy at the End of the Nineteenth Century

I. An Irrationalist Trio: Kidd - Drummond - Balfour

Hugh Mortimer Cecil

Pseudo-Philosophy at the End of the Nineteenth Century
I. An Irrationalist Trio: Kidd - Drummond - Balfour

ISBN/EAN: 9783337076269

Printed in Europe, USA, Canada, Australia, Japan

Cover: Foto ©ninafisch / pixelio.de

More available books at **www.hansebooks.com**

PSEUDO-PHILOSOPHY

AT

THE END OF THE NINETEENTH CENTURY

BY

HUGH MORTIMER CECIL

I.

AN IRRATIONALIST TRIO

KIDD—DRUMMOND—BALFOUR

LONDON
THE UNIVERSITY PRESS, LIMITED
16 JOHN STREET, BEDFORD ROW, W.C.
1897

TO THE

MEMORY OF CHARLES DARWIN.

PREFACE.

THE old conflict between religion and science has persisted down to our own time, but under a somewhat altered aspect. Neither then nor now have the combatants met on terms near enough equality to make the contest altogether a fair one. In the past, the Church, if not strong in brain, was at least powerful in arm; and if it could not convince the heretic it could at all events silence him. Then religion fought downwards upon science from the higher ground of the hillside. In our own day, thanks to the principle of compensation in the universe, the positions of the combatants have been reversed; and I am free to admit that the advantage of science is now as unfair as was the advantage of theology in the past. It is all the more unfair in that it is an advantage that science is hardly likely ever to lose again or theology ever likely again to win. There is bound to be an end, some time or other, to the dominion of brute force; and even the charming paradox of this brute force being exercised by a religion of love—by *the* religion of love, perhaps I ought to say—cannot hope to be permanently successful in retaining the world for the inquisitor and the hangman. These things have had their day, and are never likely to return. But the advantage of science is an intellectual one ; and in the long run, if barbarism and the grace of God do not overtake a nation, that course will be adopted, both in matters of opinion and in matters of practical life, that is most consonant with reason. Hence in a society in which the lower and more animal forms of strife are sinking gradually into more and more discredit, the victory tends to rest with the party of superior logic. And herein, I say, science has an unfair advantage over theology. For theology can apparently never hope to find herself again in the position of fighting from the top of the hill ; so long as men are rational, and so long as bishops confine their energies to garden parties and do not go forth with the men of war, so long will theology have to keep at the disheartening task of attacking a fortress that is quite impregnable. Hence a candid friend is prompted to ask the attacking party why the vain assault should still be kept up. The men in the citadel are in a position to dictate their own terms ; and these terms are nothing more than the modest request that the theologians will be but rational in fact as well as in appearance. Evidently, however, this is too much to ask ; and the theological party would rather make itself ridiculous in the eyes of the civilised world by its attacks on science, than take the best that science has to give it, and be grateful. If it will not be content to do this, then theology should leave the hill of reason in possession of the enemy, and settle down comfortably and bovinely on the fat plains of sentiment below. Here is pasture enough and to spare for them ; and the brains that are unfit for the conclusions of Darwin and Spencer may feed on the religious novel of Mrs. Humphry Ward, the geology of Sir J. W. Dawson, the apologetics of Mr. Gladstone, and the biographies of Jesus that are said to be in preparation by Mr. Hall Caine, Mr. Ian Maclaren, and Mr. Crockett,—three gentlemen whose capacity for sentimental fiction is the best guarantee of their fitness for such a task. Yet I fear that this cordial and disinterested recommendation to sanity of conduct will not be accepted by the party of theology. They will continue to attempt to fight Science with her own weapons, and they will continue to fail disastrously. The object of the present volume is to show how three of the modern champions of theology have fared in their attempts to capture the scientific fortress by the use of pseudo-scientific methods.

H. M. C.

January, 1897.

is an intellectual one; and in the long run, if barbarism and the grace of God do not overtake a nation, that course will be adopted, both in matters of opinion and in matters of practical life, that is most consonant with reason. Hence in a society in which the lower and more animal forms of strife are sinking gradually into more and more discredit, the victory tends to rest with the party of superior logic. And herein, I say, science has an unfair advantage over theology. For theology can apparently never hope to find herself again in the position of fighting from the top of the hill; so long as men are rational, and so long as bishops confine their energies to garden parties and do not go forth with the men of war, so long will theology have to keep at the disheartening task of attacking a fortress that is quite impregnable. Hence a candid friend is prompted to ask the attacking party why the vain assault should still be kept up. The men in the citadel are in a position to dictate their own terms; and these terms are nothing more than the modest request that the theologians will be but rational in fact as well as in appearance. Evidently, however, this is too much to ask; and the theological party would rather make itself ridiculous in the eyes of the civilised world by its attacks on science, than take the best that science has to give it, and be grateful. If it will not be content to do this, then theology should leave the hill of reason in possession of the enemy, and settle down comfortably and bovinely on the fat plains of sentiment below. Here is pasture enough and to spare for them; and the brains that are unfit for the conclusions of Darwin and Spencer may feed on the religious novel of Mrs. Humphry Ward, the geology of Sir J. W. Dawson, the apologetics of Mr. Gladstone, and the biographies of Jesus that are said to be in preparation by Mr. Hall Caine, Mr. Ian Maclaren, and Mr. Crockett,—three gentlemen whose capacity for sentimental fiction is the best guarantee of their fitness for such a task. Yet I fear that this cordial and disinterested recommendation to sanity of conduct will not be accepted by the party of theology. They will continue to attempt to fight Science with her own weapons, and they will continue to fail disastrously. The object of the present volume is to show how three of the modern champions of theology have fared in their attempts to capture the scientific fortress by the use of pseudo-scientific methods.

H. M. C.

January, 1897.

CONTENTS.

INTRODUCTION.

Object of the present volume—The significance of such works as Mr. Kidd's *Social Evolution*, Mr. Drummond's *Ascent of Man*, and Mr. Balfour's *Foundations of Belief*—Necessity for combating their errors—Nothing essentially new in these three works—Change of front of the theological party—The three modern irrationalists merely repeat, in another form, some of the oldest theological arguments—Religious apologetics almost inevitably driven into irrationalism—Mr. Kidd's thesis an old one—Illustrations from Ambrose, Savonarola, Pascal, Kant, Kaftan, Newman, and Luther.   .   *Page* 1

MR. KIDD'S *SOCIAL EVOLUTION*.

CHAPTER I.

Light thrown on Mr. Kidd's mind by his unconscious betrayals—Most of his fallacies of a purely verbal kind—His sense of his own importance and originality—The argument of the first portion of his book—Science and religion—Importance of religion in the social evolution—The conditions of human progress—Selection and rejection—No diminution of the rivalry of life in civilised societies—Man's reason antagonistic to the conditions of progress—Man's reason, as inimical to progress, held in by irrational religion—Religion secures the maintenance of the conditions of progress—Religion provides a super-rational sanction for socially-preservative action in the individual—The character of a civilisation depends upon the ethical system on which it is founded.   .   .   .   .   *Page* 15

CHAPTER II.

Mr. Kidd's intellectual type defined by his juvenile blunders—"Aggressive unbelief"—Mr. Kidd and Mr. Bradlaugh—Mr. Kidd's own book aggressive in the most pronounced degree—His misconception of the historical relations of science and religion—Scepticism as "significant" a phenomenon as religious belief—His error in supposing religious beliefs to be independent of reason—Man "*in conflict with his own reason*"—Ideas and feelings—Comte and Spencer—Mr. Kidd's psychological ignorance—His errors of phrasing and of psychology. -   .   .   .   .   .   .   *Page* 30

CHAPTER III.

Progress as the result of over-population—Mr. Kidd's argument as to the desirability of progress merely a *circulus in probando*—"Progress" cannot philosophically be defined as equivalent to "improvement"—Organism and environment—Mr. Kidd's self-contradictions and inconsistencies.
Page 39

CHAPTER IV.

"No rational sanction for the conditions of progress"—Man's individual interests subordinated by evolution to the social interests of the race—Mr. Kidd's teleology—His error in conceiving natural selection as a "force" antagonistic to man—His self-contradiction—Reason not a "force" antagonistic to natural selection, but merely one of the forces with which natural selection has to do—Mr. Kidd's misconception of evolution—The individual and the social organism—His own book a demonstration of the fatuity of his arguments. . . . . *Page* 44

CHAPTER V.

Religion as the irrational force which maintains progress—Man's "profound social instinct"—Absurdity of Mr. Kidd's thesis—More self-contradictions—His errors of the most primitive kind—Examination of his thesis as to the "ultra-rational sanctions" of religion—His verbal confusions—His own book once more a refutation of the principles he is enforcing—His spurious philosophising—His confusion of "supernatural" and "ultra-rational"—"Heart" and "head"—Mr. Kidd's real ignorance of the psychology of belief—His want of training in psychology and ethics. *Page* 52

CHAPTER VI.

Mr. Kidd's philosophy of history—Difference between Pagan and Christian society—The social virtue of Christianity—Mr. Kidd's admonishment of all previous historians—The "great problem of every progressive society"—Christianity makes for the equality of man, thus tending to bring all into the struggle for life on more equal terms—It is thus of the highest importance to the cause of progress, which demands strenuous competition, selection and rejection—Greek morality egotistical—Evolution not an intellectual movement—The high altruistic ideal of Christianity—It tends to break down caste and slavery—Our civilisation exists on an irrational basis—Mr. Kidd's historical and psychological ignorance—His misplaced regard for Mr. Froude, Mr. Lecky, and Mr. Mahaffy—The real facts as to Pagan humanitarianism—Mr. Lecky's opinion of early Christian morals—His self-contradictions—The real character of the Gospel Jesus—His intolerance—Christianity and slavery—Paine and the deists of the eighteenth century—Mr. Kidd's vulgar errors on the subject of Pagan altruism—Mr. J. A. Farrer's comparison of Christianity and Paganism—Mr. A. W. Benn on Stoicism and the idea of humanity—The innate equality of men not a Christian but a Pagan doctrine—Futility of Mr. Kidd's philosophy of history—"Destinies" and "forces"—His notion of the continuity of history—His self-contradictions—His philosophy of history a mere burlesque—His treatment of ethical developments—More absurdities—He has no conception of the real causes of moral changes—Almost stumbles upon the truth by accident. . . . . *Page* 64

CHAPTER VII.

Mr. Kidd on modern socialism—The real significance of the movement—The real impelling force is the development of the altruistic feelings—This leads to the admittance of the lower classes to the struggle for life on more equal terms with the higher classes—Mr. Kidd's confusion of mind as to selection and progress—Religion must be relied on to keep up the struggle for life in all its old intensity—Confusion as to the effect of reasoning upon mankind—Superfluity of his own book—His formulas pseudo-scientific and meaningless. . . . . *Page* 82

CHAPTER VIII.

"Human Evolution not Primarily Intellectual"—Social development and ethical codes—Religion and the intellect—No such continuous increase as we are wont to imagine in the mental development of races—Mr. Galton on the intellectual power of the ancient Greeks—The real importance of intellect as a factor in social evolution—Mr. Kidd fighting his own shadow—Secondary and primary use of intellect—Religion as the prime factor in progress—Religious character of the Teutonic peoples—The French mind irreligious—Mr. Kidd's explanation of race differences affords an illustration of his sociological ignorance—France and the limiting of the population—Mr. Kidd's own thesis self-subversive—Reason and the individual—Mr. Kidd's pseudo-scientific jargon. . . . . . *Page* 88

CHAPTER IX.

Mr. Kidd on history and universal law—"The forces at work in the evolution of society"—Evolution only concerned with the interests of the social organism as a whole—More confusion on Mr. Kidd's part—The Reformation—Latin Christianity—Evolution of the Anglo-Saxon peoples—Absurdity of speaking of our civilisation as "based upon Christianity"—Negro slavery among the "altruistic" Anglo-Saxons—Mr. Kidd's forecast of the future of civilisation—An unreliable guide—The reception of his book by the uncritical press—His "reply" to his critics—The gross paralogism of his book—Mr. J. M. Robertson's summary of it—Mr. Kidd incapable of answering even the charges of historical ignorance that were brought against him—Ten years spent in reading for *Social Evolution*—Ten weeks' reading actually embodied in it—Mr. Kidd's thesis an old one—His mental defects and his lack of adequate training—*Social Evolution* the most ignorant book of modern times. . . . . *Page* 94

MR. DRUMMOND'S *ASCENT OF MAN*.

CHAPTER I.

Theological quality of Mr. Drummond's fallacies—*Natural Law in the Spiritual World*—Mr. Drummond as the educator of the human race—Object of *The Ascent of Man*—Necessity for a re-examination of the Darwinian theory—Typical examples of Mr. Drummond's habit of thought and expression—Theological tactics in relation to the evolutionary theory—Teleological biology—"The God of evolution". . . . . . *Page* 103

CHAPTER II.

Mr. Drummond's conception of the standpoint from which evolution should be viewed—The beginning must be interpreted from the end—The evolution of man the culminating point—Mr. Drummond's absurd analogies—Error of reading a purpose into evolution—The "struggle for life" and the "struggle for the life of others"—Nutrition and reproduction—Mr. Drummond's confusion of the physiological and the ethical—Egoism and altruism—The old theistic problem of evil—Huxley on *Evolution and Ethics*—His fallacies—Mr. Drummond on evolution as the work of love—"Why was this method chosen?"—The moral purpose of evolution—Theism old and new—Browning's optimism—Romanes—Professor Knight—Professor Calderwood—The old theistic dilemma—Summary of Mr. Drummond's shortcomings up to this point—His thesis of the importance of altruism not new—Mr. Drummond's criticism of Mr. Kidd—Spencer and Huxley on altruism as a factor in the struggle for existence—The "struggle for the life of others" simply a phase of the struggle for life. . . . . . *Page* 108

CHAPTER III.

Mr. Drummond on the struggle for life—The problem of evil made by the theist—Nature and the unevolved savage—Mr. Drummond's confusion of mind—Evolution "an instrument of perfection"—The significance of weapons in early evolution—"Implements of self-preservation"—The ethical aspect of the struggle for life—Suspending judgment upon the moral meaning of evolution—Mr. Drummond as the Lady Plyant of biology—Mistake of looking upon the struggle for life as altogether painful—Theistic ethics—Omnipotence and the question of evil—Lying for the glory of God—"The object of the survival of the fittest is to produce fitness"—Confusion of Mr. Drummond's theology. . . . . *Page* 130

CHAPTER IV.

The struggle for the life of others—Mistaken notions of all previous scientists—Evolution taken as a whole is a "love-story"—Altruism and evolution—Physiological origins of egoism and altruism—Sacrifice in lower nature—Confusion of physiological and ethical terms—The ethical significance of sex—Teleological biology—Illustrations from Weismann—Fallacy of crediting Nature with "intentions"—The evolution of a mother and the evolution of a father—"The one motive of organic nature was to make mothers"—The creation of fathers—Sympathy as a factor in evolution—Monogamy and natural selection. . . . . *Page* 146

CHAPTER V.

Stigmaria and sigillaria—"Did mind, morals, men, evolve out of matter?"—A tree does not grow out of its roots—The secret of evolution lies with the environment—Environment the supreme factor—Mr. Drummond's self-contradictions and confusion—Evolutionists have always recognised the factor of environment—The cosmos as "environment"—Organism and environment purely relative terms—Mr. Drummond's confusion as to the meaning of environment—The "environment of the social tree"—Mr. Drummond nearing the rocks of folly—The physical world in reality a spiritual world—"Evolution demands a creative hand"—God accountable for the whole of nature—Love the final result of evolution—Christianity at one with evolution—The real character of the Gospel Jesus—Mr. Drummond's book as a whole. . . . . *Page* 160

MR. BALFOUR'S *FOUNDATIONS OF BELIEF*.

CHAPTER I.

Difference between Mr. Balfour and the two other irrationalists—Mr. Balfour as organism and environment—His mind and his surroundings—*The Foundations of Belief* based on the *Defence of Philosophic Doubt*—Mr. Balfour appealing to the "general reader"—Critical and uncritical receptions of the book—Comparison of Mr. Balfour's essay on "The Religion of Humanity" and "A Fragment on Progress"—"The Religion of Humanity"—Positivism emotionally inadequate, tending to despair—The "consequences" of belief—Positivism ends "in a chilling scepticism concerning the final worth of human effort"—"A Fragment on Progress"—No logical ground for the belief in a general progress of the race—Despair the note of Mr. Balfour's paper—Comparison of the two essays. . *Page* 179

CHAPTER II.

Naturalism—The "consequences" of naturalism—Naturalism and æsthetics—Mr. Balfour arguing his opponents' case for them—Naturalistic and intuitional theories of æsthetic—Mr. Balfour's tearful rhetoric—The upshot of his argument—Naturalism and ethics—Incongruity of ethical ideals and the account given by naturalism of their origin—Determinism leads to moral impoverishment—Dishonesty of Mr. Balfour's method—Example from the theory of heredity—Mr. Balfour's "pairs of contrasted propositions"—More rhetoric. . . . . *Page* 191

CHAPTER III.

Examination of the philosophic basis of naturalism—Reasons for postponing this examination until now—Mr. Balfour's metaphysical arguments and the plain man—Difficulties in the way of a purely empirical theory of things—Science and the theory of science—Mr. Balfour merely attacking the latter, not the former—The primary and secondary qualities of matter—

Amateur scepticism—Accommodating character of Mr. Balfour's scepticism —Mr. Pearson on criticism—Irrelevance of Mr. Balfour's attack—Mr. Benn on the Greek sceptics—The regularity and irregularity of nature—The principle of causation—Naturalism forcing itself into the retinue of science—Mr. Balfour's self-contradictions. . . . . *Page* 202

CHAPTER IV.

Philosophy and Rationalism—Consistency not to be purchased at famine prices —Natural and revealed religion—Reason and natural religion—" Some Causes of Belief"—Reason and authority—Fate of a society that should try to base its beliefs and actions wholly upon reason—Sophistry of the argument—Mr. Balfour on morals and authority—Mr. Balfour's warning superfluous on his own showing—Weakness of Mr. Balfour's argument in favour of authority—His own oscillation between authority and reason.
Page 212

CHAPTER V.

Mr. Balfour's "suggestions towards a provisional philosophy"—Preparing the ground for inconsistency—Different classes of belief—No distinction to be made where no relevant distinction can be discovered—Protest against the assumption that scientific beliefs stand upon a more solid platform than any others—Mr. Balfour's object in all this—The obvious criticism upon it—Mr. Balfour's anticipation of this criticism—His uncandid air of assumed candour—The "inevitableness" of certain scientific beliefs— These compared with the fundamental proposition of theology—Reasons for the universal belief in a material world—Universality and inevitableness no test of truth—"Faith or assurance in excess of, or at least independent of, reason"—Inevitable beliefs and the "state of nature"—Sophistry of the argument—" Higher" and " lower" feelings—Psychological distinction between the belief in a real world and the belief in God—Dishonesty of Mr. Balfour's dialectic—Mr. Balfour, Mr. Spencer and Spinoza—Warding off criticism—His object " not to discredit reason "—Authority and reason once more—The cause of Mr. Balfour's new-found zeal for reason—Utilises reason as an argument for theism—"Needs" and their "satisfactions"— Professor Seth on Mr. Balfour—A rational world and a rational Creator— Similarity of Mr. Balfour's argument to that of Kant—The argument "from the mere fact that we know"—The illegitimate use of the word "needs"— The logical defects of transcendentalism—Impossibility of " accounting for knowledge" except in terms of knowledge—The " mere fact that we know " does not help the argument for theism—Kant upon knowledge—Weakness of his position and of Mr. Balfour's—Fallacy of the argument about "higher" and "lower" qualities. . . . . . *Page* 224

CHAPTER VI.

Universality and inevitableness of beliefs—Sense-perceptions denied to be "the most worthy"—Action and reaction between beliefs and the formulas which express them—Difference between scientific and theological beliefs in this respect—Examples: in science the theory of heat; in theology the doctrine of the atonement—Mr. Balfour's "non-rational" beliefs in reality subconsciously rational—Beliefs and hypotheses—The "consolation" of theological beliefs—Relations between language and belief, and between belief and authority—The feminine quality of Mr. Balfour's mind—Some psychological criticisms of him—Beliefs do not exactly correspond to reality—Futility of using this fact as an argument for religion—The real ground for the rationalist's refusal to believe religious dogmas—The " needs of mankind " once more—Rationalism also " meets the needs of mankind "—Mr. Balfour's use of reason when it suits his purpose—The theistic reliance upon sentiment. . . . . *Page* 246

CHAPTER VII.

Mr. Balfour as negative and positive thinker—His failure as a constructionist—Mind and the naturalistic account of the origin of mind—Must presuppose the world to be "the work of a rational Being"—Fallacy of this argument—Meaning of right and wrong—"Atoms" and truth and error—The entanglement of Mr. Balfour's argument—The consequences of his positing a supreme reason—Failure of the attempt to reconcile religion and science—The real conflict of religion not with naturalism but with science itself—Mr. Balfour as the defender of the faith—Evasion of the problem of evil—Miracles—Psychological climates—The naturalist unfit to weigh the historic evidence for miracles—The "preferential exercise of divine power"—Argument in a circle. . . . . Page 257

CHAPTER VIII.

The question of inspiration—Reason and natural religion—Natural religion and "traditional religion"—Mr. Balfour's argument in a tangle—The inspiration of sacred books—Mr. Balfour's difficulties—Inspiration as a whole—"Divine co-operation"—Mr. Balfour's final effort—Theism *versus* naturalism—Christianity *versus* theism—The incarnation—Belief in "mysteries"—Mr. Balfour's argument might be used in behalf of any religion—Reason and the incarnation—The historical criticism of the Bible—Mr. Balfour's misrepresentations—"The ethical import of Christianity"—Ethical "needs" once more—Is Mr. Balfour a Christian?—Failure of his attack upon naturalism—Rationalism and morals—The naturalist as a moral parasite—Mr. Kidd's remarks—Our ethical code not the product of Christianity—Social ethics as cause and effect of social changes—Mr. Spencer and Mr. Balfour—Christian and rationalistic ethics in theory and practice—Mr. Balfour and Mr. Bradlaugh. . . . . Page 270

CONCLUSION.

Object of the final chapter—The reviewers of *The Foundations of Belief*—Mr. Spencer's criticism—Futility of the argument from needs to their satisfaction—The anthropocentric view of the universe—Mr. Balfour's scepticism—Fallacy of his theistic position—Reason and authority—The authority of religion decreasing, and that of science increasing—Mr. Spencer's own agnosticism—The spearing of an effigy—Examination of Mr. Balfour's criticism—Mr. Balfour merely dealing in pseud-ideas—Historical development of the God-idea—Mr. Huxley's criticism—Ancient Rome and modern Europe—Science and religion—Naturalism and Demomism—The germs of modern agnosticism in Hamilton and Mansel—Agnosticism and atheism—Mr. Balfour's definition of naturalism at once too wide and too narrow—Mr. Pearson's criticism—Christianity and statesmanship—Ambiguity of most of Mr. Balfour's terms—His confusion of naturalism, science and rationalism—Mr. Balfour's superficial acquaintance with science—The materialism of Moleschott and Büchner—The certitudes of religion and the certitudes of science—Science conceptual—Things-in-themselves—Mr. Balfour's criticism of science beside the mark—The law of causation conceptual—Authority and reason—A *reductio ad absurdum*—The Liberal press and *The Foundations of Belief*—Mr. Vamadeo Shastri's criticism—Christianity and Brahmanism—Mr. Shastri's delicate soul—Superiority of Brahmanism to Christianity—Mr. Shastri on Mr. Balfour's "needs"—"Needs" and psychological climates—One absurd religionist against another—Reaction in religion, in politics and in social life—Reason the final arbiter—Dangers of modern irrationalism. . . . . Page 283

INTRODUCTION.

THE primary object of this volume is the refutation of the fallacies and errors contained in three books—Kidd's *Social Evolution*, Drummond's *Ascent of Man*, and Balfour's *Foundations of Belief*—which at the time of their publication caused a literary sensation in England and the United States without stirring the scientific world. The ephemeral nature of these productions is so self-evident that most persons of culture and intelligence will assert that similar works do not call for a volume especially devoted to their errors, and that in a few short years they will die a natural death and go the way of all fallacy and deception. I am far from disagreeing with this criticism; on the contrary, no one could be more convinced that the vogue of these books, great as it was at first, is destined to grow smaller and smaller, until the particular form of pseudo-philosophy which they represent has passed into deserved oblivion. The path of literature is indeed malodorous with the dead bodies of their predecessors. Nevertheless, I am probably not alone in the belief that, transparent as are most of the fallacies of these books, it is not altogether superfluous to devote a volume to the consideration of them. They, and the applause which they drew forth, represent a feature of human evolution that is as interesting as it is significant. The justification of the present volume will be tolerably plain to any one who runs his eye over the past history of the conflict between religion and science, and views these modern products of irrationalism in the light of that history. He will then perceive that the problem presented by the appearance and the success of such books as these is of far greater importance than would appear upon the first glance—is, indeed, far too important to rationalism for the books to be dismissed in contemptuous silence. The books themselves—especially those of Mr. Drummond and Mr. Kidd—are perhaps the mere phenomena of a moment, and may hardly be worth detailed criticism; but the state of the intellectual world in which such works can command an enormous sale and receive almost unstinted commendation from many of the literary reviews, is undoubtedly a serious matter for rationalists. It serves to enforce the lesson, if any enforcement of it were needed, that the conflict between science and religion, between rationalism and irrationalism, is by no means a thing of the past; that it is as important now as ever it was, and that while the combatants and the weapons and the modes of warfare have changed, the conflict is as bitter, and must be as bitter, in the present as in the past. There can be no truce between the rationalist and the irrationalist; and if in these happier days the religious obscurantist has lost most of his power to inflict physical disabilities upon his opponent, none the less is it incumbent upon lovers of truth to take up arms against the hereditary foes of reason. I forbear to urge in defence of this volume the obvious argument that it is to the interest of all who value social freedom to withstand these modern forms of unreason, because of the immemorial association of religious obscurantism and political reaction. I would rather take the higher ground of arguing that intellectual error, or what we conceive to be error, should be opposed for the mere truth's sake, for the mere dignity and decency of human nature; that the spectacle of three such men as Mr. Balfour,

Mr. Kidd and Mr. Drummond playing fast and loose with reason in the cause of religious irrationalism is one that no thinking man can regard without a feeling of shame for the race; and that whatever may be our duty in respect to error as a whole, there can be no question that it is our duty to oppose to the uttermost these deliberate attempts to weaken the authority of reason in the lives and thoughts of men. Among the readers of any book on a controversial subject there are always some who, unconvinced one way or the other, are candid enough to hold their judgment in suspense upon the matters in dispute; and it is to these readers, to those who stand upon the border-line between religion and rationalism, that the appeal of such a book as the present must be made. If after reading it they are disappointed with its reasoning and fall back into the rank of the religious, be it so; they will at least have discovered their philosophy by the exercise of their own reason: while if any can be persuaded that the pseudo-philosophy of the modern apologist is just so much elaborate fallacy, rationalism will be to that extent the gainer.

It is evident at the outset, to any one who reflects for a moment, that there is nothing essentially new in the books of our three irrationalist writers. To discredit reason, to show that it is incompetent to direct the whole of our intellectual life, to place the "spiritual" above the "natural," to prove the importance of religious beliefs to the individual and to society, to justify the ways of God to man, to rebut the rationalist attack upon the benevolence of the Deity who permits so much evil in the world—these have been the objects of theologians from time immemorial; and there is nothing whatever new in the works of their modern successors, except that the defence has been altered to suit the changed method of attack. After fighting with dogged persistence for centuries, the upholders of religion have had to surrender position after position to the enemy; they have been proved wrong on point after point of history and of ethics; their sacred books have been riddled by hostile criticism, and their practical no less than their intellectual authority has almost departed from them. In our own day there has been added to the previous weapons of the sceptic the powerful weapon of the evolutionary theory, and the tactics of the religious hierarchy in face of this new attack have been consistent with all its previous modes of warfare. The theologians began with the most strenuous opposition to the evolutionary theory; they opposed to it the grotesque authority of their own sacred books; they indulged, like Bishop Wilberforce, in pointless impertinences towards better and wiser men than themselves; they declared the theory to be irreligious in itself and fatal in its consequences to morals. And how stands the matter now? The theory of evolution having conquered the intelligence of the whole of the civilised world, even theologians have no longer the hardihood to deny its truth; and the old weapon of persecution no longer lying ready to their hand, they have adopted the new method of stealing their opponents' thunder. We are now informed, in all gravity, that so far from Darwinism and the Bible being antagonistic, they are really one in principle; that so far from evolution being an irreligious invention, it has really been "God's method in creation"; and the old farce of what Mill called "suborning evidence in favour of a First Cause" has gone on apace.

Glancing cursorily at the three books, it will, as I have said, readily be seen that there is nothing essentially new in the matter of them; that they are, in fact, merely an adaptation of the old arguments, already discredited in other departments, to meet the altered attack of rationalism. When Mr. Kidd argues that reason is an anti-social force, and that an irrational element—religion—has been the prime factor in progress, we are but listening to the primitive emotionalism of earlier apologetics talking the cant of modern pseudo-science. When

Mr. Balfour argues that there is no rational basis for the system he calls naturalism, and that not reason but authority is the main arbiter of our beliefs, and when we find him turning this exceedingly naïve thesis to the uses of religion, and arguing from it that it all proves, in some mysterious way, that we ought to believe that nineteen hundred years ago a Jewish virgin gave birth to a child, we recognise that we are simply face to face once more with the same emotionalism masquerading in the garments of modern philosophy and psychology. And when Mr. Drummond, in that dreadful manner of his, that seems to be a curate's imitation of a bishop delivering a pastoral charge, regales us with his really humorous reading of evolution, when he informs us that God is Love, that the suffering attendant upon natural selection is not to be urged against the moral character of the Deity, although he has chosen to work out his scheme of evolution by this means; when we find evolution and natural selection being turned, after the manner of Browning, to the account of religious optimism, and the death of the unfit being "justified" by the survival of the fit, we see at once the affinity of these arguments with those of all the theologians of the past, who have tried to deal with the problem of evil, and who have argued either (1) that pain was necessary in order to work out a larger balance of pleasure, or (2) that if we had eyes to view the whole past, present and future of things, we should see that, as Pope put it, "all discord" is "harmony not understood," and "all partial evil, universal good". To state the case briefly, Mr. Drummond's book is just a variation upon the old theological theme that God is Love, while the works of Mr. Balfour and Mr. Kidd are variations upon the equally old theme that the emotions are nobler than the intellect, the "heart" more excellent than the "head".

There are, in fact, but three main lines on which the defence of religion against rationalism can run. The religionist must either show that rationalism is wrong in theory, that the acceptance of it involves serious consequences to the morals and the well-being of the community, or that rationalistic methods may be valid within a certain circle but invalid outside it,—invalid, that is, in the domain of theology. As to the first, theologians have suffered so many reverses that they now hesitate to meet science face to face as an avowed enemy; as to the second, that argument, such as it is, will be considered in the course of the present volume; while as to the third, one has only to glance at the theological literature of the past to see how incapable the modern apologists are of improving on their predecessors. Ever since dogma was worsted in the conflict with reason, it has claimed to emanate from a faculty that should take precedence of reason. The argument has been that the truth of certain religious dogmas, or of religion as a whole, is certified by a faculty other than reason, which reason is incompetent to criticise; while all the time that the jurisdiction of reason is being denied explicitly, it is being implicitly admitted; for the very object of the argument has been to induce conviction by means of reason. This is the fundamental fallacy of Mr. Kidd's book; and nothing could better illustrate that gentleman's incompetence than the fact of his having studied his subject for ten years, as he tells us, without discovering that his main thesis was almost as old as religious apologetics themselves. All he has done is to re-clothe the argument in the tattered garments of second-hand biology and perverted history. And as the demonstration of the antiquity of the thesis goes far to discredit Mr. Kidd *a priori*, it will be well to indicate briefly some of the main uses to which it has already been applied.

One is not surprised to come across it so early as Ambrose, whose *Non in dialectica complacuit Deo salvum facere populum suum*,[1] is the dictum of a stupid theologian who, had he lived

[1] *De Fide*, i., 5, sec. 42.

in these days, would probably have written a book like *Social Evolution*. All through the ages, indeed, and in theologians of all denominations, while faith has been held to be the passport to salvation, and while faith has been looked upon as a gift of God, theologians have been foolish enough to argue with heretics whose heresy, in the very terms of the case, must have been due to the deliberate withholding by God of the gift of faith. The process has been one of giving to reason with the one hand and taking away with the other. Reason has to be adjudged competent to make an objection against religion, but incompetent to understand the answer. Thus Savonarola, after arguing that theology is the true and only science, because while "all the others treat of special things under special aspects, theology alone treats of all under a single and universal aspect," lays it down that "for this the light of nature is not sufficient, the light of heaven being required". His real originality, says Villari, "consisted in recognising the weight of reason, experience, and conscience, in both scientific and practical questions, but without separating science from the religion in which he believed, and without admitting—as many then admitted—that man might hold one faith in philosophy, and another in religion". Savonarola, however, merely escaped this latter absurdity by falling into another. If the Christian finds that science negatives a dogma of his creed, he must either (1) give up the dogma, or (2) believe, if he can, in it *and* in the scientific doctrine that confutes it, or (3) hold that the dogma is *a priori* credible as the revealed Word of God, no matter what science may say against it. Stating it in this way, it will be seen how inevitably the Christian who does not wish to surrender his belief altogether, nor to take up the preposterous attitude of believing two contradictory propositions, is driven to the sophistical position that the truth of the dogma is certified by a higher faculty than reason, on which reason can make no impression. Thus we find Savonarola saying at one moment that "we must accept no authority save that of our own experience and reason," that "we must not run counter to reason," and at the next, that the Bible still remains the great authority in matters of opinion, and that "we may not comprehend this book by the intellect alone, but must also bring our heart and soul to the task. Thus only can we enter without peril into this infinite world of the Holy Spirit, and obtain the light needed for our salvation. *But not unto all is this gift equally granted.* From time to time God sends upon earth men favoured with a stronger light than others, and it is their part to enlighten the darkened minds of the multitude." Savonarola, of course, was one of these "favoured" men; there never was a Christian minister yet who was not firmly convinced that God had endowed him with more grace and understanding than any other minister, though he has generally had some difficulty in inducing the others to agree with him. But why, after telling his hearers that they could not comprehend the Bible by the intellect alone, should he attempt to convince them by means of an appeal to their intellect, that his reading of the Bible was the one which God intended them to adopt? And why, after making this appeal to them, and after telling them that God sent certain men upon earth "to enlighten the darkened minds of the multitude," and thus bring them into the way of salvation, should he further tell them that faith is "a supernatural gift from God"? In his work on *The Triumph of the Cross*, again, when he comes to deal with faith and natural reason, he opines that there are "things which are beyond the grasp of reason, and yet only to be known by its aid, and by admitting, or assuming as the point of departure, the necessary and supernatural works of Christ and His Church". "By reason alone," again, "we may attain to the knowledge of God's existence; but never to that of the Trinity, save by first assuming the truth of its marvellous and supernatural operations," which piece of primitive thimble-rigging is only one of Mr. Balfour's arguments in a crude and comparatively innocent form. And finally, we are not surprised to find Savonarola, after laying it down that "the force of reason cannot avail against things beyond the reach of reason," and that the Christian doctrines are "intangible to reason," proceeding to give his readers, in the usual way, the "reasons" for the Incarnation.[1]

Savonarola, then, was simply falling into the inevitable snare when he tried to show, by means of reason, that we must believe in certain doctrines because they are beyond reason. Subtler minds than his, indeed, have been driven by their religion into the same net of fallacy and self-contradiction. Compare with the above extracts, for example, the following quotations taken almost at random from Pascal's *Pensées* :—

"La dernière démarche de la raison, c'est de connaître qu'il y a une infinité de choses qui la surpassent. Elle est bien faible si elle ne va jusque-là."[2]

"Il n'y a rien de si conforme à la raison que le désaveu de la raison dans les choses qui sont de foi."[3]

"Ceux à qui Dieu a donné la religion par sentiment de cœur sont bienheureux et bien persuadés. Mais pour ceux qui ne l'ont pas, nous ne pouvons la leur procurer que par raisonnement, en attendant que Dieu la leur imprime lui-même dans le cœur; sans quoi la foi est inutile pour le salut. . . . Ce n'est pas par les agitations de notre raison, mais par le simple soumission de la raison, que nous pouvons véritablement nous connaître."[4]

"Toutes les religions et toutes les sectes du monde ont eu

---

[1] See Villari's *Savonarola*, vol. i., pp. 103, 104, 106, 108, 119, 174; and vol. ii., chaps. iii. and iv.
[2] Pascal, *Pensées*, in *Œuvres*, vol. ii., p. 257. Paris, 1819.
[3] *Ibid.*, p. 259.   [4] *Ibid.*, p. 366.

la raison naturelle pour guide. . . . Il y a trois moyens de croire ; la raison, la coutume et l'inspiration. La religion chrétienne, qui seule a la raison, n' admet pas pour ses vrais enfants ceux qui croient sans inspiration : ce n'est pas qu'elle exclue la raison et la coutume ; au contraire, il faut ouvrir son esprit aux preuves par la raison, et s'y confirmer par la coutume ; mais elle veut qu'on s'offre par l'humiliation aux inspirations, qui seules peuvent faire le vrai et salutaire effet."[1]

"Le cœur a ses raisons, que la raison ne connaît pas : on le sent en mille choses. C'est le cœur qui sent Dieu, et non la raison."[2]

Here the antithetical sharpness of statement brings into prominent relief the confusion that runs throughout the argument. One has, of course, in the case of Pascal, to consider the temperamental diathesis before passing judgment upon his system of ideas ; but it is at least certain that the Christian religion wrought for intellectual evil in him as in so many other men of dialectical acuteness, by setting him upon the suicidal course of defending doctrines which he knew were contrary to reason, by reasoning that they were above the jurisdiction of reason. And where such minds as Pascal's have gone astray, it is hardly surprising that minds like Mr. Kidd's should have become completely lost. Mr. Kidd, indeed, seems to have been doubly unfortunate ; for not only has he failed to see the manner in which he confutes himself time after time,—as when he tells us that men have not been and will not be influenced by what scientists may say as to the effect of their conduct on future generations, when all the time his own book is an attempt to influence men in this way, —but his ten years of reading have not given him any warning that other men before him have trod the same path of primi-

---

[1] Pascal, *Pensées*, in *Œuvres*, vol. ii., p. 386. Paris, 1819.
[2] *Ibid.*, p. 390.

tive fallacy. We need not pursue the historical side of the question any further. Any one who has even an average acquaintance with the history of opinions must be able to supply further evidence in the same direction. Mr. Kidd, who sometimes speaks of Kant and other philosophers with an assurance that would almost make us think he had read them, might have discovered, before he began his book, that his thesis of the inferiority of reason was merely another form of the sophistical argument by which Kant attempted to give to reason with the one hand and to take away with the other. Second-rate as well as first-rate German minds have trod the same path, and third-rate English minds have not been slow to follow them. Dr. Julius Kaftan's *Truth of the Christian Religion* is simply a more subtle form of the argument of Mr. Kidd and Mr. Balfour, done, as only a German can do it, with elaborate and futile completeness. " It strives," says Professor Flint in his introduction to the English translation, " to represent Christian faith as its own sufficient foundation. It seeks to secure for religion a domain within the sphere of feeling and practical judgment into which theoretical reason cannot intrude." The division of the human mind into the dual faculties of " practical judgment " and " theoretical reason " is, of course, simply so much Kantian apriorism. Nor does it help Dr. Kaftan in the least, for his justification of Christianity, such as it is, is merely an appeal to reason, by the argument that Christianity is justified by history, or else that the Christian consciousness of faith is sufficient proof of the truth of the religion. Bad as the reasoning is, it is still an appeal to the reason, and Dr. Kaftan's deplorable sophistry in his attempts to define " truth " so as to make it equal Christian " truth," ought to be a warning to any future theologian who attempts to discredit reason by reason. In our own day Cardinal Newman's *Grammar of Assent*, which contains almost everything that is worth noticing in Mr. Balfour's

Foundations of Belief, has striven to set religious convictions apart from others as regards their psychological genesis, and has failed. All, indeed, that the modern irrationalist can say was long ago expressed in the naïve words of Luther, that "Before faith and the knowledge of God, reason is mere darkness; but in the hands of those who believe, it is an excellent instrument. All faculties and gifts are pernicious, exercised by the impious, but most salutary when possessed by godly persons;" which amusing piece of theological impertinence is *Social Evolution* and *The Foundations of Belief* in a nutshell. Let us, however, betake ourselves to the detailed consideration of the books of the three irrationalists, commencing with that of Mr. Kidd.

MR. KIDD'S *SOCIAL EVOLUTION.*

CHAPTER I.

IN the same way that we learn more of a man's real nature from his face in those moments when he is unconscious of being observed, than in the moments when he is aware of our observation of him, we can discover the inherent weakness of a writer's mind by his unconscious betrayals no less than by his more formal fallacies. If, for example, we find him making the most elementary errors of history and of argument, and repeating them time after time, we shall have little hesitation in pronouncing him fundamentally incompetent to do any valuable work in science. It is not a question, be it observed, of writing down a man as incompetent because he does not agree with us; it is simply a question of whether a man who can perpetrate the most childish fallacies on page after page of his book and yet remain utterly unconscious of them and of their bearing upon his main positions, can be held *a priori* capable of thinking correctly for five consecutive minutes upon any subject whatever. We find Mr. Kidd, for example, falling time after time into the most elementary of all logical errors—purely verbal fallacies that strike the reader at once by their gross confusion; we find him using perfectly meaningless phrases with an air of solemn wisdom, until it becomes evident that he has been hypnotised by the mere collocation of the words; we find him setting up distinctions that do not exist, and confusing conceptions that are really distinct; and over and above all, he is utterly unconscious of the fact that the characteristics he attributes to certain human phenomena are equally predicable of other and very opposite phenomena. Apart from the intellectual quality of his argument, this spectacle defines Mr. Kidd's mental type so accurately, shows so clearly the fundamental looseness and flaccidity of his mind, that we are justified in saying at once that an intellect of this type is radically incapable of looking at any problem whatever in a thoroughly scientific manner. Let us, however, turn from the abstract to the concrete, and see the actual working of Mr. Kidd's mind as exhibited in his book.

He begins, as Professor Drummond begins, by calling attention to what he supposes to be the shortcomings of present evolutionary science. Mr. Kidd, like his fellow-irrationalist of the north, is deeply impressed by the idea that he is a Daniel come to judgment, and that it has been reserved for him at once to correct the errors and supply the deficiencies of the Darwinian theory as we have hitherto understood it, and to lay the foundations of the wiser evolutionary doctrine of the future. To say this of Mr. Kidd is not to thrust greatness upon him. His estimate of his own work is evident upon every other page of the book. He speaks in a tone of pained commiseration of the shortcomings of our present science; he draws our attention to the fact that the meaning of the development of certain epochs and the function of certain principles have not been really comprehended until now, *i.e.*, until Mr. Kidd's penetrating glance sought out their inmost being; he refers everywhere to the true scientist, the true student of human history, the true evolutionist, the biologist, in such a way that, in spite of his modesty, these terms are clearly seen to be meant for himself. Altogether, Mr. Kidd appears to have no doubt that he is a man with a mission. Unfortunately, there are certain things that even the man with a mission cannot dispense with if he wishes to bring conviction to the minds of others; he must have a better reasoning faculty than Mr. Kidd's, and he must have not only more knowledge than Mr. Kidd, but he must have acquired that knowledge at first instead of at second hand. He must not attempt to square accounts between religion and science if he is incapable of avoiding the most glaring verbal fallacies when he comes to use those words; nor must he try to philosophise upon the history of ancient and modern Europe upon the strength of a smattering of Mr. Lecky, Mr. Mahaffy, and George Henry Lewes. This is not the way great and original minds go to work upon their subject, but it is the way of Mr. Kidd. And where he is not wrong, he is so solemnly accurate that the effect is even still more grotesque. To read Mr. Kidd's carefully laboured statement of a fact which every schoolboy knows, is an education in the art of futile impressiveness; if Mr. Kidd wished to tell us, for example, that Queen Anne was dead, he would say that "the true student of history will not improbably venture to assert, with an ever-increasing conviction of the truth of his assertion, that Queen Anne is no longer living"; if he wishes us to realise that two and two make four, he will tell us that "it will not improbably be recognised by science, at no very distant date, that two and two make four". Mr. Kidd's intellectual virtues, in fact, are even more depressing than his vices, and reveal, just as effectually as these latter, the hopeless lack of alertness that is characteristic of his mind.

What is Mr. Kidd's theory of social evolution? We will find it expounded in the first five chapters of his book. Briefly, it is as follows :—

In the first chapter, "The Outlook," he lays it down that science has been quite unsuccessful in its treatment of the great question of social evolution, in that it has thrown little or no light upon the past, and can throw little or none upon the future. More especially is science to blame for her attitude towards religion. Science has never really understood the function of religious beliefs in the evolution of societies. "The general mind, so often more scientific than our current science, seems to feel that there is something wrong in the attitude of science towards the subject of religion, that the most persistent and universal class of phenomena connected with human society cannot be thus lightly disposed of, and that our religious systems must have some unexplained function to perform in the evolution which society is undergoing, and on a scale to correspond with the magnitude of the phenomena" (p. 17). It is quite an error to imagine that religious beliefs are dying out, or that they are destined to die out in the future. "No greater mistake can be made than to imagine that there is anything in evolutionary science at the end of the nineteenth century to justify such conclusions. On the contrary, if these beliefs are a factor in the development which society is undergoing, then the most notable result of the scientific revolution begun by Darwin must be to establish them on a foundation as broad, deep and lasting as any that the theologians have dreamt of. According to the laws which science has herself enunciated, these beliefs must then be expected to remain to the end a characteristic feature of our social evolution" (p. 22). Science, in fact, has dealt fairly with most products of nature, but has been exceedingly ungenerous towards religion, and "the time is certainly not far distant when she must look back with surprise, if not, indeed, with some degree of shamefacedness, to the attitude in which she has for long addressed herself to one of the highest problems in the history of life" (p. 19). "From the beginning science finds [man] under the sway of forces new to her, and with one of the strongest of these forces she herself at a very early stage comes into conflict. He holds beliefs which she asserts have no foundation in reason, and his actions are controlled by strange sanctions which she does not acknowledge" (pp. 19-20). Thus science has always been wrong in her attitude towards religion. "These religions of man form one of the most striking and persistent of the phenomena of life when encountered under its highest forms, namely, in human society. Yet, strange to say, science seems to have taken up and to have maintained, down to the present time, the extraordinary position that her only concern with them is to declare (often, it must be confessed, with the heat and bitterness of a partisan) that they are without any foundation in reason" (p. 21).

Science, however, has not only been wrong in relation to religion, it has failed to throw any real light upon the great questions of the day; and the duty of the true scientist is to investigate the evolution of man from the standpoint of all the sciences, but from that of biology in particular. "Each of the departments of knowledge which has dealt with man in society has regarded him almost exclusively from its own standpoint. To the politician he has been the mere opportunist; to the historian he has been the unit which is the sport of blind forces apparently subject to no law; to the exponent of religion he has been the creature of another world; to the political economist he has been little more than the covetous machine. The time has come, it would appear, for a better understanding and for a more radical method; for the social sciences to strengthen themselves by sending their roots deep into the soil underneath from which they spring, and for the biologist to advance over the frontier and carry the methods of his science boldly into human society, where he has but to deal with the phenomena of life where he encounters life at last under its highest and most complex aspect" (pp. 29-30).

In his second chapter, entitled "Conditions of Human Progress," Mr. Kidd will "as far as possible, unbiassed by preconceived ideas, endeavour, before we proceed further, to obtain some clear conception of what human society really is, and of the nature of the conditions which have been attendant on the progress we have made so far" (p. 31). What follows is simply a retelling of the old, old story of natural selection, of the excessive multiplication of organisms, the struggle for life, the survival of favoured variations, and "progress" as the result of it all. But Mr. Kidd is careful to insist, for his later purposes, that the laws "which have operated in shaping the development of life elsewhere have not been suspended in human society"; and that if progress is to continue, it must always proceed upon the same material as in the past, *i.e.* excessive procreation relatively to the means of subsistence must give natural selection the wherewithal to work upon. "Progress everywhere from the beginning of life has been effected in the same way, and it is possible in no other way. It is the result of selection and rejection" (p. 36). "The first condition of existence with a progressive form is, therefore, one of continual strain and stress, and along its upward path this condition is always maintained. Once begun, too, there can be no pause in the advance; for if by any combination of circumstances the rivalry and selection cease, then progress ceases with them, and the species or group cannot maintain its place; it has taken the first retrograde step, and it is immediately placed at a disadvantage with other species or with those groups of its own kind where the rivalry still goes on, and where selection, adaptation and progress continue unchecked" (p. 41). "The law of life has been always the same from the beginning—ceaseless and inevitable struggle and competition, ceaseless and inevitable selection, ceaseless and inevitable progress" (p. 42).

When man comes upon the scene the old strife is still carried on, but two new factors have come into play—man's reason and "his capacity for acting in concert with his fellows in organised societies". In war and in peace the struggle for existence always goes on. One race may oust another by exterminating it in war, or it may gradually drive it from the earth under all the forms of peace, as is being done with the Indian in North America and with the Maori in New Zealand. The one law still persists; progress is being achieved through struggle, through selection and rejection. In civilised societies, in fact, the strife is not less but greater than it was in uncivilised societies. "In the later type of civilisation the conditions of the rivalry have greatly changed; but if we look closely at what is taking place, we may see that there has been no cessation or diminution of the rivalry itself. On the contrary, the significance of the change has consisted in the tendency to raise it to a higher level, to greatly enlarge its scope and its efficiency as a cause of progress by bringing all the members of the community into it on more equal terms, and to render it freer and fairer, but, therefore, still more strenuous" (p. 57).

In his third chapter, bearing the title "There is no Rational Sanction for the Conditions of Progress," Mr. Kidd leaves the safe ground of other men's labours and begins speculation on his own account. "It becomes necessary . . . to notice for the first time a fact which, later, as we proceed, will be brought into increasing prominence. As man can only reach his highest development and employ his powers to the fullest extent in society, it follows that in the evolution we witness him undergoing throughout history his development as an individual is necessarily of less importance than his development as a social creature. In other words, although his interests as an individual may remain all-important to himself, it has become inevitable that they must henceforward be subordinated—whether he be conscious of it or not—to those larger social interests with which the forces that are shaping his development have now begun to operate" (pp. 64, 65). Thus the individual's concern is only with himself and with the present, while evolution is concerned with the social organism and with the future. "There is, therefore, one feature of the situation which cannot be gainsaid. If it had been possible at any time for all the individuals of any form of life to have secured themselves against the competition of other forms, it would, beyond doubt, have been their interest to have suspended amongst themselves those onerous conditions which thus, by sacrificing the present welfare of individuals to the larger interests of their kind in the future, prevented large numbers from reaching the fullest possibilities of life. The conditions of progress, it is true, might have been suspended, but this could not have caused the present individuals any concern. The result would, in any case, only have been visible after a prolonged period, and they could not therefore be expected to have appeared to existing members as of any importance when weighed against their own interests in the present" (pp. 66, 67). How is it, then, that man, endowed with reason, has not put an end to progress by putting an end to the struggle for life? "It would seem that a conclusion, strange and unexpected, but apparently unavoidable, must present itself. If the theories of evolutionary science have been, so far, correct, then this new factor which has been born into the world must, it would appear, have the effect of ultimately staying all further progress" (p. 67). "How is the possession of reason ever to be rendered compatible with the will to submit to conditions of existence so onerous, requiring the effective and continual subordination of the individual's welfare to the progress of a development in which he can have no personal interest whatever?" (p. 69).

There can, Mr. Kidd argues, be no rational sanction for the conditions of progress for all those upon whom the burden of natural selection presses most heavily. If the individual had followed the dictates of his own reason he would have put an end to the struggle for life (which is only of use for the development of future generations), and devoted his energies to making his own existence comfortable while it lasted. "If we ask ourselves, therefore, what course it is the interests of the masses holding political power in our advanced societies to pursue from the standpoint of reason, it seems hardly possible to escape the conclusion that they should, in self-interest, put an immediate end to existing social conditions. . . . The interest of the masses . . . appears . . . clearly to be to draw a ring fence round their borders; to abolish competition within the community; to suspend the onerous rivalry of individuals which presses so severely on all; to organise, on socialistic principles, the means of production; and lastly, and above all, to regulate the population so as to keep it always proportional to the means of comfortable existence for all. In a word, to put an end to those conditions which the evolutionist perceives to be inevitably and necessarily associated with progress now and to have been so associated with it, not only from the beginning of human society, but from the beginning of life" (pp. 80, 81).

It is a characteristic of Mr. Kidd that he repeats his arguments, and even his phrases, time after time. Not content with having stated the above dilemma, or supposed dilemma, half a dozen times already, he brings it forth once more, prefacing it this time with the remark that "the extraordinary character of the problem presented by human society begins thus slowly to come into view". "There emerges now clearly into sight a fundamental principle that underlies that social development which has been in progress throughout history, and which is proceeding with accelerated pace in our modern civilisation. It is that in this development the interests of the individual and those of the social organism to which he belongs are not identical. The teaching of reason to the individual must always be that the present time and his own interests therein are all-important to him. Yet the forces which are working out our development are primarily concerned not with these interests of the individual, but with those of the race, and more immediately with the widely different interests of a social organism subject to quite other conditions and possessed of an indefinitely longer life. . . . And in the development which is in progress it is a first principle of evolutionary science that it is these greater interests that must be always paramount. The central fact with which we are confronted in our progressive societies is, therefore, that: *The interests of the social organism and those of the individuals comprising it at any time are actually antagonistic; they can never be reconciled; they are inherently and essentially irreconcilable*" (pp. 84, 85). Thus, Mr. Kidd sums up, " there can never be found any sanction in individual reason for conduct in societies where the conditions of progress prevail ". On what, then, does progress really depend? Mr. Kidd gives the answer in his fourth chapter—" The Central Feature of Human History ".

After the usual wearisome repetitions of what he has said fifty times already, we discover that the central feature of human history is religion; and Mr. Kidd enforces this dictum by imagining the psychological effect of the sight of all our temples, churches, cathedrals and religious societies upon a visitor from another planet. " Such a visitor, at length, would not fail to be deeply impressed by what he had observed. He would be driven to conclude that he was dealing with phenomena, the laws and nature of which were little understood by the people amongst whom he found himself; and that whatever might be the meaning of these phenomena they undoubtedly constituted one of the most persistent and characteristic features of human society, and not only in past ages but at the present day " (p. 94). The visitor begins to read the various definitions of religion that have been given, from Seneca to Dr. Martineau, and finds them all wanting. At length, " there is a feature of the subject which might be expected ultimately to impress itself upon his imagination. The one idea which would slowly take possession of his mind would be that, underneath all this vast series of phenomena with which he was confronted, he beheld man in some way in conflict with his own reason. . . . It would be perceived that it was these forms of religious belief which had supplied the motive power in an extraordinary struggle which man had apparently carried on throughout his whole career against forces set in motion by his own mind—a struggle, grim, desperate, and tragic, which would stand out as one of the most pronounced features of his history" (p. 98). It is, in fact, man's religion that has supplied the antidote to his reason, and given him a sanction for social conduct. " One of the most remarkable features which the observer could not fail to notice in connection with these religions would be, that under their influence man would seem to be possessed of an instinct, the like of which he would not encounter anywhere else. This instinct, under all its forms, would be seen to have one invariable characteristic. Moved by it, man would appear to be always possessed by the desire to set up sanctions for his individual conduct, which would appear to be *super*-natural against those which were natural, sanctions which would appear to be *ultra*-rational against those which were simply rational. Everywhere he would find him clinging with the most extraordinary persistence to ideas and ideals which regulated his life under the influence of these religions, and ruthlessly punishing all those who endeavoured to convince him that these conceptions were without foundation in fact. At many periods in human history also he would have to observe that the opinion had been entertained by considerable numbers of persons, that a point had at length been reached at which it was only a question of time, until human reason finally dispelled the belief in those unseen powers which man held in control over himself. But he would find this anticipation never realised. Dislodged from one position, the human mind, he would observe, had only taken up another of the same kind, which it continued once more to hold with the same unreasoning, dogged and desperate persistence" (p. 99). And Mr. Kidd lays renewed stress on the fact that man's religious beliefs are in opposition to his reason. "The one fact which stands out clear above it all is that the forces against which man is engaged throughout the whole course of the resulting struggle are none other than those enlisted against him by his reason. . . . Throughout all the centuries in which history has him in view, we witness him driven by a profound instinct which finds expression in his religions unmistakably recognising a hostile force of some kind in his own reason" (p. 103).

The fifth chapter, "The Function of Religious Beliefs in the Evolution of Society," develops the theme of the fourth, with, of course, the usual "damnable iteration". "The pregnant question with which we found ourselves confronted was, therefore: What has then become of human reason? It would appear that the answer has, in effect, been given. The central feature of human history, the meaning of which neither science nor philosophy has hitherto fully recognised, is apparently the struggle which man, throughout the whole period of his social development, has carried on to effect the subordination of his own reason. The motive power in this struggle has undoubtedly been supplied by his religious beliefs. The conclusion towards which we seem to be carried is, therefore, that the function of these beliefs in human evolution must be to provide a *super-rational* sanction for that large class of conduct in the individual, necessary to the maintenance of the development which is proceeding, but for which there can never be, in the nature of things, any *rational* sanction" (pp. 107-108).

It necessarily follows that "there can never be . . . such

a thing as a rational religion. The essential element in all religious beliefs must apparently be the *ultra*-rational sanction which they provide for social conduct. When the fundamental nature of the problem involved in our social evolution is understood, it must become clear that that general instinct which may be distinguished in the minds of men around us is in the main correct, and that :—

"*No form of belief is capable of functioning as a religion in the evolution of society which does not provide an ultra-rational sanction for social conduct in the individual.*

" In other words :—

"*A rational religion is a scientific impossibility, representing from the nature of the case an inherent contradiction of terms*" (p. 109).

So that all previous theories of social evolution have gone astray. "The social system which constitutes an organic growth, endowed with a definite principle of life, and unfolding itself in obedience to laws which may be made the subject of exact study, is something quite different from that we have hitherto had vaguely in mind. It is not the political organisation of which we form part ; it is not the race to which we belong ; it is not even the whole human family in process of evolution. It would appear that *the organic growth endowed with a definite principle of life, and unfolding itself in obedience to law, is the social system or type of civilisation founded on a form of religious belief. . . . Throughout the existence of this system there is maintained within it a conflict of two opposing forces ; the disintegrating principle represented by the rational self-assertiveness of the individual units ; the integrating principle represented by a religious belief providing a sanction for social conduct which is always of necessity ultra-rational, and the function of which is to secure in the stress of evolution the continual subordination of the interests of the individual units to the larger interests of the longer-lived social organism to which they belong.* It is, it would appear, primarily through these social systems that natural selection must reach and act upon the race. It is from the ethical systems upon which they are founded that the resulting types of civilisation receive those specific characteristics which, in the struggle for existence, influence in a preponderating degree the peoples affected by them. It is in these ethical systems, founded on super-rational sanctions, and in the developments which they undergo, that we have the seat of a vast series of vital phenomena unfolding themselves under the control of definite laws which may be made the subject of study. The scientific investigation of these phenomena is capable, as we shall see, of throwing a flood of light not only upon the life-history of our Western civilisation in general, but upon the nature of the developmental forces underlying the complex social and political movements actually in progress in the world around us" (pp. 110, 111).

The rest of the chapter is devoted to proving that at all times and in all places the sanctions for conduct have always been ultra-rational; and Mr. Kidd proposes, in his next chapter, to apply to the history of Western civilisation this new conception of sociology. "If it is in the ethical system upon which a social type is founded that we have the seat of a vast series of vital phenomena unfolding themselves in obedience to law, then we must be able to investigate the phenomena of the past and to observe the tendencies of the current time with more profit than the study of either history or sociology has hitherto afforded. Let us see, therefore, with what prospect of success the biologist, who has carried the principles of his science so far into human society, may now address himself to the consideration of the history of that process of life in the midst of which we are living, and which we know under the name of Western civilisation" (p. 127). We will postpone, however, this fascinating excursion under the personal guidance of Mr. Kidd, until we have seen what his guidance is worth. Before going on to consider the application of his new principle to history, let us see what element of truth, if any, there is in the principle itself.

CHAPTER II.

WHEN we read, upon an early page of Mr. Kidd's book, that "the general mind, *so often more scientific than our current science, seems to feel* that there is something wrong in the attitude of science towards the subject of religion," we begin to be suspicious that we are in the presence of a mind inherently deficient in every quality that goes to make an accurate reasoner. Such a sentence as this defines at once the intellectual type; and it is an easy matter to foresee the manner in which Mr. Kidd will afterwards come to deal with the questions of religion and science, of natural selection and evolution, of progress and its cause, of the individual and society. It is evident that in every argument he brings forward he will stumble over some very simple verbal fallacies, that he will misunderstand the meaning of the words he is using, and that he will contradict and stultify himself at every turn.

So that we are not surprised, at the outset, to find him discussing the relations of science and religion in the old sweet way of the Christian Evidence advocate. He is not above referring to "the aggressive and merely destructive form of unbelief which finds expression in England in opinions like those of the late Charles Bradlaugh, and in America in the writings and addresses of Colonel Ingersoll" (p. 17). If he knew anything of the ideas of the men whose names he uses with such glib impertinence, he would know that Mr. Bradlaugh's work was constructive in the highest degree; and if he had the smallest glimmer of the faculty of self-criticism he would not fall into the vulgar fallacy of calling any new ideas " aggressive and merely destructive ". I will not waste time in showing the inanity of the current phrase " merely destructive," nor do more than point out that a " destructive " attack on a doctrine is really " constructive," in that it aims at substituting a new and presumably more correct doctrine for that which it attacks. There is little need to call attention to these very obvious points, for they are now recognised by all minds but those of the type of Mr. Kidd's. I would rather call Mr. Kidd's attention to the fact that the impertinence of his use of the word " aggressive " is equalled only by its inappropriateness. If ever there was a book which might with justice be called aggressive, it is surely his own, attacking as it does the whole received doctrine of evolution, and endeavouring to prove that all former concepts of evolution and of history are wrong. If this is not " aggressiveness " it is difficult to say what deserves that title ; and a mind of any alertness, engaged upon such a book as this, would at once have seen the absurdity of making any allusion to the " aggressive " opinions of others.

There would be little use in detaining the reader over such a trifling point as this but for the fact that it reveals, as I have said, the intellectual type. It prepares us for much that follows ; for wherever Mr. Kidd goes wrong, the error is of the same primitive kind and springs from the same primitive inability to analyse the connotations of the most ordinary words. Of this kind is his fallacy about the nature and function of religion, and its relation to science and to civilisation. And as Mr. Kidd's errors here are part and parcel of his whole argument, it is worth while to follow him somewhat more closely than the threadbare theme would otherwise warrant. A single sentence will serve the dual purpose of showing the drift of his argument and of exhibiting the congenital laxity of his mind. "The time is certainly not far distant," he writes, "when she (*i.e.* science) must look back with surprise, if not, indeed, with some degree of shamefacedness, to the attitude in which she has for long addressed herself to one of the highest problems in the history of life" (p. 19); *i.e.*, to religion and the "function" of religion in the evolution of mankind. And he goes on to argue that "she," *i.e.* science, has always been more unfair to religion than to any other mental or social phenomenon: "We live at a time when science counts nothing insignificant. She has recognised that every organ and every rudimentary organ has its utilitarian history. Every phase and attribute of life has its meaning in her eyes; nothing has come into existence by chance. What then are these religious systems which fill such a commanding place in man's life and history? What is their meaning and function in social development? To ask these questions is to find that a strange silence has fallen upon science. She has no answer. Her attitude towards them has been curious in the extreme, and widely different from that in which she has regarded any other of the phenomena of life. From an early stage in her career we find that she has been engaged in a personal quarrel with these religions, which has developed into a bitter feud. In any other circumstances it would probably have occurred to science at the outset to ask whether this struggle had not itself some meaning, and whether it was not connected with some deep-seated law of social development which it would be her duty to investigate. But this aspect of the position seems hitherto to have received scarcely any attention. These religions of man form one of the most striking and persistent of the phenomena of life when encountered under its highest forms, namely, in human society. Yet, strange to say, science seems to have taken up, and to have maintained, down to the present time, the extraordinary position that her only concern with them is to declare (often, it must be confessed, with the heat and bitterness of a partisan) that they were without any foundation in reason" (pp. 20-21).

To see the futility of writing of this kind, we have only to reverse the terms of Mr. Kidd's denunciation. Anybody might say of religion, if he were foolish enough, just what Mr. Kidd has said of science. "From an early stage in her career," we might write, "we find that religion has been engaged in a personal quarrel with science, which has developed into a bitter feud." We might say that religion should have asked "at the outset whether this struggle had not itself some meaning, and whether it was not connected with some deep-seated law of social development". We might say that science was one of the most striking and persistent of the phenomena of social life, and that all that religion has done up to the present has been to oppose science with "all the heat and bitterness of a partisan". To do this would simply be to philosophise in the manner of Mr. Kidd, and would be finally as fruitless as his own laborious demonstrations. He is very emphatic, throughout his book, on the need of the question of social evolution being taken up by really scientific minds; and on the very next page to that from which I have just quoted, he lays it down that "to *any one who has caught the spirit of Darwinian science*, it is evident that this is not the question at issue at all". As if any one with a scientific mind could talk as Mr. Kidd talks of religion and science! As a matter of fact, science—the "she" of Mr. Kidd's demonstration—has never maintained any attitude whatever towards religion, for the simple reason that science is not an entity, and cannot preserve an attitude towards anything. What Mr. Kidd is confusedly driving at is that there has always been an antagonism between men of science and men of religion; but that is a very different thing from saying that "science" has behaved with "the heat and bitterness of a partisan" towards "religion". We may say in popular language that science and religion are naturally antagonistic, just as we may say that arithmetic and bankruptcy through bad book-keeping are naturally antagonistic; but to speak in that way is merely to use a convenient formula, and no thinker would dream of basing an argument upon terms employed so loosely as this. When we come to discuss the question seriously, we have to guard ourselves against the ambiguities of words, and to state our proposition accurately. Stating it thus, we see that between the spirit represented by the religious man, which tends to repose upon tradition or a supposed revelation, and to decry human reason, and the spirit represented by the scientific man, which tends to think out all questions afresh, there always has been and always will be an antagonism. Whether the scientific men have been right or wrong has nothing to do with the matter; it still remains that Mr. Kidd is hopelessly confused when he speaks of the invariable attitude of "science" towards "religion," and that when he speaks of science looking back "with surprise, if not, indeed, with some degree of shamefacedness," to her former dealings with religion, he becomes simply absurd. Yet it is the man who is capable of philosophising in this juvenile manner who undertakes to rewrite for us the inner meaning of history, and to lay the foundations of the truly scientific theory of social evolution!

The fallacies thicken as we read. Mr. Kidd prides himself on his astuteness in perceiving that religions must have some "function" to perform in evolution, because they are among "the most striking and persistent of the phenomena of life". He does not perceive, however, that in the very terms of his own argument, unbelief, as he would call it, is equally justified by evolution. Religion itself is not a more noticeable element in human history than scepticism; and wherever we find a community most of whose members profess a certain form of religious belief, we also find some who do not share that belief. Scepticism has dogged the footsteps of religion from time immemorial, and yet, in the eyes of this founder of a new sociology, it is religion alone that forms "one of the most striking and persistent of the phenomena of life"; while unbelief is something with which, apparently, nature and evolution have had nothing to do, and which has sprung into existence through the wickedness and ignorance of men. If, as Mr. Kidd says, "we live at a time when science counts nothing insignificant," his own science might surely warn him that the persistence of the scientific attack on religion is just as universal and just as "significant" as religion itself; and if, as he writes again, "no one who approaches the subject with an unbiassed mind in the spirit of modern evolutionary science, can for a moment doubt that the beliefs represented must have some immense utilitarian function to perform in the evolution which is proceeding" (p. 23), then the utilitarian function of scepticism ought to be equally apparent to him. If nature has made the one she has made the other; it is only with Mr. Kidd that the one and not the other has "some immense utilitarian function to perform"; only with Mr. Kidd is it a case of heads, belief wins—tails, unbelief loses.

This grotesque misconception at once of religion and science appears once more when he alleges that science declares religious beliefs "to be without any foundation in reason". "From the beginning," he says, "science finds him [*i.e.*, man] under the sway of forces *new to her*, and with one of the strongest of these forces *she herself at a very early stage comes into conflict.* He holds beliefs which she asserts *have no foundation in reason;* and his actions are controlled by *strange sanctions which she does not acknowledge*" (pp. 19-20). If science ever asserted that religious beliefs had no foundation in reason, "she," as Mr. Kidd calls it, was arguing as loosely as Mr. Kidd himself; but we cannot believe so badly of science. Certainly no scientific man would ever lay it down that religious beliefs were not founded on reason; he would say, on the contrary, that they were in reality based upon reason, but upon an inaccurate and confused process of reason. He might call religion irrational, as Mr. Kidd repeatedly does, but in so doing he would be merely using that word in its popular sense; he would simply mean, for example, that the belief in the Immaculate Conception is so absurd as to be irrational in comparison with other and saner beliefs. But he would never blunder so egregiously as Mr. Kidd, and argue that religious beliefs were in no sense based on reason. He would never bring himself to set down in cold print such sentences as these:—

" . . . this extraordinary instinct which had thus driven successive generations of men to carry on such a prolonged and desperate struggle against forces set in motion by their own intellect" (p. 92).

" . . . the conflict . . . waged between these religions and the forces set in motion by human reason" (p. 93).

" . . . underneath all this vast series of phenomena . . . he beheld man in some way *in conflict with his own reason*" (p. 98).

" . . . it was these forms of religious belief which had supplied the motive power in an extraordinary struggle which man had apparently carried on throughout his whole career *against forces set in motion by his own mind*" (p. 98).

"The one fact which stands out clear above it all is that the forces against which man is engaged throughout the whole course of the resulting struggle are none other than *those enlisted against him by his reason*" (p. 103).

"Throughout all the centuries in which history has him in view, we witness him driven by *a profound instinct* which finds expression in his religions, unmistakably *recognising a hostile force of some kind in his own reason*" (p. 103).

"The central feature of human history, the meaning of

which neither science nor philosophy has hitherto fully recognised, is apparently the struggle which man, throughout the whole period of his social development, has carried on *to effect the subordination of his own reason.* The motive power in this struggle has undoubtedly been supplied by his religious beliefs" (pp. 107, 108).

It surely is hardly necessary to point out in further detail the absurdity of Mr. Kidd's application of the term "irrational" to religious beliefs. The smallest acquaintance with psychology would have shown him the folly of importing the old distinction between "instinct" and "reason" into a philosophical discussion such as this. If it is instinct that makes the religious man believe in his religion, then it is equally instinct that prompts the unbeliever to demolish the superstition; and if it is by reason that unbelief is maintained, it is none the less true that religious beliefs themselves are based upon reason. If a man does not believe in the existence of a Deity, that, according to Mr. Kidd, is due to the operation of his reason; if, however, he does believe in the existence of a Deity, that is due to an "instinct" which "recognises a hostile force of some kind in his own reason". As if the believer did not justify his belief by reason! If he believes in a God, it is because he reasons from natural phenomena to a supposed creator of them; if he believes in a future life, it is because he imagines he has some reasons for holding that the mind does not perish with the body. In neither of these cases can the belief be said to be irrational in the strict sense of the word; it is really rational, only imperfectly so. Mr. Kidd's fallacy arises from the common error of setting up "ideas" as opposed to "feelings"—the error into which Comte fell, and into which Mr. Spencer has so strangely followed him at times, losing sight of his own demonstration as to the real relations of feelings and ideas. The latter are, in the strict psychological sense, compounded out of feelings and instincts; and most of the conceptions by which our daily life is regulated are an amalgam of the three. But scientifically speaking, there is no point at which it can be said that feeling or instinct ceases and reason takes its rise; and Mr. Kidd's wholesale ascription of religion to "instinct" and of scepticism to "reason" is merely a piece of pre-scientific blundering. It bears, however, upon his whole book. To prove his main thesis at all he has to assume that while science is rational, religion is irrational; and the quality of the superstructure can be fairly well anticipated from the quality of the foundation. What the foundation is we have already seen; let us now view the superstructure. We have seen (1) that Mr. Kidd is hopelessly unscientific in the use of popular words, though all the time he is dinning it into our ears that he is the pioneer of a new science; (2) that he has no conception of the strictness necessary in the use of popular terms when a philosophical argument is in question; (3) that he misapprehends the historical relations of science and religion; (4) that he is capable of the most primitive psychological confusions, as shown in his remarks that religious beliefs are irrational, that they depend upon instinct, and that this instinct sets man "in conflict with his own reason". Such is the quality of mind, and such the attainments, of the man who tells us that there is as yet no science of sociology, and who himself undertakes to throw "a flood of light not only upon the life-history of our Western civilisation in general, but upon the nature of the developmental forces underlying the complex social and political movements actually in progress in the world around us" (p. 111). Let us follow our new guide, and see what are the wonders he is going to reveal to us.

CHAPTER III.

WE are all familiar by this time with the account given by modern science of the evolution of life upon this globe. No one now disputes the main facts of the evolutionary theory, that all organisms tend to reproduce in excess of the means of subsistence, and that some are consequently crowded out of life ; that the favoured survivors leave offspring resembling themselves, and possessing those characters that led to their survival ; and that this process has gone on through all the forms of life from time immemorial. Mr. Kidd tells us all this once more, and then draws the conclusion that since progress has been achieved by natural selection and rejection in the past, it must be achieved in the same manner in the future. He does not pause, be it observed, to define progress ; Mr. Kidd is above such small considerations as defining his words. But if he had observed this trifling preliminary he would have discovered (1) that his argument about progress is a mere *circulus in probando*, and (2) that his forecast of the future is as erroneous as his reading of the past. Let us address ourselves to his argument in detail.

Progress, presumably, means the constant survival of the fittest. This is apparent from Mr. Kidd's own words : " From time to time we find the question discussed by many who only imperfectly understood the conditions to which life is subject, as to whether progress is worth the price paid for it. But we have really no choice in the matter. Progress is a necessity from which there is simply no escape, and from which there has never been any escape since the beginning of life. Looking back through the history of life anterior to man, we find it to be a record of ceaseless progress on the one hand and ceaseless stress and competition on the other" (pp. 37, 38). Progress, then, is equivalent to the constant survival of the fittest. But progress, as distinguished from mere change, signifies a change for the better; so that when Mr. Kidd speaks of natural selection as leading to progress, he means that it leads to better forms of life. The question then arises, Better for what? What is the standard? It is evident that organism A is "better" than organism B simply because A survives while B is crowded out of life. But why is it better? Only *because* it survives. No other standard is possible. So that "better" really = more fitted to survive; "the survival of the fittest" simply = survival of the fittest to survive; and progress is simply the name for this. In other words, to speak of "progress" in organic nature is to beg the question of a standard of merit or value. Such a standard, from the very nature of things, can never be found; so that it is illegitimate to speak of evolution as a "progress" if by that word we mean "improvement". All we can scientifically assert of nature is that it is constantly changing. Mr. Kidd agrees that there is ceaseless competition among organic forces; that is, the environment is constantly acting upon the organism. In all except the highest forms of life, which can mould their own surroundings to a certain extent, the character of the environment must determine the character of the organism. If it is capable of such reaction in response to the new stimulus as will enable it to live in harmony with the changed conditions, it will survive; if it is incapable of so reacting, it will perish. But organisms being in excess of the means of subsistence, and there being innumerable slight differences between the members of the same species, it is clear that some *must* perish and some *must* survive. This does not argue any inherent "superiority," in Mr. Kidd's sense of the word, in those that survive, because the word "superiority" has here no ethical meaning; it simply implies that a given environment *selects*, so to speak, certain forms and rejects others. Since, then, an organism is called "better" merely because it survives, and since the chance of survival depends upon the environment, it is evident that progress would be a term *equally applicable to environments as well as organisms, if there were any sense in applying it to either.* The upshot of it all is that Mr. Kidd has made an initial blunder in not examining the philosophical meaning of the word "progress," and that the whole of his future argument as to there being no rational sanction for progress, and as to the functions of religious beliefs in bringing about progress, must be held to be damaged from the beginning. To tell us, as he does, that we must do certain things in order to keep progress going—no matter what it is he tells us to do—is simply to lose sight of his own previous words that " we have really no choice in the matter. *Progress is a necessity from which there is simply no escape.*" If that be so, what is the object of Mr. Kidd's book? If there *must* be progress, whether we like it or not, and whatever we do or do not do, why should Mr. Kidd be so painfully anxious to prove that we must preserve our old irrational religion, because progress depends upon irrational beliefs, and not upon reason? Even on so fundamental a question as this—fundamental, that is, for his own book—he cannot refrain from the grossest and most palpable self-contradiction. But for once he is right with one of his propositions, though it is not the one with which his argument is concerned. There will always be progress, for the simple reason that "progress" means nothing more than the survival of some organisms and the death of others.

All this, indeed, is evident from Mr. Kidd's own words—or would be evident to anybody but Mr. Kidd. "The progress of savage man, such as it is, is born strictly of the conditions in which he lives. Aimless as his history might seem when viewed from the level on which it is enacted, there can be no doubt of the progress made. But as to the nature of the progress there can also be no mistake. It is at once both inevitable and involuntary, the product of the strenuous conditions under which he lives" (p. 45). What is this but to admit that "progress" has no other meaning than that certain things that *must* happen *do* happen? We cannot pronounce the new state of things to be better than any other state, because we have no possible standard of comparison apart from our own minds; and our own minds, being products of this development, are therefore incapable of interpreting "better" in any other terms than those which lead to *our* survival. It only needs, in order to realise this, to imagine the course of evolution to have gone differently, owing to some enormous change in the physical environment. After many thousands of centuries we should have had the Mr. Kidd of those days looking back upon the past, seeing that organisms had been compelled to adapt themselves to their environment or else perish, and informing the world that evolution, *i.e.*, that particular evolution, meant constant progress. All that evolution means, however, is constant change; the survival of the fittest is not the survival of the "best," but simply of the fittest to survive. And let us suppose for a moment that Mr. Kidd's arguments up to this point have been correct; and let us further grant him his point that reason is inimical to progress, and that if we give up our irrational religious beliefs progress will come to an end. We may grant him all this, and yet it remains that his conception of progress as improvement is altogether unscientific. The contest now, be it observed, is between what we will, from courtesy, call the correct ideas of Mr. Kidd and the wrong ideas of rationalists. Suppose the latter to prevail, and to win ever more and more adherents.

What does this signify, on Mr. Kidd's own terms? Simply that since they survive while *his* ideas perish, they are therefore the better, and their survival = progress. Whether they may be philosophically right or wrong does not matter. The point is that they survive; they have been selected and his ideas rejected, and, on his own terms, this constitutes the survival of the fittest, and therefore progress. His doctrine is not even consistent with itself.

CHAPTER IV.

THE next point that calls for discussion is Mr. Kidd's assertion that "there is no rational sanction for the conditions of progress". Two new forces have made their appearance with man—"his reason and the capacity for acting, under its influence, in concert with his fellows in society". Further, "as man can only reach his highest development and employ his powers to the fullest extent in society, it follows that in the evolution which we witness him undergoing throughout history, his development as an individual is necessarily of less importance than his development as a social creature. In other words, although his interests as an individual may remain all-important to himself, it has become inevitable that they must henceforward be subordinated—whether he be conscious of it or not—to those larger social interests with which the forces that are shaping his development have now begun to operate" (pp. 64, 65).

This is a passage typical of all the defects of Mr. Kidd's mind. When he said (p. 38) that "every part, organ, or quality of these plants which calls forth admiration for its beauty or perfection . . . *has been acquired to ensure success*" in the struggle for life, we recognised at once that Mr. Kidd was addicted to those remnants of the old teleology that have survived the shock of the Darwinian theory. To speak of organs having been acquired *in order* to ensure success in the struggle for life is obviously to read nature backwards; it is not that the organs have been acquired *for* this purpose, but that when they *have* been acquired they have ensured success in the competition of life ; and the question of *how* they were produced remains still open. This is the manner in which Weismann reasons time after time ; and one can only surmise that it is a form of fallacy inseparable from the theistic mind, which runs naturally into teleological explanations even when apparently writing from the standpoint of science. But if this defect leads to such errors in an intellect like that of Weismann, the effects are still more dreadful in an intellect like that of Mr. Kidd, whose crude teleology is all the more amusing because of the talk, in the very next sentence to that quoted above, of "the evolutionist who endeavours to obtain a fundamental grasp of the problems which human society presents" —that model evolutionist, of course, being Mr. Kidd himself.

The argument now runs as follows : Progress has always and everywhere been the result of a struggle for existence, in which some have gained the victory and some have been worsened. Now " if it had been possible at any time for all the individuals of any form of life to have secured themselves against the competition of other forms, it would, beyond doubt, have been their interest to have suspended amongst themselves those onerous conditions which thus, by sacrificing the present welfare of individuals to the larger interests of their kind in the future, continually prevented large numbers of their kind from reaching the fullest possibilities of life. The conditions of progress, it is true, might have been suspended, but this could not have caused the present individuals any concern. The results would, in any case, only have been visible after a prolonged period, and they could not, therefore, be expected to have appeared to the existing members as of any importance when weighed against their own interests in the present" (pp. 66-67). And looking at man at the stage of evolution to which he has now arrived, we find him "differing in one most important respect from all that have gone before him. He is endowed with reason." And now " it would seem that a conclusion, strange and unexpected, but apparently unavoidable, must present itself. If the theories of evolutionary science have been, so far, correct, then this new factor which has been born into the world (!) must, it would appear, have the effect of ultimately staying all further progress." The reason is, that "his interests as an individual have, in fact, become further subordinated to those of a social organism, with interests immensely wider, and a life indefinitely longer than his own. How is the possession of reason ever to be rendered compatible with the will to submit to conditions of existence so onerous, requiring the effective and continual subordination of the individual's welfare to the progress of a development in which he can have no personal interest whatever?" (p. 69).

The object of all this, of course, is to lead up to the demonstration that (1) progress has not been due to a rational but to an irrational factor, and (2) that the essence of religion being irrationalism, it is religion that has really kept progress going in human societies. Now Mr. Kidd's inherent confusion of terms is apparent at the outset of his argument. " Natural selection," he practically says, " aims at the survival of the fittest, *i.e.*, progress. But this force is really antagonistic to the interests of man as he conceives them by the light of his reason. If then his reason were the main factor in evolution, he would resist natural selection, and sacrifice the future of the race to his own present." That is, Mr. Kidd conceives " natural selection " to be a " force " acting upon man against his own interests. In reality, however, the strife of evolution is not between man and natural selection, but between men themselves, and *natural selection is only the name for the result of this conflict.* Mr. Kidd's conception of the case is equivalent to saying that when a theatre is on fire, and every one rushes for the door, the balance of those who survive and those who are killed acts as an impelling "force" upon the audience. The real struggle is between man and man inside the theatre, and the balance of living and dead bodies, when all is over, is just the summing up of the result of the struggle. Mr. Kidd, in fact, in setting up "natural selection" as a force acting in one direction, and "human reason" as a force acting in another direction, is simply exhibiting once more that inherent clumsiness of mind that will always unfit him for good work in any department that requires a nice discrimination between the meanings of words, and a careful watch upon the fallacies that underlie the use of concrete terms in a purely abstract manner. He conceives man—"or the masses," as he sometimes puts it—acted upon by "natural selection" on the one side, and upon the other side by "reason," the former "force" making for progress, the latter making against it. Now he himself has already told us (p. 62) that "from these strenuous conditions of rivalry the race as a whole is powerless to escape," and again, that the racial struggle results "from deep-seated physiological causes, *the operation of which we must always remain powerless to escape*" (p. 63). This, of course, is in direct and grotesque contradiction to his future thesis, that if man's reason were allowed full play, he would put an end to these "strenuous conditions of rivalry"; for (1) if he can put an end to them, Mr. Kidd's remark that we must *always* remain powerless to escape them is simply absurd; and (2) if we cannot put an end to them, if it is really the truth that we must always be unable to escape this struggle which makes for the desirable end called "progress," then the whole of Mr. Kidd's book is a mere superfluity, being a recommendation to us not to let our reason do what it is essentially incapable of doing, in order not to stop a natural course of evolution which cannot possibly be stopped. It seems, however, that Mr. Kidd is quite unconscious of this contradiction, and we must therefore take his third chapter to mean what it really says, *viz.*, that reason, if its dictates were followed by the masses, would sacrifice the future to the present, would put an end to the struggle for existence, and would thus check progress.

Now to any one who does not lump his philosophic terms together as Mr. Kidd is in the habit of doing, it is at once apparent that so far from reason being a force antagonistic to natural selection, it is in reality only one of the forces with which natural selection has to do; it is merely one of the great contending factors of evolution, *the final result of whose contest is known as "natural selection"*. If men perversely acted upon the dictates of reason, as Mr. Kidd hopes they will not do, this would simply be adding another to the already existing elements of the struggle, and "progress" would infallibly ensue, because the actual result could not be called by any other name. And, in the second place, Mr. Kidd is once more lumping terms that ought to be carefully discriminated when he talks of it being to the interest of men to "suspend the onerous conditions of existence". The question is, To the interest of which men? Mr. Kidd ingenuously supposes all men to be on the one side, "natural selection" on the other; the men are thinking of the present, "natural selection" is thinking of the future. But the simple fact is that there is no such symmetrical ranging of the battle as this. On the contrary, the struggle is really between men of the same society,—men of different views and different interests, whose rivalry is one of the factors of evolution. "If we ask ourselves, therefore," says Mr. Kidd, "what course it is the interests of the masses holding political power in our advanced societies to pursue from the standpoint of reason, it seems hardly possible to escape the conclusion that they should in self-interest put an immediate end to existing social conditions. . . . The interest of the masses in such societies appears, therefore, clearly to be to draw a ring fence round their borders; to abolish competition within the community; to suspend the onerous rivalry of individuals which presses so severely on all; to organise, on socialistic principles, the means of production; and lastly, and above all, to regulate the population so as to keep it always proportional to the means of comfortable existence for all. In a word, to put an end to those conditions which the evolutionist [save the mark!] perceives to be inevitably and necessarily associated with progress now, and to have been so associated with it, not only from the beginning of human society, but from the beginning of life" (pp. 80-81). That is, Mr. Kidd assumes that all "the masses," if they began to think about these things, would be of one mind on the question. The notorious fact is that they are not so, and to talk as if "reason" would suggest to "the masses" the desirability of doing the things Mr. Kidd has just suggested, is to forget (1) that "the masses" do not acquiesce in the present social system because they have not reasoned about it and because a force unknown to them is carrying them on, but because a great many of them see, *by means of reason*, that their very existence depends on the existence of society, while many of them reason about the matter enough, but are restrained from unsocial action by a sense of impotence; and (2) that the argument that "self-interest" would prompt the masses to fly in the face of social conditions ignores the fact that it is actually self-interest on the part of the "classes" that has made and keeps our social conditions what they are; *i.e.*, there is no such contest as Mr. Kidd imagines, between the rational self-interest of man on the one side and the irrational forces of natural selection on the other, but that society is shaped by the contending self-interests of individuals, the biological name for the result of this contest being what is unphilosophically called "progress". Mr. Kidd's confusion is further shown in his remark (p. 84) that "the interests of the individual and those of the social organism to which he belongs are not identical ". The absurdity of speaking of individuals and the social organism as opposing entities, the interests of which are in conflict, and the absurdity of speaking of *the* individual as being pitted against the social organism, in face of the facts that there is no such thing as *the* individual, but simply individuals of varying interests and motives, and that each individual in turn, along with all the rest but one, forms the environment to that one, and so on *ad infinitum*[1]—these absurdities are so patent to any one who reflects upon the meaning of the terms which Mr. Kidd flings about in such gay irresponsibility, that it is unnecessary to labour the point any further. It is only necessary to mention what will frequently have to be mentioned in this examination—that Mr. Kidd's whole book is a practical demonstration of the fatuity of his own arguments. When he states that the interests, *i.e.*, the reason, of individuals are antagonistic to "the forces which are working out our development," he forgets that reason is just one of these forces. Then either his own book is powerless to affect the course of evolution, in which case he might have saved himself the trouble of writing it and us the trouble of reading it, or else it *is* able by its reasoning to affect the course of evolution, in which case Mr. Kidd has simply committed philosophic suicide. If, as he states (p. 86), "all

[1] Mr. Kidd remarks on the next page (84) that "if the interests of a progressive society as a whole, and those of the individuals at any time comprising it, are innately irreconcilable, it is evident," etc. What *are* the interests of a "society," as distinct from the interests of the individuals composing it, Mr. Kidd would probably find a difficulty in saying. The cause of his confusion here is, however, quite apparent. He has been speaking of the interests of the individual as being opposed to "the forces which are working out our development" (pp. 68, 83, etc.); but this abstract antagonism being insufficient for the purposes of his argument, he has, perhaps unconsciously, transformed it into a more concrete antagonism between the interests of "the individual" and those of "the social organism," never once pausing either to notice that he had changed the terms of his argument, or to ask himself what meaning, if any, those terms had.

methods and systems alike, which have endeavoured to find in the nature of things any universal rational sanction for individual conduct in a progressive society, must be ultimately fruitless," then the writing of his own book has been a trebly futile performance; for is not its avowed object to teach men the true principles of evolution, to prevent them checking over-population and the struggle for existence, and so to afford a "rational sanction" for this kind of individual conduct? And if he succeeds in doing this, if he succeeds in inducing men to be irrational, and to give in to natural selection in the old style, under the seductive influence of the reasoning of his own book, what is this but showing that reason is not only not antagonistic to progress, but is a very important factor in it?. And if he really thinks, as he says on page 75, that "men never have been, and are not now, influenced in the least by the opinion of scientists or any other class of persons, however wise, as to what the result of present conduct, apparently calculated to benefit themselves, may be on generations yet unborn," we may reply with the question whether men are influenced by "the opinions of scientists or any other class of persons" as to what the result of present conduct, apparently calculated *not* to benefit themselves, may be on generations yet unborn. If they are not so influenced, what can be the use of Mr. Kidd's book—placing him, for the sake of argument, among the "scientists or any other class of persons, however wise"? and if they are so influenced, then clearly reason is precisely that motive force in evolution which Mr. Kidd has been striving so laboriously to prove it is not. Either way his position is an absurdity.

CHAPTER V.

THE object of Mr. Kidd's third chapter has been to show that progress depends not upon a rational, but upon an irrational force. The object of the next two chapters, entitled respectively "The Central Feature of Human History" and "The Function of Religious Beliefs in the Evolution of Society," is to prove that this irrational force is religion, which alone can be relied upon to keep up the progress of the race. He finds what he rightly calls "the extraordinary spectacle of man, moved by a profound social instinct, continually endeavouring, in the interests of his social progress, to check and control the tendency of his own reason to suspend and reverse the conditions which are producing this progress". Here the humble inquirer may be tempted to ask: What is this "social instinct," and what is its purpose in evolution? Mr. Kidd's argument is that man's reason, concerned solely with the happiness of the individual and of the present moment, would stop progress if it were not for this "profound social instinct," which makes him play into the hands of evolution, so to speak, by acting irrationally. Then why is this social instinct a good one, and why should we be expected to bow down and worship it? And what are the "interests of social progress"? Either the "interests of social progress" means the happiness of mankind or not. If not, why should Mr. Kidd wish us to be so anxious about them? If yes, then what becomes of Mr. Kidd's contention that this irrational social instinct is necessary *in order to counteract the influence of reason, which would sacrifice progress to happiness?* For surely even Mr. Kidd, with all his passion for abstract biology, and all his confusion of terms, would not write an elaborate book merely to persuade men that they ought to sacrifice their own happiness of the moment for a purely abstract state of affairs which he calls "the interests of social progress". And on his own showing, be it observed, these "interests of social progress," which we are so sedulously to guard, are a mere chimæra. He himself has argued that evolution can never cease, that natural selection must always go on, and that the social misery attendant upon the process must therefore always continue. On these terms, then, the next generation will not be one whit the better for any self-abnegation on our part. If we check the foolish dictates of reason, that prompt us to put an end to the dreadful strife, and make the best of the world while we are in it, the next generation will simply be delivered over, bound hand and foot, to the tender mercies of natural selection; and if Mr. Kidd's advice is still acted on, generation after generation will be born into the same conditions of struggle and of misery. Then what, in the name of common sense, is Mr. Kidd's precept good for? Accepting his argument as true, does he seriously think men will calmly lie down to external natural selection in the future, as they have had to do in the past, and put up with perpetual misery, in order—not to alleviate the misery of any future race of men, but to keep "progress" going, to subserve some mysterious "interests of social progress," which are not the interests of any individual or any mass of individuals, but simply the abstract interests of an abstract process called "evolution," ending in an abstract result called "progress"? We are to refrain from eating our cake now, not in order that some one else may be able to eat it in the future, but in order that there may always be the abstract cake to be eaten by an abstract humanity in the future that never comes! This is the upshot of Mr. Kidd's brilliant argument about "social instincts".

The gist of these two chapters is, briefly, that religious beliefs have always existed among men, that they have been the central feature of history, that they are super-rational, that they thus provide a sanction for individual conduct which reason cannot provide, and that their function is thus to check the disintegrating influence of reason, and so to keep progress going. A few characteristic extracts, showing Mr. Kidd's conception of psychological processes, are worth quoting here (some of them for the second time), as illustrating the grossly unscientific way in which he sets about to prove a most important part of his theory.

". . . this extraordinary instinct which had thus driven successive generations of men to carry on such a prolonged and desperate struggle against forces set in motion by their own intellect" (p. 92).

". . . the conflict . . . waged between these religions and the forces set in motion by human reason" (p. 93).

Religious movements are "not only independent of, but in direct conflict with the intellectual forces" (p. 94).

"The one idea which would slowly take possession of his mind would be that, underneath all these vast series of phenomena with which he was confronted, he beheld man in some way in conflict with his own reason" (p. 98).

"The one fact which stands out clear above it all is that the forces against which man is engaged throughout the whole course of the resulting struggle are none other than those enlisted against him by his reason" (p. 103).

"Throughout all the centuries in which history has him in view, we witness him driven by a profound instinct which finds expression in his religions, unmistakably recognising a hostile force of some kind in his own reason" (p. 103).

"The central feature of human history, the meaning of

which neither science nor philosophy has hitherto fully recognised, is, apparently, the struggle which man, throughout the whole period of his social development, has carried on to effect the subordination of his own reason" (pp. 107, 108).

It would be discourteous to any reader's intelligence to deal in detail with such utterances as these, with their amateur psychology, their loose phrasing and their reiteration of a meaningless cant formula of which Mr. Kidd either cannot or will not see the futility. To any reader of average intelligence, indeed, the question must inevitably suggest itself: How can any man who is capable of philosophising in this primitive manner undertake, as Mr. Kidd has done, to lay afresh the whole foundations of sociological science, and to elucidate for us the whole past history of the human race? For Mr. Kidd's errors are not those of a great inquirer feeling his way darkly and painfully along a hitherto untrodden path. New as he thinks his theory is, it and his errors are simply the vulgar fallacies of the man in the street, stumbling over his own words, and building up elaborate edifices of argument on the sandy foundation of a mere misconception of his terms. Never once in the whole course of his inquiry has Mr. Kidd paused to inform his reader, or indeed himself, what he means by such words as "progress," "society," "social instinct," "reason," "super-rational," "ethical sanction"—words upon the precise definition of which his whole theory depends, and through whose confusion of meanings that theory becomes such a hodge-podge of wasted argument. Nowhere is it more important to define one's terms than in the case of words which are part of the every-day language of men, and which have consequently a score of meanings or shades of meaning enclosed within them. Phrases like "the social organism," for example, which are merely the rough-and-ready symbols of ordinary conversation, need to be defined with the most rigorous precision when they are made the basis of a sociological argument. Yet Mr. Kidd pursues his happy, ingenuous way among them, much as the proverbial bull pursued his way through the proverbial china-shop, and handles the most evasive philosophical terms much as a hodman might handle a delicate electrical instrument.

It has already been pointed out that Mr. Kidd, in speaking of religion as being one of the most universal and characteristic features of social evolution, ignores the fact that scepticism is no less universal and no less characteristic; and that the sociologist who attempts to build up a theory upon the one fact while ignoring the other, who regards the prevalence of religious beliefs as proving that they have some "function" to perform, while scepticism has no such function, is simply making argument a farce. Here we find Mr. Kidd conducting his thesis in a similar manner. He argues as if the "instinct"—convenient word!—that leads men to believe in religion were something universal, while all the time his very argument implies that a great number of the race do not possess this instinct. "Moved by it," he writes (p. 99), "man would appear to be always possessed by the desire to set up sanctions for his individual conduct, which would appear to be *super*-natural against those which were natural, sanctions which would appear to be *ultra*-rational against those which were simply rational." Now this, if it means anything, means that "man" holds these beliefs *quâ* man; that is, they are or ought to be the common property of all men. This seems to be the argument as Mr. Kidd originally intended it, a view of the case which is borne out by his next chapter, in which he tells us that, from the lowest savage to the most civilised races of the present, socially preservative actions have depended upon religious beliefs.[1] But even Mr. Kidd is bound to be aware that in every society there have been men who rejected

[1] See, for example, p. 115: "But if, on the one hand, we find primitive man thus everywhere under the sway of customs," etc.

the current religion; and so, in the very next sentence to that quoted above, he proceeds to get his argument into the customary tangle. "Everywhere he would find him clinging with the most extraordinary persistence to ideas and ideals which regulated his life under the influence of these religions, and ruthlessly punishing all those who endeavoured to convince him that these conceptions were without foundation in fact" (p. 99).

Thus calmly does Mr. Kidd sweep aside every tendency that makes against the symmetry of his theory. According to him, these persecuted beings and the opinions they represent have simply nothing whatever to do with evolution, which is apparently kept going entirely by those who hold the current religious beliefs. These justify the utility of their beliefs, and at the same time preserve the standard of morality intact (for Mr. Kidd informs us that he agrees with Mr. Lecky that utilitarian theories are "profoundly immoral"), by slaying and persecuting all who do not share the religious opinions of the majority,—which is quite a new light on ethics. "Man" holds the religious beliefs by instinct, and "he" (whoever "he" may be) persecutes those who do not agree with him. As Mr. Kidd goes on to remark, "At many periods in human history also, he would have to observe that the opinions had been entertained by considerable numbers of persons, that a point had at length been reached, at which it was only a question of time, until human reason finally dispelled the belief in those unseen powers which man held in control over himself (*sic*). But he would find this anticipation never realised. Dislodged from one position, *the human mind*,[1] he would observe, had only taken up another of the same kind, which it continued once more to hold with the same unreasoning, dogged and desperate persistence" (pp. 99, 100). Here Mr. Kidd has come to the length of denying to sceptics even

[1] Italics mine.

a human mind! Who it is does the dislodging, and what it is that is dislodged, is not quite clear. If "the human mind" will not give up its religious beliefs, whose minds are they that embrace scepticism? If sceptics exist, as Mr. Kidd admits, what does he mean by saying that the human mind will never give up its religious beliefs? And, crowning absurdity of all, if in spite of all attempts to dislodge the human mind from its fortress of super-rational beliefs, it only continues to hold this fortress with "unreasoning, dogged and desperate persistence," is not Mr. Kidd's book—the object of which is to make people stick to these beliefs—something of a superfluity, a generous but unnecessary helping of a machine that went on triumphantly for ages before Mr. Kidd's book was written, and will go on triumphantly for ages after it is forgotten? And once more, if Mr. Kidd holds that his book is not a superfluity, that by its reasoning it *may* induce people to be religious and so save "progress," then men are not helping out evolution by "the social instinct" and the rest of it, but by reason pure and simple, and Mr. Kidd's thesis about the disintegrating force of reason has gone the way of all absurdity.

It will be admitted that Mr. Kidd has here got his argument into a very pretty tangle. Satisfied with it, however—as is evident from his complacent remark that "there is not, it is believed, anything which is unreal or exaggerated in this view of one of the chief phases of human evolution,"—he proceeds to elucidate for us, in still closer detail, "the function of religious beliefs in the evolution of society". As was to be expected, he stumbles at the very beginning over that constant pitfall of the amateur sociologist—the false analogy between the life of the individual and the life of a society. He agrees with the historian,[1] "the popular imagination," and "public

---

[1] "It may be observed, too," he writes, "that this idea of the life, growth, and decline of peoples is deeply rooted. It is always present in the mind of the historian" (p. 106). *The historian* is characteristic of Mr. Kidd.

speakers and writers in the daily press,"—a sweet concourse of authorities!—that "social systems are endowed with a definite principle of life,"—which is hardly the sort of expression we would expect to hear from one who prides himself on his scientific intelligence. Gold, we presume, is similarly endowed with a definite principle of aureity, and water with a definite principle of aquosity. But Mr. Kidd, in that inexorable, lucid way of his, sets himself now to inform us what this "definite principle of life" really is. In his own words, he is going to "open up a new and almost unexplored territory". Premising that "*no form of belief is capable of functioning as a religion in the evolution of society which does not provide an ultra-rational sanction for social conduct in the individual*"; or "*in other words, a rational religion is a scientific impossibility, representing from the nature of the case an inherent contradiction of terms*" (pp. 109, 110), he proceeds thus: "We come, it would appear, in sight of the explanation why science, if social systems are organic growths, has hitherto failed to enunciate the laws of their development, and has accordingly left us almost entirely in the dark as to the nature of the developmental forces and tendencies at work beneath the varied and complex political and social phenomena of our time. The social system which constitutes an organic growth, endowed with a definite principle of life, and unfolding itself in obedience to laws which may be made the subject of exact study, is something quite different from that we have hitherto had vaguely in mind. It is not the political organisation of which we form part; it is not the race to which we belong; it is not even the whole human family in process of evolution. It would appear that: *The organic growth endowed with a definite principle of life, and unfolding itself in obedience to law, is the social system or type of civilisation founded on a form of religious belief.* It would also appear that it may be stated as a law that: *Throughout the existence of this system there is maintained within it a conflict of two opposing forces; the disintegrating principle represented by the rational self-assertiveness of the individual units; the integrating principle represented by a religious belief providing a sanction for social conduct which is always of necessity ultra-rational, and the function of which is to secure in the stress of evolution the continual subordination of the interests of the individual units to the larger interests of the longer-lived social organism to which they belong*" (pp. 110, 111).

Observe here the looseness and inexactitude of the phrasing, just where the argument ought to be expressed in the clearest and most rigid terms it is possible to find. We have "social systems" which are "organic growths," endowed with "a definite principle of life"; these social systems, again, are "founded" on a form of religious belief, and within them there is an "integrating principle" pulling one way, and a "disintegrating principle" pulling another way. Can any one seriously believe that the writer who is capable, at this time of the nineteenth century, of framing a proposition in this way, and then claiming that he is talking science where all other men have only talked vanity, is fit to do proper scientific work in any department whatever of human thought? These sentences, which are the very corner-stone of Mr. Kidd's book, are simply the merest shoddy, the pseudo-science of the half-educated curate instructing an evening class at a Y. M. C. A. Mr. Kidd's pet phrase is on a par with that of the man who should say that the individual is a system endowed with a definite principle of life, founded on a form of activity, and the scene of a conflict between two opposing forces,—a disintegrating principle tending to the discontinuance of life, and an integrating principle tending to its continuance. The hollowness of a proposition like this is seen when applied to an individual organism; it is only when it is applied to the "social organism" that its very emptiness gives it a factitious appearance of profundity, and earns for those who indulge in this style of verbosity the reputation of new and original thinkers on sociology.

The remainder of Mr. Kidd's fifth chapter is a monument of confusion of terms and fallacy of reasoning. He himself is apparently never conscious that he begins with the word "supernatural" as characteristic of religious beliefs, and afterwards uses his favourite word "ultra-rational" as if it bore precisely the same meaning. He has, of course, no difficulty in showing to his own satisfaction that all religions have originated in beliefs in the supernatural; but this is a very different matter from showing that these beliefs are ultra-rational. If a savage believes in the existence of ghosts, he does so because he has *reasons* for his beliefs; to repeat the argument that has already been used, he believes in ghosts not because he does not reason, but because he reasons badly. In the strict psychological sense his belief is founded as much on rational processes as the contrary belief that ghosts do not exist. Similarly, the belief of a Theist in the existence of a Supreme Being, the belief of a Christian in the Immaculate Conception, are beliefs in a supernatural, but are not ultra-rational beliefs. This is the simple distinction which Mr. Kidd is incapable of making; this is the primitive verbal confusion on which he has elected to build an important section of his argument. When he quotes his favourite Mr. Lecky to the effect that "all religions which have governed mankind have done so . . . by speaking, as common religious language describes it, to the heart," and not to the intellect, he is simply using the cant formulas of everyday life to prove a philosophical proposition. A little preliminary psychological analysis would show him that the distinction between "heart" and "head" is purely fanciful; that there are no beliefs springing from the one without any participation from the other; and that either the belief in a Deity is as "rational" as most of our beliefs, or the term "ultra-rational"—used as distinguishing the so-called instinctive perceptions from the so-called intellectual perceptions—must be applied to a vast number of everyday beliefs as well as those of religion. But it is characteristic of Mr. Kidd to base an important argument on a mere indistinctness of terms that any intelligent schoolboy could have made clear for him; and it is also characteristic of such a mind that it should tell us that " the deep-seated instincts of society have a truer scientific basis than our current science ". Once more, it is not from an intellect of this type that a revolution in sociology is to come. Further analysis of this chapter of Mr. Kidd's book is superfluous. " However these beliefs may differ from each other or from the religions of the past," he writes, " they have the one feature in common that they all assert uncompromisingly that the essential doctrines which they teach are beyond reason, that the rules of conduct which they enjoin have an ultra-rational sanction, and that right and wrong are right and wrong by divine or supernatural enactment outside of, and independent of, any other cause whatever" (pp. 122, 123). That religions have a *supernatural* element in them is sufficient proof for Mr. Kidd's accommodating mind that their codes of ethics are wholly *ultra-rational*. Of the " significance," as he would call it, of the fact that religious systems of ethics are so largely based upon intuitive theories, Mr. Kidd seems to have no scientific perception. He appears to know as little of the psychological and social genesis of moral sentiments, and theories of moral sentiments, as he does of biology or history or sociology. A quotation from that dubious authority, Mr. Lecky, a few primitive confusions of terms, and a comprehensive ignorance of the labours of hundreds of writers who have gone before him—these are sufficient for Mr. Kidd to build up a new theory in any department of human thought. No one, of course, quarrels with him for his imperfections of mind or temperament; but it is surely permissible for us to protest against his writing a book from the depths of these imperfections, against his complacent remarks that no previous writer has understood this or that problem of human evolution, and against his no less complacent references to himself as "the evolutionist," "the thinker who has caught the true spirit of evolutionary science," and the rest.

CHAPTER VI.

THIS, then, is the end of Mr. Kidd's introduction to his work. He has given us the theoretical bases; he now proceeds to apply these principles, and to elucidate the history of Western Europe by them. This is the purpose of his sixth and seventh chapters.

Briefly, his argument is this: our civilisation, "as a continuous growth," begins "its life-history" in "the early centuries of our era". That is, there is an immense difference between Greek and Roman and modern civilisation, and the latter begins with Christianity. The Roman world was everywhere decaying, until there came "the new force which was born into the world with the Christian religion" (p. 133). This "new force" was indeed a marvel among forces. "The original impetus was immense. The amorphous vigour of life was so great that several centuries have to pass away before any clear idea can be obtained of even the outlines of the growth which it was destined to build up out of the dead elements around it. From the beginning the constructive principle of life was unmistakable; men seemed to be transformed; the ordinary motives of the individual mind appeared to be extinguished. . . . Amid the corruption of the time the new life flourished as a thing apart; it took the disintegrated units and built them up into the new order, drawing strength from the decay which was in progress around it" (pp. 133, 134). And "we have to note also that the new force was in no way the product of reason or of the intellect. No impetus came from this quarter. As in all movements of the kind, the intellectual forces of the time were directly in opposition" (pp. 134, 135). This gigantic force carries all before it, until in the fourteenth century all Europe exhibits the spectacle of " the growth and development of a stupendous system of otherworldliness. The conflict against reason had been successful to a degree never before equalled in the history of the world. The super-rational sanction for conduct had attained a strength and universality unknown in the Roman and Greek civilisations" (p. 139).

Ignorant historians, who have not had the inestimable advantage of being taught their history by Mr. Kidd, are now admonished of their error in speaking of the dark ages as "a time of death and barrenness". This is "to totally misunderstand the nature of the movement we are dealing with. The period was barren only in the sense that every period of vigorous but immature growth is barren. The fruit was in the centuries to come. Science has yet scarcely learned to look at the question of our social evolution from any standpoint other than that of the rationalism of the individual; whereas, we undoubtedly have in these centuries a period in the lifetime of the social organism when the welfare, *not only of isolated individuals, but of all the individuals of a long series of generations*, was sacrificed to the larger interests of generations at a later and more mature stage" (p. 140). Now, " it will have been evident from the last chapter, if the conclusions there arrived at were correct, that we may state it as an historical law that: *The great problem with which every progressive society stands continually confronted is: How to retain the highest operative ultra-rational sanction for those onerous conditions of life which are essential to its progress; and at one and the same time to allow the freest play to those intellectual forces which, while tending to come into conflict with this sanction, contribute nevertheless to raise to the highest de-*

gree of social efficiency the whole of the members" (p. 141). These two desirable tendencies find full freedom in Christianity, or, as Mr. Kidd calls it in his scientific way, "the ethical system upon which our civilisation is founded". Ancient society was one of caste to a great extent, and wide altruistic and humanitarian sentiments were almost foreign to it. "As for any conception of duty or responsibility to others outside the community," says Mr. Kidd glibly of the Greek state, "it did not exist. Morality was of the narrowest and most egotistical kind. It never, among the Greeks, embraced any conception of humanity; no Greek, says George Henry Lewes, ever attained to the sublimity of such a point of view" (p. 145).

Under the conditions of life as they held in the Greek and Roman states there could never be any progress; this has been brought about by Christianity, which is possessed of a fund of altruistic feeling which has tended to make men equal, thus ensuring a greater stress of competition, and a consequently higher level of the race through natural selection. " Nothing can be more obvious, however, as soon as we begin to understand the nature of the process of evolution in progress around us, than that the moving force behind it is not the intellect, and that the development as a whole is not in any true sense an intellectual movement" (p. 157). The movement has really been super-rational, deriving its force from the Christian religion. This, as Mr. Kidd goes on to repeat, brought into Europe an altruistic ideal infinitely higher than any of which the world had previously had knowledge. It was, indeed, this excess of virtue that led to the persecution of the early Christians by the Roman state.[1]

---

[1] Mr. Kidd has achieved some good things in the comic writing of history, but he has nowhere surpassed these pages on the persecution of the early Christians. "What it is, however," he writes, " of the highest importance to note here is that it was those same altruistic ideals, which seem so altogether exemplary in our eyes, that filled the minds of the lower classes of the Roman population (who were not permeated with the intellectual scepticism of the

And since the time when Christianity came to itself, so to speak, and really began to do its proper work in society, it has been consistently helping evolution along. With its immense fund of altruistic feeling it abolished caste, it abolished slavery; it is always breaking down the power of the governing and wealthy classes, and strengthening the hands of the masses. Thus it is working towards the time when there shall be no social distinctions, when all shall be admitted to the struggle of life on terms of equality, when the competition will be fiercer and more strenuous, and when natural selection will have a really good opportunity of picking out the fittest and slaying the unfit, all in the cause of progress. And as the sanctions of Christianity are not rational but super-rational, our civilisation is built upon a super-rational basis. "The conception of the native equality of men which has played so great a part in the social development that has taken place in our civilisation is essentially irrational. It receives no sanction from reason or experience; it is the characteristic product of that ultra-rational system of ethics upon which our civilisation is founded" (p. 197).

Such is Mr. Kidd's summary of the history and the developmental tendencies of the Europe of the last twenty-five centuries. There is nothing new in it; new as he fondly imagines it to be, it is what we have heard for many a year past from the average Christian Evidence lecturer. One hardly knows what to be most surprised at in Mr. Kidd's exposition—the amazing historical and psychological ignor-

educated classes) with vague but deep-seated distrust and hatred of the new religion and its adherents. *The profound social instincts of the masses of the people—then, as nearly always, possessing a truer scientific basis than the merely intellectual insight of the educated classes*—recognised, in fact, in the new ideals which were moving the minds of men, a force, not only different in nature and potentiality to any of which the ancient world had previous experience, but one which was fundamentally antagonistic to the forces which had hitherto held together that organisation of society which had culminated in the Empire" (p. 162).

ance which it displays, or the audacity with which this schoolboy's composition is put forward as a philosophical account of the evolution of European society. Nowhere is Mr. Kidd's lack of adequate training for his task more noticeable than here. For his sweeping generalisation on the characteristics of pagan and Christian civilisation, he relies altogether on the precarious authorities of Mr. Froude, Mr. Lecky and Mr. Mahaffy, unconscious all the while of the logical defects of the first, and the hopelessly subversive contradictions of the second and the third. There is not a shred of evidence that Mr. Kidd has made any first-hand study of the ancient civilisations which he so glibly disparages, while there is every possible evidence to the contrary. What are the facts as to the humanitarian feelings in ancient Greece and Rome and Christian Europe? Mr. Kidd has told us, on the authority of Mr. Lecky's *History of European Morals*, that Christianity brought a new force into the world; that "the new religion evoked, to a degree before unexampled in the world, an enthusiastic devotion to its corporate welfare, analogous to that which the patriot bears to his country"; that "there sprang from it a stern, aggressive, and at the same time disciplined enthusiasm, wholly unlike any other that had been witnessed upon earth"; that "amid the corruption of the time the new life flourished as a thing apart"; that "there has probably never existed upon earth a community whose members were bound to one another by a deeper or purer affection than the Christians in the days of the persecution. Self seemed to be annihilated. The boundaries of classes and even of nationalities and of races went down before the new affinities, which overmastered the strongest instincts of men's minds;" that with Christianity "a spirit of utter self-abnegation had been born into the world"; that in ancient Greece, "as for any conception of duty or responsibility to others outside the community, it did not exist. Morality was of the narrowest and most egotistical kind. It never among the Greeks embraced any conception of humanity;" that the Christian movement "involved from its inception the very highest conception of the altruistic ideal to which the human mind has in any general sense ever obtained"; that "any impartial observer would describe the most distinctive virtue referred to in the New Testament as love, charity or philanthropy. It is the spirit of charity, pity and infinite compassion which breathes through the Gospels. The new religion was from the outset . . . a proclamation of the universal brotherhood of man;" that "the noble system of ethics, the affection which the members bore to each other, the devotion of all to the corporate welfare, the spirit of infinite tolerance for every weakness and inequality, the consequent tendency to the dissolution of social and class barriers of every kind, beginning with those between slave and master, and the presence everywhere of the feeling of actual brotherhood were the outward features of all the early Christian societies"; that "in the altruistic conceptions of Christianity all the bonds of race, nationality and class were dissolved"; that it proclaimed "the uncompromising doctrine of the innate equality of men"; that "compared with ours even the noblest Greek ethics were of the narrowest kind, and Greek morality, as already observed, at no period embraced any conception of humanity"; that "the two doctrines which contributed most to producing the extinction of slavery were the doctrine of salvation and the doctrine of the equality of all men before the Deity," and so on.

As to the beautiful characters of the early Christians, their love for each other, their devotion to the common welfare, let Mr. Lecky's own self-contradictory pages and the Pauline Epistles serve for answer. As to the proclamation of the brotherhood of man, which the Gospels are said to contain, does it require to be pointed out that the religion there proclaimed is an essentially exclusive one, granting salvation to those only who will believe in Jesus, and damning all the rest; that Jesus himself exhibited at times the narrowest sectarian spirit; that he made a distinction between the Jews and the Gentiles; that he expressly forbade his disciples on one occasion to preach the Gospel to the Gentiles and the Samaritans;[1] and that he threatened with the most dreadful punishment the cities that would not accept the teaching of twelve ignorant fishermen? As to the point about slavery, the writer who at this time of day can point to Christianity as the motive force in its abolition is almost past arguing with. "Mr. Kidd," writes one critic, "shows that he is aware that slavery has flourished down almost into our own times under the auspices . . . of an Anglo-Saxon community; but the knowledge has no effect on his sociology. As little is that affected by the knowledge he has presumably gathered from Mr. Lecky, that in the Christianised Roman empire, living under the flawlessly irrational creed of salvation, there were probably more slaves than under paganism, and not more manumissions. It is needless, therefore, to inquire whether he knows that the first decisive modern blow at slavery was dealt by the French Revolution, at a time when the Christian doctrine of salvation had nearly as little hold on the minds of those actively concerned as it has on the minds of French politicians to-day. In this case, perhaps, Mr. Kidd would withdraw the trump card of 'salvation' and play that of 'equality of all men before the Deity,' making out that the 'aggressive' Paine and the devout Robespierre in their different ways were thus after all satisfactorily irrational,

---

[1] I am well aware of the existence of the text commanding the disciples to go forth and teach all nations; but apart from any critical theories as to the date of this text, the Christian apologist obviously has to reconcile it with those mentioned above. If the character of the Gospel Jesus is a composite one, and his utterances contradictory, so much the worse for the Christian.

though Paine's fellow-deists in the United States were not irrational enough to take up his testimony against slavery."

And finally, as to the thesis that altruistic and humanitarian feelings, in their widest aspect, are purely outgrowths from Christianity, the slightest acquaintance with pagan literature would have shown Mr. Kidd that he was merely talking the vulgarest commonplaces of the vulgarest school of Christian apologists. He has stated that Greek morality never rose to a conception of humanity; and in a stricture of this kind he must of course be understood as including Roman morality in his condemnation, as his argument is that world-wide altruism is the specific product of Christianity. What, then, are the facts? The facts are that pagan literature is superior to the sacred Christian books in their precepts of this kind, just as the pagan moralists as a whole were superior to the early Christian writers in almost every quality of humanism, of serenity, of toleration; and that the very idea of the innate equality of all men, which Mr. Kidd so ignorantly ascribes to Christianity, was Stoic in its origin. Though the labouring of these points is simply the retelling of a thrice-told tale, I am constrained to give some evidence for them, selecting, as the most convenient and most concise summary, the comparison of pagan and Christian morality in Mr. J. A. Farrer's *Paganism and Christianity*:—

"To live as if he knew himself born for others," says Mr. Farrer, "has already been alluded to as one of the characteristics in Seneca's picture of the ideal Stoic; and his other references to the subject deserve attention. 'It is required of a man to be of benefit to man, to many if he can, failing that to a few, failing that to those nearest him, failing those to himself. No man can live happily who regards himself alone, who turns everything to his own advantage; it behoves you to live for another, if you would live for yourself.' And, comparing the Stoic with the Epicurean views of happiness, he says: 'Our pleasure is to benefit others, even at our own labour, provided we lighten the labour of others; or at our own peril, provided we save others from peril; or at our own loss of fortune, provided we alleviate the necessities and distresses of others'. . . . Aurelius, too, never wearies of reminding himself that man is by nature a rational and social animal, whose function and true work is to labour for his fellow-man, his fellow-kinsman, as the child of the same God. It is utterly false to say that this idea of the brotherhood of all men rests on the teaching of Christianity. It was one of the dominant ideas of philosophy, especially of Stoicism, long before the foundations of the Church were laid. Marcus Aurelius rises from the conception of the political community to that of the wider community of humanity with a breadth of spirit that at no time of her history has belonged to the Church, regarding, as she ever has done, all who are ignorant of or indifferent to her teaching as aliens and enemies and outcasts. 'The whole world is in a manner a state,' he concludes; and 'my city and country as far as I am Antoninus is Rome, but so far as I am a man it is the world. The things then which are useful to these cities are alone useful to me.' The idea of humanity as a whole, of all mankind as one fraternity, independent of all barriers of race or language, was first grasped by the philosophers; the hold of it was rather relaxed than tightened by the Church; and the narrow nationalism of modern Europe contrasts poorly with the cosmopolitanism of the pre-Christian world. The supreme pontiff of pagan Rome offered up prayers for the whole human race. We have the testimony of Plutarch that the pagan priests prayed not only for whole communities, but for the whole state of mankind. It was Cicero, and no Christian, who said: 'Nature ordains that a man should wish the good of every man whoever he may be, and for this very reason, that he is a man'. When Socrates was asked to what city he belonged, he answered, 'To the world'; nor was his conception of moral duty as conterminous with humanity ever afterwards lost. It was upheld by Diogenes the Cynic, as by Zeno the Stoic. Seneca only professed an axiom of philosophy when he wrote : ' We ought to devote our soul to no particular place. This is the conviction with which we must each live. I was not born for one corner, my country is the whole world.' Plutarch, speaking of the lost work of Zeno, called the *Republic*, says: ' The much admired *Republic* of Zeno aimed singly at this, that neither in cities nor towns we should live under distinct laws one from another, but should look on all men as our fellow-countrymen and citizens, observing one manner of life and kind of order, like a flock feeding together with equal rights in common pasture '." [1]

Passages like these might of course be greatly multiplied, but sufficient has been said to show the absurd ignorance of Mr. Kidd's statement that pre-Christian ethics were narrow and egotistical compared with Christian ethics. And while we are at this point, it may be worth while to show in greater detail the error of supposing that the doctrine of the innate equality and brotherhood of men emanated from Christianity. For this purpose I quote from the section on Stoicism in Mr. Benn's *Greek Philosophers* :—

" The third great idea of Stoicism was its doctrine of humanity. Men are all children of one Father, and citizens of one state; the highest moral law is, Follow Nature, and Nature has made them to be social and to love one another; the private interest of each is, or should be, identified with the universal interest; we should live for others that we may live for ourselves ; even to our enemies we should show love, and not anger; the unnaturalness of passion is proved by nothing more clearly than by its anti-social and destructive tendencies. Here, also, the three great Stoics of the Roman empire— Seneca, Epictetus, and Marcus Aurelius—rather than the

[1] *Paganism and Christianity*, pp. 173-176.

founders of the school, must be our authorities; whether it be because their lessons correspond to a more developed state of thought, or simply because they have been more perfectly preserved. The former explanation is, perhaps, the more generally accepted. There seems, however, good reason for believing that the idea of universal love—the highest of all philosophical ideas next to that of the universe itself—dates further back than is commonly supposed. It can hardly be due to Seneca, who had evidently far more capacity for popularising and applying the thoughts of others than for original speculation, and who on this subject expresses himself with a rhetorical fluency not usually characterising the exposition of new discoveries. The same remark applies to his illustrious successors, who, while agreeing with him in tone, do not seem to have drawn on his writings for their philosophy. It is also clear that the idea in question springs from two essentially Stoic conceptions: the objective conception of a unified world, a cosmos to which all men belong; and the subjective conception of a rational nature common to them all. These, again, are rooted in early Greek thought, and were already merging into distinctness at the time of Socrates. Accordingly we find that Plato, having to compose a characteristic speech for the Sophist Hippias, makes him say that likeminded men are by nature kinsmen and friends to one another. . . . The most one can say is that the fiction of original liberty was imported into Roman jurisprudence through the agency of Stoic lawyers, and helped to familiarise men's minds with the idea of universal emancipation [*i.e.* from slavery] before political and economical conditions permitted it to be made a reality." [1]

So much, then, for Mr. Kidd's knowledge of the history of morals—a knowledge likely to impress only those who can still regard Mr. Lecky as an authority on the question. Of

[1] Benn's *Greek Philosophers*, vol. ii., pp. 36-40.

Mr. Kidd's philosophy and history, however, nothing can be said that would do justice to its futility. If you ask him why the wonderful "force" which came into the world with Christianity took so long to do any good, why it plunged Europe for twelve centuries into the appalling misery and ignorance of the dark ages, he answers that this was necessary "for the sake of the future," that these centuries were "a period in the lifetime of the social organism *when the welfare, not only of isolated individuals, but of all the individuals of a long series of generations, was sacrificed to the larger interests of generations at a later and more mature stage*" (p. 140); which is more grotesque as an explanation of an historical sequence than anything that even Kingsley perpetrated; or he will tell us that the ethical system of Christianity was "*at a later stage in suitable conditions* calculated to raise the people coming under its influence to the highest state of social efficiency ever attained". He will speak of "the social revolution which it is the destiny of our civilisation to accomplish"; and he will tell us that this "must proceed by the most orderly stages, and must reach its completest expression" among the peoples with whom the Reformation movement "followed its natural order": as if the Reformation had not followed in each country its "natural order," that is, the only order possible to it under those particular circumstances; as if, it being our "destiny" to accomplish a certain social revolution, we could do anything else but accomplish it; and as if his own book were not, on these lines, a pure superfluity. But Mr. Kidd is strong on destinies and forces. In these he lives and moves and has his being. "It is in the period of the post-Reformation development," he tells us, "that it became *the destiny* of the religious system, upon which our civilisation is founded, to *release into the practical life of the world the characteristic product which constitutes such a powerful motive influence enlisted in the cause of progress*"

(p. 199); which is perhaps the most humorous sentence in a book that is brimful of humorous things.[1] Particularly grotesque, too, are Mr. Kidd's notions of the continuity of history; his utterances on this point are instructive as coming from the writer who speaks of himself as the student of human history, the biologist, the evolutionist, and who undertakes to bring a vain and erring pseudo-scientific world to a comprehension of the true course of things. First of all he begins with the assumption that "our civilisation," as he calls it, dates from the beginning of the Christian era. Of the influence of pre-Christian thought and civilisation upon modern Europe, he has apparently no conception whatever, though he tells us plainly that in order to understand the last hundred years at all we must study the centuries that have gone before—which is a respectable proposition not open to dispute, though not, perhaps, very new or very illuminative. "It would appear that those who think about these problems, while rightly perceiving that we in reality live in the midst of the most rapid change and progress, forthwith become so impressed with the magnitude of the change, that they overlook the connection between the present and the past, and form no true conception of the depth and strength of the impression which the centuries that have preceded our own have produced on the age in which we are living" (p. 130); which would be very distressing if it were true. The only man who "overlooks the connection between the present and the past," however, is Mr. Kidd himself. He speaks of "the essential unity and continuity of the vital process which has been in progress in our civilisation from the beginning," as if this process were not continuous with processes that were in existence *before* the

---

[1] In the earlier editions of Mr. Kidd's book it was even worse. It read thus: " . . . to release into the practical life of the world that product which constitutes the most powerful motive influence ever enlisted in the cause of progress ".

Christian era; while only eight lines later he is actually capable of saying that "in the French nation of the present day we have the extraordinary spectacle of a whole people *who have cut themselves off from the past in the world of thought, almost as completely as they have done in the world of politics,*" the "essential unity and continuity of the vital process" having here apparently come to grief, ceasing to be essential, one and continuous. He polishes off the complex history of twelve centuries in á paragraph, with the jaunty formula: "We reach at length the twelfth century;" and now we learn that "the triumphs of the ancient civilisation are as though they had never existed; they are not only forgotten; *there is simply no organic continuity between the old life and that which has replaced it*" (p. 138). Once more the essential unity and continuity of the vital process has become rather erratic in its conduct.

Then, in a momentary aberration into correctness, Mr. Kidd gravely tells us that "so far from our civilisation tending to produce an interruption of, or an exception to, the cosmic process which has been in progress from the beginning of life, its distinctive and characteristic feature, he[1] observes, must be found in the exceptional degree to which it has furthered it" (p. 153). It is, at all events, consoling, after some of Mr. Kidd's utterances, to be assured that the cosmic process is going on all right, and is not in any immediate danger; and we duly appreciate his warning to some persons, though we cannot say to whom his warning is addressed, to think of the social revolution as one, "the significance of which is perceived to lie, not, *as is often supposed*, in its tendency to bring about *a condition of society in which the laws of previous development are to be suspended;* but in the fact that it constitutes the last orderly stage in the same cosmic process which has been in

---

[1] The "he" is "the evolutionist," who, as he "ponders on this process of development," gradually perceives "its immense significance".

progress in the world from the beginning of life" (p. 159). This also is consoling. But why should a writer so unswervingly, so austerely scientific as this, speak of Christianity as "a force . . . different in nature and potentiality to any of which the ancient world had previous experience" (p. 162)? Why, after telling us that the French Revolution has not "in any way added to or taken from the developmental forces that are shaping" the modern world, should he tell us, only ten lines later, that here was "a force utterly unlike any of which the ancient world had experience" (p. 183), and speak of this humanitarianism as being "a force" peculiar to *our* civilisation from the beginning, "a force" different in character from any that moved the ancient world (p. 186) ; as if in the ancient world, as well as the modern, there were not thousands of the power-holding classes who sympathised with the hard fate of the poor and lowly ? Why, again, after speaking of the essential unity and continuity of history, should he say of France that "the process of social development therein, although rapid, has been *too irregular*, and *its people have too completely broken with the past* to allow of an exact comparison of the relationship to each other of the developmental forces at present at work" (p. 207)? Why, after setting Germany, France, and the United States aside in this manner, as being examples of "irregular" and "disorderly" evolution, outside the line of "orderly" evolution which England has taken, should he tell us that : "Once we have grasped the conception of our civilisation as *a developing, organic growth, with a life-history which must be studied as a whole*, we perceive how irrational it is to regard any of the units as independent of the influence of a process which has operated upon society for so many centuries" (p. 258)? Contradictions and lapses of this sort are common enough in Mr. Kidd's book, and when helped out by an accommodating ignorance of the philosophy of history, go to make an exceedingly interesting study of pretentious fallacy. As one of his critics says: "To keep this theory [of the beneficial influence of Christianity upon civilisation] in countenance, the thousand years of Chinese Christianity in Byzantium, the absolute stagnation of Christian Abyssinia, and the collapse of Christian Egypt, Africa, Syria, and Spain, before Islam, are sublimely ignored. Mr. Kidd will prove his case if only you let him ignore two-thirds of the leading facts of history, and handle the rest in a fashion which reduces evolutionary science to burlesque."

Nor is Mr. Kidd any happier in his discussion of ethical developments. Instead of trying to find a scientific reason for the growth of humanitarianism, he calmly attributes it all to Christianity, and speaks of "the religious beliefs upon which our social system is founded," and of "the *fund of altruism* with which our civilisation is equipped". Of the real causes of the ethical changes that take place during the evolution of society he could scarcely be expected to know much, these being so obscure as to tax the powers of men of greater learning and finer logical training than he. But he might at least have learned something from Buckle that would have saved him from writing such a passage as this: "It has been the custom to attribute the progress and the success of the movement by which the working classes have already obtained a larger share of political power, and through which they are now laying the foundation of a more equal social state, to a variety of causes,—to the spread of education, to the growth of intelligence, to the development of the influence of the press, to the progress of industrialism, to the annihilation of space by the improved means of communication and the increased opportunities for organisation resulting, and generally to 'economic tendencies' of all kinds. *But it is primarily due to none of these things. It has its roots in a single cause, namely, the development of the humanitarian feelings, and the deepening and softening of character that has taken place amongst the Western peoples"* (pp. 194-195). Or, as he puts it in another place, "the real impelling force ... has its seat in the development the altruistic feelings have attained amongst us" (p. 214). Ask him what has made the altruistic and humanitarian feelings develop in this way, and he can only reply that Christianity has "equipped" our civilisation with a "fund" of them, which fund acts as a "force" when it is "let loose". This is indeed sublime, and when he tells us, at a later stage, that "one of the most marked and characteristic features of the evolutionary process which has been in progress in our Western civilisation appears to be *its tendency to restrain intellectual development*" (p. 275), we are compelled to regard him as a melancholy example of the truth of at least one part of his theory. But we can only reiterate that no man is compelled to write a book on social evolution without knowing the labours of those who have gone before him. "It is so hard to write a play in five acts," said the weary Frenchman, "and so easy not to write one." It is so hard to write a good book on social evolution, and so easy not to write one, we may say to Mr. Kidd. If only he had read Buckle it would have dawned upon him slowly that there are reasons—physical, social, commercial, industrial, military, intellectual—for the changes in ethical ideals and ethical practice. He himself seems to have been within measurable distance of stumbling upon the truth by accident in one place. We have already seen that he shuffles away from the difficulty as to the dark ages by saying that Christianity had not yet worked out its "destiny,"—that the times were unpropitious for it, and so on. Yet when he is compelled to face the fact that in Christian Europe the proletariat were as poor, as miserable, as oppressed as ever they were in pagan Europe, he gets an inkling of something like the real cause, or one of the causes. "No glamour," he writes, "can hide the wretchedness of the masses of the people throughout the early stages of the history of the present European peoples. Their position was, at best, but one of slavery slightly modified. The worse than animal conditions to which they were subject, the unwholesome food on which they fared, and the state of general destitution in which they lived, must, in all probability, be held to be associated with the general prevalence in Europe late into the middle ages of widely prevalent diseases that have since become extinct. The terrible 'plague' epidemics periodically devastated Europe on a scale and to an extent which the modern world has no experience of, and which we can only very imperfectly realise" (pp. 234, 235). It is in actual concrete forces like these that we must seek the reasons for the fact that altruism did not spread in those days as it has done in the last two centuries, and not in such pseudo-explanations as that the fund of altruism with which our civilisation is equipped has only just had a fair chance to do something. And if Mr. Kidd had pursued his investigation along these lines he would probably have discovered that the inventions of science and the growth of commerce have had far more to do with the growth of humanitarianism than the moral precepts of half a dozen ancient pious forgeries.

CHAPTER VII.

THERE is all the less need to dwell more minutely upon the absurdities of Mr. Kidd's philosophy of history, as many of his critics have called him to task upon the same score. No one, I imagine, with more than a schoolboy's knowledge of history, could be impressed by the chapters in which Mr. Kidd undertakes to prove that a new era began with Christianity, that this introduced a new "force" into the world, which by reason of its "fund of altruism" tended to bring more and more people into the rivalry of life on conditions of equality, and that Christianity has possessed this virtue by reason of its super-rational qualities. The argument is as futile as the history is *à priori*, and one may well ask whether Mr. Kidd has the slightest understanding of the words he uses, when we find him referring to "the success of those forms which have contributed to the fullest working out of that cosmic process which is proceeding throughout human existence, just as it has been proceeding from the beginning of life" (p. 206); as if there were some forms that did *not* contribute to the "working out of the cosmic process". Let us, however, proceed to the consideration of Mr. Kidd's eighth chapter, on "Modern Socialism".

"The uprising," he says, "known throughout Europe and in America as the Socialist movement, is the most characteristic product of our time." Few people, however, understand the true meaning and realise the full significance of this movement. Mr. Kidd will enlighten them. While the masses on the one hand are acquiring more extended political and economic rights, the position of the power-holding classes is being silently undermined by the "fund of altruism". "The real impelling force which lies behind the political advance that we ... have been making in recent times, has its seat in the development the altruistic feelings have attained amongst us, and in the deepening and softening of character which has accompanied the change" (p. 214). As to what makes the altruistic feelings delevop, Mr. Kidd has of course no reply other than that the "fund" of them with which Christianity supplied "our civilisation" is now being "let loose". Under this influence the lower and weaker members of the community are being gradually raised into a better position for the struggle for life; and "the question which now presents itself is: What is the significance of this situation, and of that remarkable period of transition through which political life in England, as in most countries where our civilisation has reached an advanced stage, is passing?"

The fallacies begin the moment Mr. Kidd attempts to answer his own question. "At the outset," he remarks, "underneath all socialist ideals, there yawns the problem of population. Progress so far in life has always been ... necessarily associated with the inexorable natural law *over which man has no control, and over which he can never hope to have any control*, which renders selection necessary, and which, therefore, keeps up the stress of life by compelling every type, as the first condition of progress, to continually press upon and tend to outrun the conditions of existence for the time being" (p. 222). Remembering this, we read on, and find on the next page that "it is not necessary ... to deal at length with the fate of any people" amongst whom restriction of population is practised. "*The conditions of selection being suspended*, such a people could not in any case avoid progressive degeneration, even if we could imagine them escaping more direct consequences." So that such a community would suspend the inexorable law over which we can never hope to have any control! It would check progress, although progress "is a necessity from which there is simply no escape"! Mr. Kidd apparently does not perceive that whether a country produces a hundred thousand or a million new organisms per annum is quite a matter of indifference, so far as natural selection is concerned. The hundred thousand, no less than the million, will react to the stimulus of the environment in varying degrees—some efficiently, others inefficiently; and natural selection will still be the name of the process by which the latter tend to be eliminated at the expense of the former. This, indeed, follows logically enough from Mr. Kidd's own words as to the inexorable nature of selection and progress; he only blunders when he imagines that any community, by restricting its numbers, can put an end to the law of natural selection.

The object of the fallacy, however, is easily seen. Mr. Kidd intends in this way to show that only the non-rational forces of religion can be trusted to maintain the struggle for life in all its old crudity and bitterness, and so ensure the continuance of what he calls progress. Thus he is careful to point out that it is no real objection to socialism that it "could not last". "These are the mere commonplaces which only bring us to the crux of the subject. Impressive as such considerations may be to those who have caught the import of the evolutionary science of the time, no greater mistake can be made than to think that they form any practical answer to the arguments of those who would lead us on to socialism. Why? *For the simple reason that, as we have throughout insisted, men are not now and never have been in the least concerned with or influenced by the estimates which scientists or any other class of persons may form of the probable effects of their present conduct on unborn generations*" (p. 225), which is indeed an amazing admission for Mr. Kidd to make. He is arguing that to begin a socialist state for the benefit of the individuals of the present generation, would check the stream of progress; that men will act only in the interests of the present so long as they use their reason on the facts of life, and that the interests of future generations must therefore be secured by a submission to the irrational force of religion. Now either men can be induced, by an appeal to their reason, to act in the interests of future generations, or they cannot. If they can, then Mr. Kidd's thesis is gone; if they cannot, then what is the meaning of his own book, which is a reasoned appeal to them to do certain things rather than others? This is not a new fallacy for Mr. Kidd. He has already said that arguments as to the hurtful character, in the long run, of certain social forms, "have never been of the slightest practical importance; for ... men in such circumstances are everywhere dominated, not by calculations of the supposed effects of their acts or their institutions on unborn generations, but by more immediate considerations of their own personal advantage" (p. 179). And his contention is that it was the non-rational forces of religion that made away with slavery. Be it so, if Mr. Kidd will have it so; but it only serves to make his own position worse. If the non-rational forces of religion are going to keep a nation from the suicidal policy of limiting its population, let them do so; but to tell the nation that it *ought not to adopt* this course, is to appeal to the reason of men, to argue with them that it is *more rational* to keep the population increasing than to let it decrease. What is Mr. Kidd's book but an attempt to induce men to act "by calculation of the effects of their acts on unborn generations"? And if he wrote his book knowing that his arguments could not possibly be "of the slightest practical importance," we can only make once more the comment that he supplies an invidious personal example of one of his own theses, that the tendency of religion is to restrain intellectual development. The fallacy occurs again and again; we meet with it on page 254, where we are told that "the intellect has no power to effect the subordination" of the interests of the individual to the race, all the while that Mr. Kidd is making an appeal to the intellect; and again on page 318, where we are told that "the eternal forces that are working out the destiny of the race are continually effecting the subordination of the interests of successive generations of men to those larger interests *to which the individual is indifferent*, . . ." Mr. Kidd apparently forgetting that the mere writing of his own book is evidence that *he* at least is not indifferent to these larger social interests, and that to endeavour to convince other men that they should follow a certain course of development is a confutation of his own thesis, that the "eternal forces" are of themselves working out this development in antagonism to the reason of the indifferent individual.

We need not follow Mr. Kidd through all the weary pages in which he expounds what he imagines to be the true significance of modern socialism. He sums up that the future development of society "must complete the process of evolution in progress by eventually bringing all the people into the rivalry of life, not only on a footing of political equality, *but on conditions of equal social opportunities*. This is the end which the developmental forces at work in our civilisation are apparently destined to achieve in the social life of those people amongst whom it is allowed to follow its natural and normal course uninterrupted by disturbing causes" (p. 242). It would be unkind to ask Mr. Kidd what he means by developmental forces, and by the natural course of social development. Let us rather hasten on with him to the conclusion that "we are entering on a new era," in which the people shall have won not only political, but social enfranchisement. It will not, however, be a socialistic era. "The avowed aim of socialism is to suspend that personal rivalry and competition of life which not only is now, but has been from the beginning of life, the fundamental impetus behind (*sic*) all progress. The inherent tendency of the process of social development now taking place amongst us is (as it has been from the beginning of our civilisation) to raise this rivalry to the very highest degree of efficiency as a condition of progress, by bringing all the people into it on a footing of equality, etc. . . . This is the meaning of that evolutional process which has been slowly proceeding through the history of the Western peoples" (p. 253). So that Mr. Kidd not only knows what the future constitution of society will be, but also sees that our society has had an "inherent tendency" from "the beginning of our civilisation" to carry us to this condition. Then is not his own book somewhat superfluous? Or if he still holds to it that his book may be of use in helping evolution along, are we to suppose that the birth of Mr. Kidd was one of the facts of history which point, as Mr. Balfour would say, to "preferential action" on the part of God? For if the "inherent tendency" of evolution cannot be trusted, alone, to carry us whither it is bound to carry us, the author of *Social Evolution* must surely have been designed to assist the inherent tendency to do what it is inherently incapable of doing.

Nor need we dwell upon the facts that religion is not now, and never has been, by any means synonymous with altruism, and that the great fund of altruism of which Mr. Kidd speaks only seems to have become a great fund in the century when the power of religion is decaying. To this he would probably reply, in his profound philosophical way, that the fund has always been there, but latent; and that it has only lately been liberated by the developmental process. Mr. Kidd, I need hardly say, is at liberty to write anything he likes; but he must not impose upon his readers the difficult task of discovering meanings in phrases that are "full of sound and fury, signifying nothing".

CHAPTER VIII.

I HAVE already had occasion to remark upon Mr. Kidd's unfortunate habit of repetition. His next chapter—entitled " Human Evolution is not Primarily Intellectual "—is so far a mere repetition of all that he has previously said on the subject of social development that we need not spend much time over its details. He argues, in a curiously inverted way, that those nations have advanced most which have had the best ethical systems; forgetting (1) that ethical systems are as much the product of a civilisation as *vice versâ;* (2) that since all the nations of Europe have practically the same ethical system, there must be some more specific causes for the differences in their civilisations. When he writes again that " it has not been understood or taken into account that the great deep-seated evolutionary forces at work in society are not operating against religious influences and in favour of the uncontrolled sway of the intellect. On the contrary, it seems to be clear that these religious influences have been always and everywhere triumphant in the past, and that it is a first principle of our social development that they must continue to be in the ascendant to the end, whatever the future may have in store for us," he is very badly confused indeed. If he means that religion is not being undermined by rationalism, he is welcome to that consoling belief, though he will get very few of the clergy to agree with him; while if he really means that religion is bound " to be in the ascendant to the end," he might surely have left the "great deep-seated evolutionary forces" to do their own work without his feeble assistance.

The rest of his chapter is mainly concerned with showing that there has not been that continuous increase in mental development which evolution would lead us to expect. He cites Mr. Galton as to the high intellectual development of the ancient Greeks, and remarks that "if the average mental development reached by the Greeks was so superior to ours as this, we have here a fact the import of which in human evolution has not yet been clearly perceived. If the intellectual ability of the people who developed this extinct civilisation is to be taken as being not only in excess of that of those modern Europeans whose civilisation is winning such an ascendancy in the world to-day, but as being as far above it as the mental ability of these latter is above that of some of the lowest of the peoples whom they have displaced through the operation of natural selection, then it seems extremely difficult to reconcile this fact with an unshaken belief in any theory according to which intellectual development must be taken as the dominant factor in human evolution" (pp. 272, 273). The delicious gravity of it! and the delicious stupidity! Who, in the name of all that is holy, ever contended that the most intellectual nation was bound to survive? Evolution proceeds on many lines, and it is no uncommon thing for a highly educated and refined race to go down before barbarism, or before a more highly organised military state. When a sociologist speaks of the importance of intellect in evolution, he simply means that intellect is a powerful factor in the struggle for life; it is one of the most efficient means of securing wider correspondence between the organism and the environment. He never for a moment imagines that a small and pacific race of high artistic development will be able, in the absence of a good military organisation, to withstand the aggression of a powerful and warlike neighbour. Mr. Kidd is simply fighting his own shadow. And if he had examined his thesis more closely he would have seen that intellect is in reality just as powerful a factor in the social as in the individual struggle for life. Other things being equal, the savage with a quicker and stronger brain has the advantage of his duller fellows; and other things being equal, the nation with a good average brain development has an advantage over nations with a lower brain capacity. And in our modern societies the mass of men can exist, so to speak, on the brains of others. A scientific invention such as the lucifer match can be understood and utilised by a million Europeans who would never be capable of inventing such a thing themselves; and the power to utilise inventions of this kind, though it implies no more intrinsic brain capacity than that of the savage, gives the European a very decided advantage in the securing of a correspondence between himself and his environment. Curiously enough, Mr. Kidd has seen, or partially seen, this very point, but without noticing its implications. He has shown that the civilised man can count so much better than the savage, not because his brain is any better, but because our scale of numbers is really a " kind of mental tape-measure, with which we are provided ready-made by the society to which we belong "—that is, something equivalent to the mechanical inventions which we can all use when once they have been invented. He quotes with approval the words of Mr. Bellamy: " Nine hundred and ninety-nine parts out of the thousand of every man's produce are the result of his social inheritance and environment;" and adds: " This is so; and it is, if possible, even more true of the work of our brains than of the work of our hands ". Mr. Kidd recognises this, but turns it to the account of the altogether indefensible proposition that something else than intellect is the secret of the ascendancy of the Western nations; while if anything follows *from his own demonstration*, it is that the second-hand knowledge of the universe which we derive from the brains of other men is almost as valuable in the struggle for life as if we had obtained it by our own effort, and that this constitutes in the secondary, though perhaps not in the primary, sense an advantage over the savage who possesses no social heritage of this kind. Mr. Kidd's absurd explanation of the difference between civilised and uncivilised races is that the former possess "high social qualities," while the latter do not—which is really no explanation at all, but simply an inverted form of the fact to be explained. To say that we have a high civilisation because we possess qualities that tend to social efficiency, is equivalent to saying that a man is healthy because he has a body that tends to be strong.

Mr. Kidd is, of course, leading up to the conclusion that religion has been the prime factor in progress. He imagines that "the Teutonic peoples undoubtedly possess certain equally characteristic qualities, not in themselves intellectual, which contribute in a higher degree to social efficiency, and which—having in view the manner in which natural selection is operating and the direction in which the evolution of the race is proceeding—must apparently be pronounced to be greatly more important than these merely intellectual qualities" (p. 299). The English and the Germans, in fact, are more religious than the French, while in the French mind "there is an indefinite something . . . of a distinctly high intellectual order which is not native to either the German or the English peoples". To explain racial differences by the fact of race is now generally recognised to be what John Stuart Mill said it was—the most vulgar of all ways of evading the real question as to what has made races different. Mr. Kidd's pages are yet another illustration that he has still to learn the very elements of his subject; and while no one would think of arguing against so absurd a set of propositions at this time of day, all will join in the wish that Mr. Kidd, before he began to write on sociology, had learned something of the work of sociologists.

France is of course taken as an example of the dreadful effects of intellectual prudence, as shown in the voluntary keeping of the population within due limits. Mr. Kidd blindly assumes that France is of "lower social efficiency" than Germany or England, being evidently ignorant of the state of civilisation in France—or anywhere else for that matter—and of the real concrete causes that have made the population question press upon France earlier than upon us. In his hodman's way he disposes of the whole question by the mere application of one senseless formula—that we are more socially efficient than the French because we have qualities that tend to greater social efficiency, these qualities being at bottom religious and irrational. And in any case Mr. Kidd's own arguments are self-subversive. He speaks of the checking of the population as due to the "enlightened selfishness in the individual which must always lead him to rank his own interests, or those of his immediate belongings, in the actual present before the wider and entirely different interests of the longer-lived social organism to which he belongs"; as if the population were not checked in France as much in the interest of future generations as of the present. As for the phrase about the "interests of the social organism," we have already seen that to be meaningless, the interest of the "social organism" having no existence apart from the interests of the individuals composing it. And finally, if reason should not be used in social matters, since reason tends to make us take thought for the morrow, and so impede the "inexorable law" of progress, how is the situation bettered by Mr. Kidd's book? He tells us, in the interests of the future, that we must not reason about the future; he tells us that the only way to be sure we are in line with the cosmic process is not to reason about it, although he has to reason with us to get us to see that we must not reason ; and his own way of securing the continuance of progress, *i.e.*, of taking thought for the morrow, is to recommend us not to take thought for the morrow. And when, at the conclusion of the chapter, he gravely talks some portentous nonsense about the anabolism and katabolism of societies, we are compelled to admonish him that a profound scientific theory is not to be built up in these days by combining a smattering of scientific terms, that might be picked up any evening by a sharp boy at a mechanics' institute, with a capacity for illogical error that would disgrace any of Mr. Kidd's most admired historians.

CHAPTER IX.

THOUGH there remains yet another chapter in Mr. Kidd's book, it contains practically nothing that he has not said too many times already. He imagines that "when the application of the principles of evolutionary science to history comes to be *fully* understood," *i.e.*, as it is by Mr. Benjamin Kidd, there will be a great revolution in our ideas of human development; and he exhibits once more his own ignorance of history and sociology by supposing that until now men have regarded human history "as a bewildering exception to the reign of universal law". He repeats his argument that "the forces which are at work in the evolution of society are certainly, on the whole, working out the greatest good of the greatest number in a progressive community. But . . . the greatest good which the evolutionary forces . . . are working out, is the good of the social organism as a whole. *The greatest number in this sense is comprised of the members of generations yet unborn, or unthought of, to whose interests the existing individuals are absolutely indifferent*" (p. 313). One finally wearies of pointing out the imbecile—there is no other word for them—self-contradictions of Mr. Kidd. For the last time, if the evolutionary forces are working out the good of the social organism, they can very well be left alone at their task; if these forces are "certainly, on the whole," carrying out the work they have been engaged on since the beginning of life, nothing that we can do will hinder them; if Mr. Kidd thinks of the interests of unborn generations, they cannot be said to be unthought of; if he cares about their interests, it cannot be said that existing individuals are absolutely indifferent to them; and if he induces other people to think about the future, after telling them that they must not think of the future, if he hopes to induce men to be guided by his reasoning in those actions which affect future generations, after laying it down that men are not and never have been influenced in these matters by any thought of the future, he is simply confuting his own book and holding himself up to ridicule.

Thus the dreary stream of fallacy and absurdity flows on. He explains the process of development in the modern world by the fact that the process of development has produced this development (p. 319). He speaks of "the release into our social life of an immense and all-pervading (*sic*) fund of altruistic feeling, which has provided the real motive force behind the whole onward movement with which our age is identified" (p. 321), while all the time his own argument against "the self-asserting rationalism of the individual" implies that this "fund" is anything but "all-pervading". He imagines that this abundance of altruism has been generated in us by Christianity, and that what distinguishes Christianity from all other religions is the essential (*sic*) spirit that underlies (*sic*) it (p. 320). I cheerfully admit that a religion which has its essence underneath it is indeed something distinct from all others. And after all his talk about Christianity and altruism, and of the extent to which the latter is indebted to the former, it turns out that "when we turn to those peoples amongst whom the religious movement of the sixteenth century was interrupted or suppressed, and amongst whom the Latin form of Christianity prevails, we find that the situation is not exactly the same. Amongst these people the idea of the innate equality of all men, with the consequent conception of the fundamental right of all to equal opportunities, which is the peculiar product of the ethical system on which our civilisation is founded, has practically reached the same development as elsewhere. But the profound change *in social character* which has accompanied this development, amongst the Anglo-Saxon peoples, for instance, has not proceeded so far. The deepening of individual character, resulting in a certain inbred sense of integrity, which has rendered the sense of wrong intolerable, and the softening process which has made the Anglo-Saxon peoples so sensitive to the sight of misery or suffering, have not progressed to the same extent" (p. 324). The handsome tribute to the Anglo-Saxon race, to which, by a curious coincidence, Mr. Kidd himself belongs, may be passed over as so much vulgar clap-trap; but what are we to think of a writer who tells us in one breath that Christianity is the motive force behind civilisation, and in the next that Christianity has only wrought for high civilisation in some places and not in others? Thus on his own admission, Christianity, though the "principle of life" that was destined to work out the progress of the Western nations, failed to produce anything but stagnation for many hundreds of years, and then produces an altruistic civilisation only in that race which has the good fortune to claim Mr. Kidd as its own. Any one not incurably stupid would have seen that, on such terms as these, it is rank nonsense to speak of Western civilisation as being "based" on the ethical system of Christianity; and when Mr. Kidd tells us that the English people alone have undergone "a natural and orderly development," while among other nations the development has been neither natural nor orderly, he is talking such sheer nonsense that one apologises for reprinting it. His remarks on the different histories of the nations since the Reformation are a perpetual see-saw of ignorance and fatuity. It was among the Anglo-Saxons alone, apparently, that the altruistic religion followed its "natural course"; yet it was among these self-same Anglo-Saxons that negro slavery began and ultimately grew to such enormous proportions. Mr. Kidd imagines that what made the slave trade finally intolerable and led to its suppression was the altruism generated in the Anglo-Saxon race by Christianity; what had become of Christian altruism during the years when the slave trade flourished, he apparently has no wish to tell us. If the question were put to him, he would probably reply that Christianity has only just begun to fulfil its "destiny".

But enough of Mr. Kidd's fallacies. The remainder of his final chapter is occupied with a forecast of the future state of civilisation, in which the Anglo-Saxon race is to be predominant, and the tropics are to be administered from the temperate zones. Of the concrete physical and physiological causes of the decline of the lower races before the higher in some quarters of the globe, he has of course not a shadow of an idea. He would explain the dying-out of the Maoris, for example, by the fact that they are not socially so efficient as the English, a form of the *circulus in probando* to which Mr. Kidd is very much addicted. And we may safely decline to follow him in his prognostications of the future of the world. The man who can turn out such a book as his on the history of the past is not exactly the most reliable guide as to the future. In any case it is time we took leave of him. His book has had almost unbroken praise from one reviewer after another, which is in itself a sign of the ease with which any system of fallacy, so long as it is made to serve the interests of religion, will still be swallowed by the average Anglo-Saxon. In a sense, then, Mr. Kidd was right when, in a lucubration which he facetiously called a reply to his critics,[1] he told us that there was no sociology in England at present. If that remark be taken to apply to the bulk of those who reviewed his book so eulogistically, it is certainly correct.

[1] In the *Nineteenth Century* for February, 1895.

The fallacies of it lie so nakedly on the surface that any one who is unable to see them must be as fundamentally illogical as Mr. Kidd himself; while those who failed to see the grotesque absurdity of his philosophy of history are indeed hopeless. What is the upshot of his book? I give it in the concise summary of Mr. Robertson:—

"*People who carefully apply reason to their way of life, like the ancient Greeks and the modern French, tend to decline in power and to die out. To prevent the application of reason to the problems of life, then, is the course seen by reason to be rational; and in order to succeed in this course we must reasonably maintain an unreasonable religious system. Systematic socialism and systematic individualism are alike ruinously rational, being alike the expression of the wish of the individual to better his lot, which wish always prevents future betterment. We must therefore take thought for the morrow by not taking thought for the morrow, but follow those blind instincts which our other instincts tell us ought not to be followed; and to keep everything on right lines we must believe in a religion which we have no reason for believing.*"

It is the writer who has so laboriously made himself ridiculous who tells us that the time has not yet come to answer his critics. There has been, he says, "scarcely any attempt to deal with the book as an organic unity"; though he admits that many critics have attacked certain positions in detail. Yet he neither attempts to deal with these, nor to answer the few who *have*, on his own admission, dealt with the book "as an organic unity". The only inference possible is that he is simply incapable of answering them. He was told by many that his history was just second-hand ignorance; yet he makes no attempt to prove his critics wrong, or to justify his own historical philosophy. And the reader who has been exasperated at Mr. Kidd's ignorance of history, and at the blind eagerness with which he snatches at any dictum from Mr.

Lecky or Mr. Mahaffy that may help to prove his point, heedless of the other dicta in which these writers contradict the first, must learn with amazement that Mr. Kidd had been studying his subject for ten years before he wrote upon it. It is safe to say that such reading as he has done could be got through by any fairly intelligent man in less than ten weeks; and in that time he would certainly have seen that the thesis of *Social Evolution*, instead of being the discovery Mr. Kidd imagines it to be, is as old as reaction itself. As I have pointed out, it is nothing more than a resuscitation, in the garb of modern pseudo-science, of the old antithesis between the intellect and the emotions, between the head and the heart. Mr. Kidd must have read singularly little in his ten years of study if he failed to become aware of this; and as it lies on the face of his book that he knows absolutely nothing at first hand of Greek, Roman, or mediæval civilisation, that he is as ignorant of psychology as if that science were not yet born, and that he is quite unable even to see when he is contradicting himself, one can only sum him up by saying that such a mind as his is essentially incapable of any scientific work whatever. Professor Sidgwick concluded that Mr. Kidd had left social science where he found it;[1] to which criticism the only objection is that Mr. Kidd never did find it. His book is indeed what one of his critics has called it—the most ignorant book of modern times.

[1] See *National Review*, December, 1894.

MR. DRUMMOND'S *ASCENT OF MAN*.

CHAPTER I.

To pass from Mr. Kidd to Mr. Henry Drummond is to pass from the atmosphere of mere fallacy to the atmosphere of theological fallacy, which, if it is somewhat denser, has the compensating quality of being infinitely more exhilarating—to the non-theological mind. Eleven years ago Mr. Drummond distinguished himself by the publication of his *Natural Law in the Spiritual World*—a volume which was assiduously boomed at the time by the orthodox press, and which has now deservedly gone the way of all fustian. His present performance is easily recognisable as having come from the same brain; it exhibits the same gift for expounding the scientific doctrines of other men, the same faculty of cheerful paralogism, the same breadth and serenity of fallacy. Altogether, Mr. Drummond is decidedly more interesting reading than Mr. Kidd. The latter's errors are merely those of a well-meaning man utterly unfitted by nature and by training to write a thoughtful book; Mr. Drummond's fallacies have a charm that is only found in the books that have a distinctly theological purpose. Of which, however, more anon.

Mr. Drummond, like Mr. Kidd, begins by mounting the tripod and flinging his prophetic garment round him in folds of majestic severity. He also has to complain that up to the time when, unable to keep any longer from the public the great thoughts that were gestating within him, he resolved to write and publish *The Ascent of Man*, our reading of evolution was painfully and hopelessly inadequate. " Though its standpoint is evolution and its subject man," he writes in his preface, "this book is far from being designed to prove that man has relations, compromising or otherwise, with lower animals. Its theme is ascent, not descent. It is a history, not an argument. And evolution, in the narrow sense in which it is often used when applied to man, plays little part in the drama outlined here. So far as the general scheme of evolution is introduced, . . . the object is the important one of pointing out how its nature has been misconceived—indeed how its greatest factor has been overlooked in almost all contemporary scientific thinking. Evolution was given to the modern world out of focus, was first seen by it out of focus, and has remained out of focus to the present hour. Its general basis has never been re-examined since the time of Mr. Darwin; and not only such speculative sciences as teleology, but working sciences like sociology, have been led astray by a fundamental omission. An evolution theory drawn to scale, and with the lights and shadows properly adjusted—adjusted to the whole truth and reality of nature and of man—is needed at present as a standard for modern thought; and though a reconstruction of such magnitude is not here presumed, a primary object of these pages is to supply at least the accents for such a scheme." And, as he complains a little further on, "singular though the omission may seem, no connected outline of this great drama [of evolution] has yet been given us" (p. 2).

Here again, as in the case of Mr. Kidd, it will not be unprofitable to inquire what are the qualifications of the writer who thus condemns the work of his predecessors, and volunteers to give us the true key to the comprehension of the drama of the universe. Of Mr. Drummond's former ludicrous performance—*Natural Law in the Spiritual World*—it is charity at this time of day to say nothing; but the selection of a few sentences from the present volume, typical of Mr. Drummond's habit of thought, will perhaps afford the reader an opportunity of judging of the scope and quality of his mind, and thence a means of forecasting the likelihood of such a mind completing the ambitious task that has been set it. Mr. Drummond's method of exposition is, if anything, even more aggravating than Mr. Grant Allen's; if the latter's method is, as one of his reviewers said of it, that of a certificated science teacher lecturing to a mechanics' institute, Mr. Drummond's is that of a curate with a fatal felicity in vapid epigram talking to the debating society of a Young Men's Christian Association. Here are some characteristic examples:—

"Every step in the proof of the oneness in a universal evolutionary process of this divine humanity of ours is a step in the proof of the divinity of all lower things" (p. 3). Anybody but Mr. Drummond would see that if everything is divine nothing is divine.

"Evolution involves not so much a change of opinion as a change in man's whole view of the world and of life. It is not the statement of a mathematical proposition which men are called upon to declare true or false. It is a method of looking upon nature. Science for centuries devoted itself to the cataloguing of facts and the discovery of laws. Each worker toiled in his own little place—the geologist in his quarry, the botanist in his garden, the biologist in his laboratory, the astronomer in his observatory, the historian in his library, the archæologist in his museum. Suddenly these workers looked up; they spoke to one another; they had each discovered a law; they whispered its name. It was Evolution. Henceforth their work was one, science was one, the world was one, and mind, which discovered the oneness, was one" (p. 11). From which it would appear that Mr. Drummond cannot even write a paragraph of platitudes and fatuities without being melodramatic.

"That the struggle for life has been a prominent actor in the drama is certain. Further research has only deepened the impression of the magnitude and universality of this great and far-reaching law. But that it is the sole or even the main agent in the process of Evolution must be denied. *Creation is a drama, and no drama was ever put upon the stage with only one actor. The struggle for life is the 'Villain' of the piece, no more; and, like the 'Villain' in the play, its chief function is to react upon the other players for higher ends*" (p. 17); which is the epigrammatic curate with a vengeance.

"*There* [*i.e.*, in the hour of birth] *is the opportunity of Evolution. There is an opening appointed in the physical order for the introduction of a moral order.* If there is more in nature than the selfish struggle for life *the secret can now be told.* Hitherto, the world belonged to the food-seeker, the self-seeker, the struggler for life, the father. *Now is the hour of the mother*" (p. 22).

"The struggle for the life of others is sunk as deep in the 'cosmic process' as the struggle for life;[1] the struggle for life has a share in the 'ethical process' as much as the struggle for the life of others. Both are cosmic processes; both are ethical processes; *both are both cosmical and ethical processes*" (p. 30).

"But what if morality be the main product of the cosmical system—of *even* the cosmical system? What if it can be shown that it is the essential and not the incidental result of it, and that so far from being a by-product, it is *im*morality that is the by-product?" (p. 33).

"If Evolution is simply a method of creation, why was this very extraordinary method *chosen*?" (p. 47).

These few elegant extracts, culled at random from the introduction to Mr. Drummond's book, are typical of him.

---

[1] This, be it remembered, after the preceding rhapsody about altruism coming in with mothers, about "the opportunity of evolution," and about the "opening appointed in the physical order for the introduction of a moral order".

Here again, as in the case of Mr. Kidd, we may feel inclined to ask at the outset what are the chances of a mind of this order throwing any new light on the theory of evolution, or even of seeing what light already exists. After the anxious exordium of the preface, in which Mr. Drummond, weary of the errors of all preceding evolutionists, yearns to reconstruct the whole theory on its true basis, one really feels somewhat disappointed at meeting in the first fifty pages with fatuities like those quoted above. Yet this is not to be understood as implying that Mr. Drummond's theories are not interesting. They have an interest all their own, and are well worth looking at as a study in theological biology. For Mr. Drummond courageously accepts the whole main body of evolutionary science as quite proven. In the early Darwinian days it was the theological fashion to deride the theory of evolution and to insult its adherents, as when the vulgar bishop brought upon himself the dignified rebuke of Huxley. But the times are changed. The theologians, learning the folly of denying what every one else is asserting, have not only accepted the evolutionary theory in its entirety, but have come to claim it as their own; the very God in whose name evolution was denied has now become the "God of evolution"; and theologians like Mr. Lyman Abbott are not above assuring us that God himself is subject to the evolutionary process. To this school of contrition, then, Mr. Drummond may be said to belong. It being impossible to deny evolution now as it was denied thirty years ago, the only alternative is to accept it in its scientific aspect and quarrel with its philosophy. That religion should have been worsted in this its latest conflict with science is rather distressing, but the day may yet be won, a defeat may yet be turned into a victory, by enlisting biology in the service of teleology, by turning evolution to the account of religion. Let us follow Mr. Drummond in his attempted performance of this feat.

CHAPTER II.

"IF, evolution can be proved to include man," he begins by remarking, "the whole course of evolution and the whole scheme of nature from that moment assume a new significance. The beginning must then be interpreted from the end, not the end from the beginning. An engineering workshop is unintelligible until we reach the room where the completed engine stands. Everything culminates in that final product, is contained in it, is explained by it. The evolution of man is also the complement *and corrective* (*sic*) of all other forms of evolution. From this height only is there a full view, a true perspective, a consistent world. The whole mistake of naturalism has been to interpret nature from the standpoint of the atom—to study the machinery which drives this great moving world simply as machinery, forgetting that the ship has any passengers, or the passengers any captain, or the captain any course" (p. 12). Thus early and thus ingenuously, by means of a couple of analogies, does Mr. Drummond begin his task of making biology teleological. Surely it scarcely needs to be pointed out that Mr. Drummond's analogies have the common defect of all analogical reasoning, together with other defects of their own? For there is absolutely no analogy between the machine and the workroom on one hand and man and nature on the other, or between the course of evolution and the course of a ship. The essence of the former illustration is that we know the *purpose* of the machine because we are external to it, and because the machine is made in obedience to *our* purpose, to supply the end for which we designed it. In the case of the ship, again, its course is definite and comprehensible, because *we* have arranged it with the end already in our minds. But who can look upon evolution, upon nature and man in this way? We are not external to the course of evolution, as we are external to the ship, but part and parcel of it—part of a process which began ages before man existed upon the globe, and which will continue ages after he has vanished from it. We are not the final shapely fruit of nature, as the machine is the final shapely form of the shapeless fragments in the workshop, but merely one among a million other forms, superior to them in the one faculty of mind, but, like them, the product and the battle-ground of impersonal cosmic forces, and of no more importance in the story of cosmic evolution as a whole than they are. And to talk of obtaining from the present stage of development of man "a full view, a true perspective" of evolution, is to ignore the fact that man himself is still evolving along with all the other forms of life, and that whatever ground there might be for a hypothetical last man indulging in reflections upon the inner meaning of human evolution, the indulgence in such reflections on our part is a mere form of imaginative recreation. So that when Mr. Drummond says that "the mistake of naturalism has been to interpret nature from the standpoint of the atom," instead of beginning with "the final product, man," he is simply confusing his analogies in the interests of his religion. Naturalism merely "interprets nature from the standpoint of the atom" in that it reduces to scientific form our varied knowledge of the universe, and arguing back from effect to cause, from complex to simple, finds in "the atom," as Mr. Drummond calls it, a point from which we can run lines of connection through everything that exists. With "interpretation," in the teleological sense in which Mr. Drummond uses the word, naturalism has simply nothing to do. Interpretations of this sort come only from the theist, who, accustomed as he is to reading a divine purpose into everything, must needs assume an intimate acquaintance with the intentions of the Great Artificer, and point to man as the final point up to which evolution has all along been working. But if the ordinary theistic reading of a purpose into the order of events in the cosmos is illegitimate, it is none the less illegitimate when the object is to show that because we are accustomed to look upon man as the "highest" product of evolution, therefore through him can be comprehended the "meaning" of the cosmic life. The very words "meaning" and "interpretation" are themselves illegitimate.

"But it is not so much in ignoring man," Mr. Drummond continues, "that evolutionary philosophy has gone astray; for of that error it has seriously begun to repent. What we have now to charge against it, what is a main object of these pages to point out, is, that it has misread nature itself. In 'fixing on a part' whereby to 'reconstruct the ultimate,' it has fixed upon a part which is not the most vital part, and the reconstructions, therefore, have come to be wholly out of focus" (p. 15). This error has consisted in regarding the struggle for life as "the governing factor in development". There is, however, "a *second* factor, which one might venture to call the *struggle for the life of others*, which plays an equally important part. Even in the early stages of development its contribution is as real, while in the world's later progress, under the name of altruism, it assumes a sovereignty before which the earlier struggle sinks into insignificance. That this second form of struggle should all but have escaped the notice of evolutionists is the more unaccountable, since it arises, like the first, out of those fundamental functions of living organisms which it is the main business of biological science to investigate. The functions discharged by all living things, plant and animal, are two in number. The first is nutrition, the second is reproduction. The first is the basis of the struggle for life; the second, of the struggle for the life of others. These two functions run their parallel course—or spiral course, for they continuously intertwine—from the very dawn of life. They are involved in the fundamental nature of protoplasm itself.... Yet, in constructing the fabric of evolution, one of these has been taken, the other left" (pp. 17, 18).

This is Mr. Drummond's short and easy method with biology. Because when an organism feeds itself it feeds itself, and when it reproduces another organism it reproduces another, the first of these processes is purely egoistic, the second purely altruistic! You have only got to assume, as blandly as Mr. Drummond, that nutrition is wholly self-regarding, and reproduction wholly other-regarding, and the trick is done; you have assumed all you have to prove, and the course of the argument is henceforth smooth. Even Mr. Drummond, in an unusually thoughtful moment, becomes aware that reproduction, *quâ* reproduction, scarcely deserves all the good things he has said of it. "To say that reproduction is synonymous with the struggle for the life of others conveys at first little meaning, for the physiological aspects of the function persist in the mind, and make even a glimpse of its true character difficult.... Suffice it for the moment to say that the physiological aspects of the struggle for the life of others are so overshadowed even towards the close of the animal kingdom by the psychical and ethical that it is scarcely necessary to emphasise the former at all. One's first and natural association with the struggle for the life of others is with something done for posterity—in the plant the struggle to produce seeds, in the animal to beget young. But this is a preliminary which, compared with what directly and indirectly rises out of it, may be almost passed over. The significant note is ethical, the development of other-ism, as altruism—its immediate and inevitable outcome" (pp. 21, 22). In other and less sophistical words, while nutrition is always egoistic, reproduction is *not* always altruistic—although Mr. Drummond's argument, if it is to be worth anything whatever, ought to prove that as nutrition is egoistic, *quâ* nutrition, reproduction is altruistic, *quâ* reproduction. Altruism has an ethical meaning, or it has no meaning at all; and if Mr. Drummond wishes us to believe that altruism has its root in the reproductive function, he should give us some evidence in support of his theory. Instead of doing that, he first of all makes the bland assumption that nutrition = egoism and reproduction = altruism, and then calmly assures us that reproduction is not really altruism,—*i.e.*, ethical in content—until we come to otherwise ethical beings! In all but the lower plant and animal kingdoms "the physiological aspects of the struggle for the life of others are so overshadowed . . . by the psychical and ethical that it is scarcely necessary to emphasise the former at all"! And the purely physiological, *i.e.*, non-ethical, character of reproduction in the lower organisms is "a preliminary which may be almost passed over"! And though the "significant note is ethical," this "significant note" is not heard at the beginning of the music, but only towards the end, where it has already begun to be sounded by other instruments than the one of which it is supposed to be the significant note! And all the while, be it observed, Mr. Drummond has not given a word of evidence in support of the theory that egoism is the concomitant of nutrition and altruism of reproduction; nor has he noticed the futility of speaking of altruism as "ethical"—as if egoism were not equally an ethical factor.

"All along the line," he goes on, "through the whole course of the development, these two functions act and react upon one another; and continually as they co-operate to produce a single result, their specific differences are never lost. The first, the struggle for life, is, throughout, the self-regarding function; the second, the other-regarding function. The first, in lower nature, obeying the law of self-preservation, devotes its energies to feed itself; the other, obeying the law of species-preservation, to feed its young. While the first develops the active virtues of strength and courage, the other lays the basis for the passive virtues, sympathy and love. In the later world one seeks its end in personal aggrandisement, the other in ministration. One begets competition, self-assertion, war; the other unselfishness, self-effacement, peace. One is individualism, the other altruism" (pp. 24, 25).

Here the confusion of terms is more than ever apparent. Why is it so confidently laid down that nutrition engenders egoism, and reproduction altruism? Let us take a concrete case. A tigress seeks her food, and finds it in an antelope. That, according to Mr. Drummond, is the struggle for life,—mere egoism. The tigress then produces cubs. This, Mr. Drummond tells us, is the struggle for the 'life of others,—altruism, or at any rate the stuff out of which altruism is afterwards made. But every fresh case of reproduction simply involves another struggle for nutrition, *i.e.*, implies more egoism, as Mr. Drummond would put it. For how are the tiger-cubs to be kept alive? By food. And where and how is the food to be obtained? By the parent's filching it from other tigers, or by preying upon weaker organisms. This is certainly altruism with a vengeance! And when the tiger-cubs grow up, the old struggle for life becomes keener than ever. On the terms of Mr. Drummond's argument, the more cubs the more altruism. But since the cubs must have food, it follows that the more cubs the more egoism! And if all other organisms go on reproducing to their fullest, *i.e.*, giving full play to their altruistic instincts, the conflict will be all the keener, and the result will be an increase of egoism!

Nay, a too altruistic tiger, that forbore to dismember an antelope, would soon perish and make way for a tiger not so afflicted with other-ism. Mr. Drummond's identification of nutrition with egoism, and reproduction with altruism, is in fact a mere confusion of terms, due to the use of the unfortunate phrase "*struggle* for the life of others". Why struggle? The struggle for self is conceivably a characteristic of organic nature. But what is the struggle for others, so far as this is "synonymous with reproduction"? Who are the "others," in the first place? If tiger A preys upon antelope B, where is the altruism in A producing offspring to prey upon the offspring of B? To call this an altruistic struggle for the life of others is simply to blunder over the meanings both of "struggle" and of "others".

This, of course, involves no denial of the fact that altruism, or the physiological elements from which altruism develops, has a place in the lower organisms. It simply means that Mr. Drummond's argument is illegitimate, in that it crudely identifies nutrition with one ethical factor and reproduction with another, and puts an extraneous ethical interpretation upon a purely physiological function by using the phrase "*struggle* for the life of *others*". He only shows that reproduction is altruistic by assuming it; he only shows that it is "other-regarding" by saying it is equivalent to struggling for others. And his attempt at scientific completeness in the phrase that both tendencies spring from the same protoplasm is simply superfluous futility. Where else could they conceivably spring from?

"To say that no ethical content," he continues, "can be put into the discharge of either function in the earlier reaches of Nature goes without saying. But the moment we reach a certain height in the development, ethical implications begin to arise. These, in the case of the first, have been read into Nature, lower as well as higher, with an exaggerated and merciless malevolence. The other side has received almost no expression. The final result is a picture of Nature wholly painted in shadow—a picture so dark as to be a challenge to its Maker, an unanswered problem to philosophy, an abiding offence to the moral nature of man. The world has been held up to us as one great battlefield heaped up with the slain, an Inferno of infinite suffering, a slaughter-house resounding with the cries of a ceaseless agony" (p. 25).

Here, it will be observed, Mr. Drummond is beginning to tread upon dangerous ground; he is upon the old crux of all theisms—the problem of evil and suffering. How he evades the difficulty will appear in the sequel. His first move is to turn upon Huxley, and make out part of his own case by playing off upon each other the unfortunate fallacies of the unfortunate lecture on *Evolution and Ethics*. That lecture, which contained errors worthy of Mr. Drummond himself, is now quoted as a support to Mr. Drummond's own theory of ethical evolution. When Huxley said that "social progress means a checking of the cosmic process at every step, and the substitution for it of another, which may be called the ethical process,"[1] he forgot that the "cosmic process" cannot be checked, that when we attempt to check something which we assume to be the cosmic process, that attempt is itself simply *part* of the cosmic process, and that the ethical process is not something distinct from the cosmic process, but merely one phase of it, just as egoism is another phase. He seems indeed to have recognised the fallacy of his position, for in a note he reminds himself that, "strictly speaking, social life and the ethical process, in virtue of which it advances towards perfection, are part and parcel of the general process of evolution"; but he was weak enough to leave the text as it stood, though seemingly conscious that it was illogical. Huxley's lecture, indeed, is of practically no importance in the discus-

[1] *Evolution and Ethics*, p. 33.

sion on evolution and ethics, and its only interest, from the intellectual side, is this fundamental fallacy of assuming the ethical process to be distinct from the cosmic process. Mr. Drummond of course has no difficulty in pointing out the fallacy, which must surely have been apparent to all who read the lecture. He is thus right in his plea that Nature should be regarded as a whole; right in his protest against looking upon Nature, "as far as the plant, animal, and savage levels," as being "synonymous with the struggle for life". That is, avoiding the verbal pitfalls that make his phrases so dangerous to the unwary, egoism is not the "cosmic process," and altruism an antagonistic process, but both are factors in the one universal movement of life from the beginning of time.

Mr. Drummond, however, not satisfied with having stated an obvious truism, must needs turn it to the account of teleology by attempting to discover the "purpose" of the cosmic process. "What is the valid answer? Of course that Nature has put in her own ends if we would take the trouble to look for them. . . . Hitherto the evolutionist has had practically no other basis than the struggle for life. Suppose even we leave that untouched, the addition of an other-regarding basis makes an infinite difference. For when it is then asked on which of them the process turns, and the answer is given 'On both,' we perceive that it is neither by the one alone, nor by the other alone, that the process is to be interpreted, but by a higher unity which resolves and embraces all. And as both are equally necessary to the antinomy, even that of the two which seems irreconcilable with higher ends is seen to be necessary. Viewed *simpliciter*, the struggle for life appears irreconcilable with ethical ends, a prodigious anomaly in a moral world; but viewed in continuous reaction with the struggle for the life of others, it discloses itself as an instrument of perfection the most subtle and far-reaching that reason could devise" (pp. 35-37). And as evolution goes on, "the one struggle waxes and the other wanes.... Lest the alleged *waning* of the struggle for life convey a wrong impression, let it be added that of course the word is to be taken qualitatively. The struggle in itself can never cease. What ceases is its so-called anti-ethical character.... The path of progress and the path of altruism are one. Evolution is nothing but the involution of love, the revelation of infinite spirit, the eternal life returning to itself" (pp. 45, 46).

Here at last the cloven hoof appears. The object of Mr. Drummond's insistence upon the fundamental character of altruism in the scheme of evolution has been to work in the old Theistic argument that evil is not real, but only apparent. He shows his hand, indeed, immediately after the passages just quoted, when he gives to the next section of his introduction the heading "Why was evolution the method *chosen?*" Here at once he commits himself to the position that there is a Deity who has deliberately selected evolution as the best manner of working out the perfection of the universe. This is Mr. Drummond's proof of the proposition :—

"If evolution is simply a method of creation, why was this very extraordinary method chosen? Creation *tout d'un coup* might have produced the same result; an instantaneous act or an age-long process would both have given us the world as it is. The answer of modern natural theology has been that the evolutionary method is the infinitely nobler scheme. A spectacular act, it is said, savours of the magician. As a mere exhibition of power it appeals to the lower nature; but a process of growth suggests to the reason the work of an intelligent mind. No doubt this intellectual gain is real. While a catastrophe puts the universe to confusion at the start, a gradual rise makes the beginning of nature harmonious with its end" (p. 47). Mr. Drummond, however, will have none of these fatuities of natural theology; he prefers a fatuity of his own. As thus :—

"But can an intellectual answer satisfy us any more than the mechanical answer which it replaced? *As there was clearly a moral purpose in the end to be achieved by evolution, should we not expect to find some similar purpose in the means? Can we perceive no high design in selecting this particular design, no worthy ethical result which should justify the conception as well as the execution of evolution?* We go too far, perhaps, in expecting answers to questions so transcendent. But one at least suggests itself, whose practical value is apology enough for venturing to advance it. *Whenever the scheme was planned, it must have been foreseen that the time would come when the directing of part of the course of evolution would pass into the hands of man.* A spectator of the drama for ages, too ignorant to see that it was a drama, and too impotent to do more than play his little part, the discovery must sooner or later break upon him that Nature meant him to become a partner in her task and share the responsibility of the closing acts. . . . Nature may have entrusted the further building to mankind, but the plan has never left her hands. The lines of the future are to be learned from her past, and her fellow-helpers can most easily, most loyally and most perfectly do their part by studying closely the architecture of the earlier world, and continuing the half-finished structure symmetrically to the top. The information necessary to complete the work with architectural consistency lies in Nature. We might expect that it should be there. *When a business is transferred, or a partner assumed, the books are shown, the methods of the business explained, its future developments pointed out. All this is now done for the evolution of mankind. In evolution Creation has shown her hand.* To have kept the secret from man would have imperilled the further evolution. To have revealed it sooner had been premature. Love must come before knowledge, for knowledge is the instrument of love, and useless till it arrives. But now that there is altruism enough in the world to begin the new era, there must be wisdom enough to direct it. To make Nature spell out her own career, to embody the key to the development in the very development itself, so that the key might be handed over along with the work, was to make the transference of responsibility possible and rational. . . . The past of Nature is a working model of how worlds can be made. The probabilities are there is no better way of making them. If man does as well it will be enough. In any case he can only begin where Nature left off, and work with such tools as are put into his hands. If the new partner had been intended merely to experiment with world-making, no such legacy of useful law had ever been given him. And if he had been meant to begin *de novo* on a totally different plan, it is unlikely either that that should not have been hinted at, or that in his touching and beautiful endeavour he should be embarrassed and thrown off the track by the old plan. As a child set to complete some fine embroidery is shown the stitches, the colours and the outline traced upon the canvas, so the great mother in setting their difficult task to her later children, provides them with one superb part finished to show the pattern" (pp. 48, 49, 50, 51, 52).

This is the great philosophy of evolution for which we have been carefully prepared, and which is now sprung upon us. The jargon is the jargon of pseudo-science, but the ideas are the ideas of the curate at the Y.M.C.A. And what are these ideas but a re-hash of the old theistic apologies for God, simply translated into the language of modern evolution? The older theologians used to argue that evil would cease to appear evil to us if only we could know the purpose of it. The modern theologian argues that God, supposing him to be the author of evolution, is not to be blamed for the suffering which evolution involves, because this suffering is an instrument in the working out of higher perfection. "Viewed *simpliciter,*" as Mr. Drummond has said in a passage already quoted, "the struggle for life appears irreconcilable with ethical ends, a prodigious anomaly in a moral world; but viewed in continuous reaction with the struggle for the life of others, it discloses itself as an instrument of perfection the most subtle and far-reaching that reason could devise."

These, alas, are not new ideas. They are as old as theology itself, and will live as long as theism, simply changing from age to age as the form of the scientific attack changes. It is just the argument of Browning, in the passage from *The Ring and the Book* which Mr. Drummond quotes:—

> I can believe, this dread machinery
> Of sin and sorrow, would confound me else,
> Devised—all pain, at most expenditure
> Of pain by who devised pain—to evolve,
> By new machinery in counterpart,
> The moral qualities of man—how else?—
> To make him love in turn, and be beloved;
> Creative and self-sacrificing too,
> And thus eventually God-like.

It is the argument by which the vacillating Romanes sought to square his science and his theology: "'The fair order of nature is only acquired by a wholesale waste and sacrifice'. Granted. But if the 'wholesale waste and sacrifice,' as antecedent, leads to a 'fair order of nature' as its consequent, how can it be said that the 'wholesale waste and struggle' has been a failure?"[1]

It is the argument of Professor Knight: "A larger good is evolved through the winnowing process by which physical nature casts its weaker products aside," etc.[2]

It is the argument of Professor Calderwood: "Not the death in the world, but the life in it, thus becomes the object most conspicuous, showing the grand purpose served through

---

[1] Romanes, *Thoughts on Religion*, p. 92.
[2] Knight, *Aspects of Theism*, pp. 184-186.

all conflict. If animal life is being strangely sacrificed, it is in order that a stronger life may fill a larger place."[1]

It is, in fact, simply the latest form of the ancient theistic attempt to justify the ways of God to man; and, like all former attempts, it is involved in the old dilemma of how to reconcile the supposed love and omnipotence of the Deity with the universal pain which he permits. No Theist has ever been able to overcome this difficulty, and no Theist ever will overcome it. If God can prevent the suffering and will not, he is not good; if he would prevent it but cannot, he is not omnipotent. The rejoinder to this argument, that if we could see the whole process and understand the whole meaning of life, the apparent evil would turn out to be real good, involves the error of supposing that we can ever dissociate ourselves from Nature as a whole. Either God designed the whole of Nature or he did not; if he did not, Theism is absurd at its very foundations; if he did, then he designed the objector to Theism as much as he designed the Theist; if he designed the evil for an ultimately good purpose, then he equally designed the moral repugnance with which we regard this evil, and the moral opprobrium which we attach to the creator of it. To this old dilemma Theism can give no rational answer, because it starts out with the fundamental fallacy of positing a Deity who is at once omnipotent and all-loving, and who yet permits evil to exist which he might remove. On foundations like these no rational philosophy can be built; and the attempt to justify the struggle for life by the newer method is no more successful than the attempts of old. For if God is omnipotent he could very well have made a perfect universe to begin with. To this Mr. Drummond would reply that it is infinitely grander to have given the universe evolution as its principle of perfection, because of the moral discipline and education it gives to man. As if, supposing the universe to have been

[1] Calderwood, *Evolution and Man's Place in Nature*, p. 12.

made perfect at the outset, there would have been any one to have regretted that he had not been made imperfect, on account of the discipline afforded by struggle! We only talk of the beauty of struggle because the struggle is unavoidable, and the only thing we can do is to make the best of a very bad constitution of things. Pain is good, said the older Theists, because it disciplines and chastens us, and makes us realise all the more our blessedness when we are free from pain. But for what does pain discipline us? Simply to endure more pain. The argument is a mere circle. Nor is the attempt to show that the struggle for life is good because it leads to the survival of the fittest any more successful. The closer examination of that theory must be reserved for a later stage of this criticism; here it is only necessary to point out that to philosophise in this manner is simply to read evolution backwards. The struggle for life is *not* an instrument of perfection. One might as well say that certain sides of the dice are the more perfect because they happen to be uppermost in the fall. What survives as the result of the struggle is not the most perfect, in any ethical sense, but simply the fittest; that is, just as when iron and wood are thrown upon water, the one sinks while the other floats, through the action of the same force of gravitation upon differently constituted bodies, so in the struggle for life one organism perishes and another survives, simply because one can withstand better than the other the combination of opposing forces which happens to be dominant at the moment. But to call the one organism "better" or "more perfect" than the other is as absurd as to call the wood more perfect than the iron. And as for Mr. Drummond's argument that God deliberately chose the method of evolution because he "foresaw" that "the time would come when the directing of part of the course of evolution would pass into the hands of man," that is really almost too absurd for serious criticism. The spectacle of a Deity, anxious to make a perfect world, carefully making it imperfect, and then leaving it to struggle for countless ages in pain and misery, until the earth is once more swallowed up in night, is too grotesque for anything.

Reviewing, then, Mr. Drummond's arguments up to this point, we may summarise our criticism thus :—

1. He volunteers to bring biology and sociology up in the way they should go, yet his great new principle turns out on examination to be simply the old theistic fallacy in a new form.

2. Even this fallacy is not original, for it is shared by almost every theistic writer of the day who has dabbled in evolution.

3. There is no value in his argument that we ought to seek the meaning of evolution in its end, not in its beginning, in man, not in the atom, for the reason that we do not know the end of evolution as yet; and for the reason that while we are external to the atom we are not external to ourselves, and so cannot avoid the egoistic fallacy of interpreting the universe in terms of ourselves.

4. In the same way, his analogies about the machine and the workshop, and the ship and its course, are quite invalid, for the reason that there is simply no true analogy between these and the course of evolution.

5. He has blindly assumed that egoism has its birth in nutrition, and altruism its birth in reproduction. He has credited the mere physiological function of reproduction with the ethical attributes of altruism, in spite of his own disingenuous protestations that he is aware such a crediting ought not to be made.

6. His very phrase, "struggle for the life of others," is hopelessly unscientific, in that it (*a*) gives wrong connotations to the word "struggle," (*b*) gives wrong connotations to the word "others," and (*c*) overlooks the difficulty that reproduc-

tion is more egoistic than altruistic, because it is simply another phase of the struggle for life itself.

7. His teleology is no more successful than the older teleology, in that it evades the old difficulties of (*a*) whether a Deity actually made the world, (*b*) whether the Deity, if he made the world, is all-good, (*c*) whether an all-good Deity would create evil, (*d*) whether the Deity is also omnipotent, and (*e*) whether an omnipotent Deity who permits evil can be regarded as all-good.

8. His argument that the struggle for life was consciously designed as an "instrument of perfection" is open to all the objections that have from time immemorial been urged against the theistic contention that pain was meant by God to be an instrument of perfection.

Two more points only remain to be touched upon at this stage of the discussion : (1) Mr. Drummond maintains that his thesis of the importance of altruism, and its fundamental character as part of the cosmic process, is in substance new ; and he has of course no difficulty in making whatever capital there is to be made out of the astonishing fallacies and self-contradictions of Huxley's lecture on *Evolution and Ethics*. But he himself is constrained to admit, upon reflection, that the thesis is not quite so new as he at first alleged it to be ; and he mentions casually the names of " Fiske, Littré, Romanes, Le Conte, L. Büchner, Miss Buckley, and Prince Kropotkin," together with Messrs. Geddes and Thomson and Mr. Herbert Spencer, as writers who "have expressed themselves partly in the same direction" (p. 43). They have, indeed ; the principle of the importance of altruism in organic and social development is so self-evident that it would have been a wonder had any thinker failed to perceive it. But if, when Mr. Drummond says that these writers "have expressed themselves *partly* in the same direction," he means that they have avoided his peculiar errors and assumptions on the subject, there will be none to gainsay him. (2) He quarrels with Mr. Kidd for maintaining that altruism must have an ultra-rational sanction, and justly exposes that gentleman's ignorance of Mr. Herbert Spencer's *Principles of Ethics*—a book which Mr. Kidd, though he frequently takes Mr. Spencer's name in vain, has probably never seen. And Mr. Drummond disposes of his fellow-irrationalist thus:—

"What Mr. Kidd has succeeded, and splendidly succeeded, in doing is to show that nature, *as interpreted in terms of the struggle for life*, contains no sanction either for morality or for social progress. But instead of giving up Nature and reason at this point, he should have given up Darwin. The struggle for life is *not* 'the supreme fact up to which biology has slowly advanced'. It is the fact to which Darwin advanced ; but if biology had been thoroughly consulted it could not have given so maimed an account of itself. With the final conclusion reached by Mr. Kidd we have no quarrel. Eliminate the errors due to an unrevised acceptance of Mr. Darwin's interpretation of Nature, and his work remains the most important contribution to social evolution which the last decade has seen. But what startles us is his method. To put the future of social science on an ultra-rational basis is practically to give it up. Unless thinking men have some sense of the consistency of a method they cannot work with it, and if there is no guarantee of the stability of the results it would not be worth while. . . . We believe with Mr. Kidd that 'the process of social development which has been taking place, and which is still in progress in our Western civilisation, is not the product of the intellect, but the motive force behind it has had its seat and origin in the *fund of altruistic feeling* with which our civilisation has become equipped'. But we shall endeavour to show that this fund of altruistic feeling has been slowly funded in the race by Nature, or through Nature, and as the direct and inevitable result of that struggle for the life of others, which has been from all time a condition of existence" (pp. 68, 71, 72).

This is typical of Mr. Drummond's confusion of thought. As against Mr. Kidd's absurd contention that we must be irrational in order to progress, he is of course right; but how does he proceed to correct Mr. Kidd's view of the case? First he thinks it necessary to inform us that this "fund of altruistic feeling has been slowly funded in the race by Nature"—as if any rational man would think of disputing the proposition that "Nature" had made us altruistic. Then he lays it down that this "funding" has gone on as "the direct and inevitable result" of the struggle for the life of others. Previously he had told us that the struggle for the life of others had its root in reproduction, of which "the significant note is ethical, the development of other-ism, as altruism" (p. 21)—"sympathy, tenderness, unselfishness, and the long list of virtues which make up altruism," being "the direct outcome and essential accompaniment of the reproductive process" (p. 22). If, then, altruism is the "essential accompaniment" of the reproductive process, how comes it that at a certain epoch there is more of it than there was in previous times? How has it been "funded," and in whom? And if egoism is the essential accompaniment of the nutritive process, on the terms of Mr. Drummond's argument, how is it that this is diminishing as he says? If nutrition = egoism, and reproduction = altruism, how is it that altruism is increasing at the expense of egoism, when there must always be at least as much nutrition as reproduction? The conception of egoism and altruism as "forces" or "funds," one of which increases while the other decreases, is simply the grossest blundering, the apotheosis of bastard argument. If altruism has increased in the modern world, there are concrete causes for it, and writers like Mr. Kidd and Mr. Drummond, who are content to ascribe this increase to the "funding" of altruism by religion, which is the "motive force behind our civilisation," or to the reproductive process pure and simple, are merely reducing science to the grotesque. And all the while the principle of the struggle for life, at which Mr. Drummond turns up the white of a clerical eye, is quite competent to take upon itself the whole of the burden and the whole of the credit of evolution. For the struggle for the life of others, to use Mr. Drummond's jargon, if it helps to determine which organisms or societies shall survive and which shall perish, is simply *a phase of the struggle for life*. "In a moral world," he himself tells us, "the fittest are the weak, the pitiable, the poor" (p. 268); that is, to strip the phrase of its theological exaggeration, there comes a time when the physically weak are not hastily weeded out in the struggle for life, but are kept alive and nourished and cared for by the altruism and self-sacrifice of others. But so far from this process being a negation of the struggle for life, it is simply part and parcel of it. The care for others, *i.e.*, altruism, always has been a factor in the preservation of societies. As Mr. Spencer has put it: "The most general conclusion is that in order of obligation the preservation of the species takes precedence of the preservation of the individual. It is true that the species has no existence save as an aggregate of individuals; and it is true that, therefore, the welfare of the species is an end to be subserved only as subserving the welfare of individuals. But since disappearance of the species, implying absolute disappearance of all individuals, involves absolute failure in achieving the end, whereas disappearance of individuals, though carried to a great extent, may leave outstanding such numbers as can, by continuance of the species, make subsequent fulfilment of the end possible; the preservation of the individual must, in a variable degree according to circumstances, be subordinated to the preservation of the species, where the two conflict."[1] And even Huxley's own

[1] *Principles of Ethics*, ii., 6.

illogical assertion that "the practice of that which is ethically best—what we call goodness or virtue—involves a course of conduct which, in all respects, is opposed to that which leads to success in the cosmic struggle for existence. In place of ruthless self-assertion it demands self-restraint," etc.[1]—even this is refuted by his own previous argument that a pack of wolves could not exist for a single winter unless "ruthless self-assertion" were subordinated to "self-restraint". There never has been, in fact, a time when the world was all egoism—this being the "cosmic process"; and altruism is not a new "force" which has suddenly come in to counteract this cosmic process. And to say, as Mr. Drummond says, that "Love is not a late arrival, an after-thought, with Creation. It is not a novelty of a romantic civilisation. . . . Its roots began to grow with the first cell of life which budded on this earth" (p. 276); and then to tell us, only five pages later, that "from self-ism to other-ism is the supreme transition of history," and then once more, on the next page, that "even at its dawn life is receiver and giver; even in protoplasm is self-ism and other-ism"; to see-saw like this is merely to pay the penalty of clinging obstinately to a self-contradictory theory that is flawed with paralogism at its very foundation. If the first cell of life contained egoism and altruism, or the potentiality of them, what, we may once more ask, has made the latter grow at the expense of the former? To rhapsodise about the "opportunities" and the "purposes" of evolution, and the "love" that is at the back of evolution, is simply to offer the thinnest theological sentiment in place of a scientific explanation. If altruism is increasing, it is because those societies which, from a variety of causes, have been able to practise it and develop it have had, *ceteris paribus*, a very real advantage in the struggle for life over societies in which the internecine

---

[1] *Evolution and Ethics*, p. 33. See again his note on pp. 56-57, which is once more contradictory.

struggle was fiercer and more prolonged; that is, altruism, or the struggle for the life of others, as Mr. Drummond calls it, is simply one factor among many others in the struggle for life, and the struggle for life is *the* principle of evolution, of which nutrition and reproduction, egoism and altruism, and all other modes of action and reaction, are but so many phases.

CHAPTER III.

WITH the first, second, third, fourth, and fifth chapters of Mr. Drummond's book—entitled respectively, " The Ascent of the Body," " The Scaffolding Left in the Body," " The Arrest of the Body," " The Dawn of Mind," and " The Evolution of Language "—we have no immediate concern. They are simply a *résumé* of the best-known facts of evolution—interesting enough in its way, and rather agreeably done on the whole, but containing nothing new, and therefore not calling for any criticism. Our task begins again with his sixth chapter, entitled " The Struggle for Life "—an interesting chapter, because it shows to what depths of intellectual dishonesty a worthy man can descend in his efforts to defend the moral character of his Deity. The difficulty, be it observed, is entirely of his own making, just as the old problem of evil, which has always beset the path of the Theist, has been made a problem by the Theist himself. To posit a " problem of evil " is to assume that somehow, or at some time or other, the problem might be solved. The problem of evil, however, is essentially incapable of solution. To adduce one reason alone in proof of this, neither good nor evil is an absolute term, admitting of accurate and universal definition. Each is purely relative. For example: a hungry tiger chases an antelope for his dinner. Two things may happen: (1) the tiger, being in good health, may catch the antelope and make his meal of him; (2) the tiger, being in ill-health, may be unable to catch the antelope. In the first case, the tiger will regard his healthy condition during the chase as a good thing, while the antelope will regard it as an evil thing; in the second case, the antelope will call the tiger's ill-health good, the tiger will call it evil. Evidently opinions of good and evil are purely relative, depending very much on the point of view of the moralist. Here, then, for the Theist to hope to solve the "problem of evil" is to forget that it is quite impossible for us to know what good and evil are from a universal standpoint, and therefore what the problem is. So that a rational man is content to recognise the relative characters of good and evil, and not to confuse the matter still further by introducing, as the author of this system of good and evil, a Being to whom he attributes the quality of infinite goodness. On these terms the Theist may well have his "great and dark problem of evil," for from premises so contradictory as these nothing but contradiction can come. The problem, such as it is, is altogether of his own making.

Similarly, when Mr. Drummond begins to justify the ways of God to man in relation to the struggle for life, we feel constrained to admonish him, in all friendliness, that there is really no need to attempt any such task. Evolution is evolution, and the struggle for life we all implicitly, if not explicitly, condemn. If, then, Mr. Drummond chooses to say that an all-good, all-wise, and all-loving Father has deliberately selected the struggle for life as his instrument for working out the evolution of mankind, he must surely be aware that it will be no easy matter to reconcile the known facts of evolution with the hypothetical character of his Deity. An attempted reconciliation of this kind can be done only by sophistry—and, I fear I must add, by a sophistry that is not always unconscious and involuntary. Nevertheless, such attempts are always interesting. If they throw no light on the subject of evolution, they throw a very powerful light on the mental and moral processes of their authors. They are not exactly science, but they constitute a human document.

Mr. Drummond begins his criticism of the struggle for life with one of those curate-at-the-Y.M.C.A. forms of exposition in which he has such a fatal facility.

"Start with a comparatively unevolved savage, and see what the struggle for life will do for him. When we meet him first he is sitting, we shall suppose, in the sun. Let us also suppose—and it requires no imagination to suppose it—that he has no wish to do anything else than sit in the sun, and that he is perfectly contented and perfectly happy. Nature around him, visible and invisible, is as still as he is, as inert apparently, as unconcerned. Neither molests the other; they have no connection with each other. Yet it is not so. That savage is the victim of a conspiracy. Nature has designs upon him (*sic*), wants to do something to him. That something is to move him. Why does it wish to move him? Because (*sic*) movement is work, and work is exercise, and exercise may mean a further evolution of the part of him that is exercised. How does it set about moving him? By moving itself. Everything else being in motion, it is impossible for him to resist. The sun moves away to the west, and he must move or freeze with cold. As the sun continues to move, twilight falls, and wild animals move from their lairs, and he must move or be eaten." And so on, and so on, in the most approved curatese. "Multiply these movements, and you multiply him. Make him do things he has never done before, and he will become what he never was before. . . . The universe has to be so ordered that that which man would not have done alone he should be compelled to do. In other words, it was necessary (*sic*) to introduce into Nature, and into human nature, some such principle as the struggle for life" (pp. 243-245).

Here we are already in the thick of Mr. Drummond's

method. First of all " Nature," which = man plus the rest of the universe, is separated from "man," who apparently is not part of Nature. Then Nature, which is really our name for that which undergoes evolution, "wants" to bring about a little evolution on its own account. It "has designs upon" man. It moves him, in order to make him—want to be moved!—which is indeed a luminous piece of philosophising. If " Nature" really acts in this manner, like Mr. Spencer's man in the street who "must do something" when things would go along much better if he would only refrain from doing something, she is really very much to blame and the savage very much to be pitied. She might as well have left the poor devil sitting on his rock "in the sun"—to conjure up Mr. Drummond's arcadian picture of him—with no wish to do anything else than sit in the sun, perfectly contented, perfectly happy. If he is in this condition he is indeed well circumstanced. But Nature has designs on him—wants to move him. Baby is doing nothing, in fact, and the fond mother comes along to tell him not to. He *must* be moved. What happens when he is moved? He begins, says Mr. Drummond, to exercise muscles which he otherwise would not have exercised. " He must either move away, and move away very fast, to find the sun again; or he must chase, and also very fast, some thick-furred animal, and kill it, and clothe himself with its skin. Thus from a man he has become a hunter, a different kind of a man, a further man. He did not wish to become a hunter; he *had* to become a hunter. All that he wished to do was to sit in the sun and be let alone, and but for a Nature around him which would not rest, or let him alone, he would have sat on there till he died." And what if he had? He would at least never have known the unhappiness of struggle, which is all that "Nature," on Mr. Drummond's terms, gives him. He is to become a hunter in order that he may hunt, and he must hunt because he is hungry, and he is hungry because Nature "moves," as Mr. Drummond puts it, the meal he has had in the morning. That is, I bring a friend into my room. He is sitting there quietly and harmlessly, when suddenly I run a knife into him. I then proceed to philosophise to him in the manner of Mr. Drummond. I tell him that it is not good for him to sit there, " perfectly contented, perfectly happy ". He must be moved—for his own good; and the way to move him is to move something else into him, a knife for preference. Now if he does not move, I tell him, he will bleed to death ; so he must move and discover things which will stop the bleeding, and other things which will heal the wound. "Thus," I tell him, "from a man you have become a medical man, a different kind of a man, a further man. You did not wish to become a medical man; you *had* to become a medical man. . . . In other words, if ever you were to learn the important art of curing wounds, it was necessary first to give you a wound." To this he might reply, not unreasonably, that he had no ambition whatever to become an expert wound-dresser ; that rather than have a wound in order to teach him how to dress wounds, he would rather, if it was all the same to me, not have a wound at all. And to Mr. Drummond we may say that to tell us that man *had* to become this or that in order to be this or that, is simply to explain things backwards; and to say that "it was necessary" to introduce the struggle for life into the universe is to raise the questions : (1) Necessary for whom ? (2) Necessary for what purpose? (3) If the struggle for life had *not* been inaugurated, and men had never been set in a never-ending round of conflict and misery, would they ever have been conscious of having missed anything ? It is as absurd as to say that we must not all commit simultaneous suicide, because then there would be nobody alive to carry on the business of the world. If there was nobody alive, obviously no one could feel very much aggrieved.

Mr. Drummond proceeds to sketch the evolution of man so far as this has depended on the struggle for life; and we must constantly bear in mind the plea he has already urged in justification of evolution, that it was "an instrument of perfection the most subtle and far-reaching that reason could devise". Remembering this, let us follow the theologian in his exposition of the struggle for life, and its ethical function in the scheme of things. He shows how certain things—the erect posture, the prehensile hand, for example—have aided him in the struggle, and how the club has been an important element in evolution. Then he sketches the development of weapons both of offence and defence, and finally gives us the philosophy of these things. "These primitive weapons are the pathetic expression of the world's first struggle. As the earliest contribution of mankind to solve its still fundamental difficulty—the problem of nutrition—they are of enduring interest to the human race" (p. 251). These weapons, that is, are of use in enabling man to get the better of his fellow-men or of animals, and the erect posture is particularly advantageous, because it enables him the better to club his fellows. At this point Mr. Drummond, with unusual thoughtfulness, becomes aware that this is not altogether a testimonial to the God of Love. So he informs us that we must not misconceive the real meaning of this development. As for these weapons, "*so far from being, as one might suppose, mere implements of destruction, they are implements of self-preservation; they entered the world not from hate of man, but from love of life;*" which is about the most humorously Jesuitical justification of murder which I have yet seen. Mr. Drummond's words are words of balm and comfort to all those whose hands are raised against their fellows; they can plead that when their life-preserver cracks a householder's skull the motive is not hate of man, but love of life. *The Ascent of Man* is really one of those books no burglar's library should be without.

But Mr. Drummond now plunges deeper and deeper into the mire. "We see now, perhaps, more clearly why evolution at the dawn of life entered into league with so strange an ally as *want*. The evolution of mankind was too great a thing to entrust to any uncertain hand. The advantage of attaching human progress to the struggle for life is that you can always depend upon it. Hunger never fails" (p. 255). Nature, we see, is still there, at the post of duty, pale and anxious, but brave and steadfast, assiduously "moving" man for his own good, a sort of policeman among a loafing humanity, an Irish nurse waking the patient at the stated hour in order to make him take his sleeping draught. And now Mr. Drummond begins to finger his brief, and rises to exculpate his client, the Deity, from the charge of murdering his own creatures.

"The association of the struggle for life with the physiological function of nutrition must be continually borne in mind. For the essential nature of the principle has been greatly obscured by the very name which Mr. Darwin gave to it. Probably no other was possible; but the effect has been that men have emphasised the almost ethical substantive 'struggle,' and ignored the biological term 'life'." As for Mr. Drummond's own phrase, "struggle for the life of others," there is of course no objection to emphasising the ethical substantive "struggle" to the fullest degree. You must only refrain from this emphasis when it is apt to make theology look foolish. "A secondary implication of the process has thus been elevated into the prime one; and this, exaggerated by the imagination, has led to Nature being conceived of as a vast murderous machine for the annihilation of the majority and the survival of the few. *But the struggle for life, in the first instance, is simply living itself (sic); at the best, it is living under a healthily normal maximum of pressure; at the worst, under an abnormal maximum.*" That is all; if you are handicapped by poverty and disease in the struggle for life, and you find yourself being painfully and ignominiously snuffed out like a candle that has been lit in mistake, you are not to raise vain hands to heaven and curse him who flung your poor body to the wolves of his world; you are to buy, beg, borrow or steal a copy of *The Ascent of Man*, and having learnt that all that is the matter with you is that you are under an abnormal maximum of pressure, you are to console yourself with this great thought, you are to congratulate Mr. Drummond on his faculty for euphemism, and then make the best end that is possible for you. For "as we have seen," says Mr. Drummond, "initially, [the struggle for life] is but another name for the discharge of the supreme physiological function of nutrition. If life is to go on at all, this function *must* be discharged, and continually discharged. . . . Whatever man came ultimately to wish and to achieve for himself, it was essential at first that such arrangements should be made for him. The machinery for his development had not only to be put into Nature, *but he had to be placed in the machine and held there, and brought back there as often as he tried to evade it.* To say that man evolved himself, nevertheless, is as absurd as to say that a newspaper prints itself. To say even that the machinery evolved him is as preposterous as to say of a poem that the printing press made it. The ultimate problem is, who made the machine? and who thought the poem that was to be printed?" (pp. 255-258).

Mr. Drummond, it will be seen, is most anxious that we should realise that it is not evolution that causes the struggle for life, but God. He goes on: "If you say that you do not unreservedly approve of the machine, that it lacerates as well as binds, the difficulty is more real. *But it is a principle in the study of history to suspend judgment both of the meaning and of the value of a policy until the chain of sequences it sets in motion should be worked out to its last fulfilment. When the full tale of the struggle for life is told, when the record of its victories is closed, when the balance of its gains and losses has been struck, and especially when it has been proved that there actually have been losses, it will be time to pass judgment on its moral value.*" This from the man who all along has jauntily given his verdict of approval upon the struggle for life; who has told us that it, along with the struggle for the life of others, was the most perfect instrument which reason could devise! He is to slobber as he likes over the love and wisdom of the Deity, but when you point to the merciless and unending conflict which, on his own showing, the Deity has imposed upon mankind, you are told to suspend *your* judgment "until the chain of sequences shall be worked out to its last fulfilment"—that is, until you reach the other side of eternity.

Mr. Drummond, indeed, sees for a moment the absurdity of his position. "Of course," he writes, "this principle cuts both ways; it warns off a favourable as well as an unfavourable verdict on the beneficence of the system of things." And yet he is inconsistent enough once more to presume to give the verdict in favour of "the beneficence of the system of things". "But evolution is a study in history, and its results are largely known. And it would be affectation to deny that on the whole the results are good, and appear the worthier the more we penetrate into their inner meaning. Men forget when they denounce the struggle for life that it is to be judged not only on the ground of sentiment, but of reason (*sic*), that not its local or surface effects only, but its permanent influence on the order of the world, must be taken into account" (pp. 258, 259). "That is," says Mr. Drummond, "the struggle for life is good; yet, if you come to look at it, there is something bad about it too. So that the best thing we can do is to suspend our judgment upon the matter at present, since from the very nature of things we are not in a position to give a proper opinion upon it. When I say *we* must suspend our judgment, however, I mean that *you* must; I am competent to give my opinion here and now; and, looking at the matter in a way impossible to you—*i.e.*, rationally—I lay it down that evolution *is* good after all, and my previous words are not to be used in evidence against me." Mr. Drummond as the Hamlet of evolution—funny without being vulgar—is amusing enough; but Mr. Drummond as the Lady Plyant of theology is the very essence of humour.

But Mr. Drummond's further remarks on this theme must be quoted in full; no selection could do them justice :—

"Even on the lower ranges of Nature the unfavourable implications of the struggle for life have probably been exaggerated. While it is essential to an understanding of the course of evolution to retain in the imagination a vivid sense of the struggle itself, we must beware of over-colouring the representation, or flooding it with accompaniments of emotion borrowed from our own sensations. The word struggle at all in this connection *is little more than a metaphor*. When it is said that an animal struggles, *all that is really meant is that it lives*. An animal, that is to say, does not, in addition to all its other activities, have to employ a vast number of special activities, to the exercise of which the term struggle is to be applied. *It is life itself which is the struggle:* and the whole life, and the whole of the activities and powers which make up life, are involved in it. To speak of struggle in the sense of some special and separate struggle, to conceive of battle, or even a series of battles, is misleading *where all is struggle and all is battle*. Especially must we beware of reading into it our personal ideas with regard to accompaniments of pain. The probabilities are that the struggle for life *in the lower creation* is, to say the least, *less painful than it looks*. Whether we regard the dulness of the states of consciousness among lower animals, or the fact that the condition of danger must become habitual, or that death when it comes is sudden and unaccompanied by that anticipation which gives it its chief dread to man, we must assume that whatever the struggle for life subjectively means to the lower animals, it can never approach in terror what it means to us. *And as to putting any moral content into it until a late stage in the world's development, that is not to be thought of.* Judged of even by later standards, there is much to relieve one's first unfavourable impression. *With exceptions, the fight is a fair fight. As a rule there is no hate in it, but only hunger.* It is seldom prolonged, and seldom wanton. As to the manner of death, it is generally sudden. As to the fact of death, all animals must die. As to the meaning of an existence prematurely closed, *it is better to be to be eaten than not to be at all.* And, as to the last result, it is better to be eaten out of the world and, dying, help another to live, than pollute the world by lingering decay. The most, after all, that can be done with life is to give it to others. Till Nature taught her own creatures of their own free will to offer the sacrifice, is it strange that she took it by force?" (pp. 259-261).

This extraordinary passage is well worth examining at once for its logic and its ethics. First of all we are told that we must not allow our emotions to pass moral judgment upon the slaughter that attends the struggle for life. To speak of it as a struggle, in fact, is somewhat to misunderstand it; "to conceive of battle . . . is misleading, where all is struggle and all is battle;" that is, an animal's life is not a struggle because it is *all* struggle. If a man's head is pounded for five minutes, that constitutes assault and battery; but if it is pounded regularly every day there is no assault nor battery in the case! And especially must we beware of reading our own ideas of pleasure and pain into the struggle for life, and of putting a moral content into it. That is, whether animals suffer or not in the struggle for existence, their creator has no responsibility in the matter, and we have no right to pass a moral judgment upon him; though if a human being acted in the same manner we should be justified in calling his conduct infamous. Thus does theology make for righteousness.

But following immediately upon Mr. Drummond's protest that we must not introduce ethical ideas into the discussion, he proceeds to introduce ethical ideas of his own into it, by arguing that after all the fight is not so bad as it looks. Calmly he sweeps aside the whole of what he calls "the lower creation," on the plea that they really cannot suffer as much as we suffer. As if that were the point at issue! The question is not whether animals suffer little or much, but whether it is consistent with the wisdom which Mr. Drummond attributes to his Deity that he should choose so clumsy and roundabout a method of working out "perfection," and whether it is consistent with his attribute of goodness that he should deliberately and foreknowingly inaugurate a scheme that means death and suffering and frustration for so many millions of his creatures. Does any human being think that the creator of a worm has no moral responsibility towards a worm, simply because it is not a man? Would Mr. Drummond, to put the question pertinently, claim such exemption from responsibility for himself? And if not, why should he claim it for a God who is supposed to be better and wiser and more compassionate than he?

And notice the theologian's defence of the struggle among the higher animals. "*With exceptions*, the fight is a fair fight." As if the question were whether the animals were fighting fairly or unfairly, and not whether a God of Love is justified in setting his creatures on earth to fight! And the "*with exceptions*" is positively charming, as are also the other reservations of Mr. Drummond's argument. "*As a rule*, there is no hate in it, but only hunger. It is *seldom* prolonged, and *seldom* wanton. . . . *It is better to be to be eaten than not to be at all.*"

I cannot find words to express my opinion of the man who can write such a sentence as this last, or of the theological system that makes such writing possible. That any man should descend to such depths of immoral sophistry, and all in the name of religion, all with the plea of subserving a moral purpose, is something too infinitely saddening for anger. This is the man who speaks serenely of the " lower animals," conscious, apparently, of his own superiority! As if any ape or tiger, with the lust of murder in its eye, were half so cruel a satire upon this world and the wisdom of its Maker as the modern theologian who thus prostitutes himself in the cause of his religion. To look upon a moral type like this, and to know that religion is breeding thousands like it, is almost to despair of human nature. For a man to watch the slow agony of a mouse in the paws of a cat, or of a man fighting his pathetic fight with the micro-organisms of consumption, and then, in order to save the reputation of his God, to tell us that the fight is a fair fight, that there is no hate in it, but only hunger, and that it is better to exist to be eaten than not to exist at all—to do this and not to be conscious that he is guilty of wilful and deliberate sophistry is something more than I can believe. And this lying for the glory of God is justified because of its services to morals!

"There is another side to this principle," continues Mr. Drummond, " from which its higher significance becomes still more apparent. It follows from the struggle for life that those animals which struggle most successfully will prosper, while the less successful will disappear—hence the well-known principle of natural selection, or the survival of the fittest. Waiving the discussion of this law in general, and the varying meanings which 'fitness' assumes as we rise in the scale of being, observe the *rôle* it plays in Nature. *The object of the survival of the fittest is to produce (sic) fitness.* And it does so both negatively and positively. In the first place it produces fitness by killing off the unfit. Without the rigorous weeding out of the imperfect, the progress of the world had not been possible. . . . It is only when one considers the working of the struggle for life on the large scale, and realises its necessity to the evolution of the world as a whole, that one can even begin to discuss its ethical or teleological meanings. To make a fit world, the unfit at every stage must be made to disappear; and if any self-acting law can bring this about, though its bearing upon this or that individual case may seem unjust, its necessity for the world as a whole is vindicated.[1] If more of any given species are born into the world than can possibly find food, and if a given number must die, that number must be singled out upon some principle; and we cannot quarrel with the principle in physical nature which condemns to death the worst. By placing the death penalty upon the slightest shortcoming, natural selection so discourages imperfection as practically to eliminate it from the world. *The fact that any given animal is alive at all is almost a token of its perfectness. Nothing living can be wholly a failure"* (pp. 263-265).

The inanity of the last two sentences, and their fatuous contradiction with all that has gone before, may be passed over in charitable silence. But the ethic of the remainder of the passage is certainly a precious light upon the theistic mind. Why, in the name of common sense, are the imperfect organisms made at all by a Creator who is supposed to know his own mind and to be capable of getting what he wants? The spectacle of an all-wise and all-powerful Deity deliberately blundering in this manner, making ten organisms in order to kill off five of them, and for the sole reason of keeping the other five alive, is too grotesque even to arouse a decent spirit of contempt. If God's purpose is "to make a fit world," why should he be foolish enough to make millions of

---

[1] How it can be vindicated as being good for the world "as a whole," when in "this or that individual case" it is admitted to be bad, is more than the uninstructed mind of the sceptic can understand.

the unfit only to kill them? "Natural selection," says Mr. Drummond, "discourages imperfection." Then what, in the name of reason, encourages it? And if the Deity is so foolish as to construct a world on these principles, what is to be thought of the theologians who affect to find in it evidences of his wisdom and foresight? For, be it noted, Mr. Drummond finally makes his God out to be stupid as well as wicked. The object of natural selection, he says, is to produce fitness by weeding out the unfit. Yet he himself argues in other places (1) that "natural selection" by no means invariably works in the direction of progress; in parasites, for example, it has "consummated almost utter degeneration," so that here God's chosen instrument has apparently failed to do its work; (2) that natural selection must always go on—in which case there will *always* be the unfit as well as the fit; and (3) that if natural selection were to cease stagnation would ensue. Therefore, on the lines of Mr. Drummond's own argument, either the perfection God is aiming at can never come, or if it does come it can only = stagnation. And while to suppose that God started the world and then let things drift is bad enough in all conscience, to suppose that he does all the murder of his own creatures for a conscious and deliberate purpose is to make him out a worse monster than ever. He is simply wicked without being charming.

So much, then, for Mr. Drummond's treatise upon the struggle for life. It is full of the most amazing contradictions, the most amazing logic, and the most amazing ethic. He feels that the struggle for life is an evil, on the supposition that a good God made the world, and yet he will not admit it. He tells us that we cannot pronounce moral judgment upon evolution "till the full tale is told," yet he immediately proceeds to give his own judgment upon it. He repeats all the fallacies of the old "design" argument, and adds to them a few of his own; and he finishes up with a display of ethical perversion that is indeed no new thing in the history of religion, but is a peculiarly repulsive thing from the point of view of rationalist morals. Let us now follow him in the remainder of his devious course. Having expounded the philosophy of the struggle for life, he will now expound the philosophy of what he calls the struggle for the life of others.

CHAPTER IV.

MR. DRUMMOND accommodatingly begins with a few fallacies that reveal at once the weakness and the confusion of his argument. "We now open a wholly new, and by far the most important, chapter in the evolution of man," he writes. " Up to this time we have found for him a body, and the rudiments of mind. But man is not a body, nor a mind. The temple still awaits its final tenant—the higher human soul. With a body alone, man is an animal : the highest animal, yet a pure animal ; struggling for its own narrow life, living for its small and sordid ends. Add a mind to that and the advance is infinite. The struggle for life assumes the august form of a struggle for light : he who was once a savage, pursuing the arts of the chase, realises Aristotle's ideal man, 'a hunter after truth'. Yet this is not the end. Experience tells us that man's true life is neither lived in the material tracts of the body, nor in the higher altitudes of the intellect, but in the warm world of the affections. *Till he is equipped with these, man is not human.* He reaches his full height only when love becomes to him the breath of life, the energy of will, the summit of desire" (pp. 275, 276).

This is the primitive psychology of the theological college, which we do not argue against at this time of day ; we smile at it, and let it pass. But it is upon this primitive psychology that Mr. Drummond actually chooses to base the remainder of his argument. He hovers about for a moment between the thesis that love is co-eternal with life, and the opposite thesis that love came in at some time or other to complete the life of man, who until that time was only an animal. Vacillations of this kind, however, are what we are accustomed to from reasoners like Mr. Drummond; and we are also accustomed to his beating of the big drum as a preliminary to the announcement that he will expound to us a principle which science up to now has strangely and inexplicably overlooked. " As the story of evolution is usually told," he writes, "love—the evolved form, as we shall see, of the struggle for the life of others—has not even a place. Almost the whole emphasis of science has fallen upon the opposite—the animal struggle for life. Hunger was early seen by the naturalists to be the first and most imperious appetite of all living things, and the course of Nature came to be erroneously interpreted in terms of a never-ending strife. Since there are vastly more creatures born than can ever survive, since for every morsel of food provided a hundred claimants appear, life to an animal was described to us as one long tragedy; and poetry, borrowing the imperfect creed, pictured Nature only as a blood-red fang. Before we can go on to trace the higher progress of love itself, it is necessary to correct this misconception. And no words can be thrown away if they serve, in whatever imperfect measure, to restore to honour what is in reality the supreme factor in the evolution of the world. . . . The first chapter or two of the story of evolution may be headed the struggle for life; but take the book as a whole and it is not a tale of battle. It is a love-story" (pp. 277-279).

With the latter conclusion we shall have to deal later on. But it is necessary to point out here the extraordinary confusion of Mr. Drummond's ideas upon evolution. Does he seriously think there ever was a time in the history of the higher animals when the struggle for life was entirely what he calls an "animal" struggle, without any admixture of altruism? If his words do not mean this they mean nothing at all; and, judging from some of the specimens we have had of his faculty for verbose fatuity, the latter supposition is not improbably the correct one. But when he lays it down that "science" has not taken account of altruism in its reading of evolution, what has become of his own earlier admission that writer after writer had expressly included this factor? He himself mentioned Mr. Herbert Spencer and Messrs. Geddes and Thomson, along with "Fiske, Littré, Romanes, Le Conte, L. Büchner, Miss Buckley, and Prince Kropotkin," and these are assuredly not all. Has he forgotten his own quotation from Mr. Spencer? "What is the ethical aspect of these [altruistic] principles? In the first place, animal life of all but the lowest kinds has been maintained by virtue of them. Excluding the *protozoa*, among which their operation is scarcely discernible, we see that without *gratis* benefits to offspring and earned benefits to adults, life could not have continued. In the second place, by virtue of them life has gradually evolved into higher forms. By care of offspring, which has become greater with advancing organisation, and by survival of the fittest in the competition among adults, which has become habitual with advancing organisation, superiority has been perpetually fostered and further advances caused."[1] Has he forgotten his own quotation from Messrs. Geddes and Thomson's *Evolution of Sex*, when he so serenely informs us that science has been almost ignorant of the great principle of altruism in evolution? The thesis of the importance of the altruistic emotions in the evolution of animal life is to be found almost everywhere in the writings of evolutionists; but what these have done is simply to avoid the primitive fallacies of Mr. Drummond.

Briefly, his argument is this: the two fundamental functions of organic life are nutrition and reproduction. From the former we get egoism—the struggle for life; from the

[1] *Principles of Ethics*, ii., 5.

latter we get altruism—the struggle for the life of others. The way in which a primitive unicellular organism reproduces—*i.e.*, by fission—is an example of self-sacrifice on the lowest ranges of organic life. "There is no reproduction in plant, animal, or man which does not involve self-sacrifice. All that is moral and social and other-regarding has come along the line of this function. Sacrifice, moreover, as these physiological facts disclose, is not an accident, nor an accompaniment of reproduction, but an inevitable part of it. It is the universal law and the universal condition of life" (p. 290). But above and beyond this there are "other gifts which reproduction has bestowed upon the world. . . . All the arrangements in plant life which concern the flower are the creations of the struggle for the life of others. For reproduction alone the flower is created; when the process is over it returns to the dust. This miracle of beauty *is a miracle of love.* Its splendour of colour, its variegations, its form, its symmetry, its perfume, its honey, its very texture, are all notes of love—love-calls or love-lures or love-provisions for the insect world." And not only flowers but foods are the products of love. "What are these grains? Seeds—stores of starch or albumen which, *in the perfect forethought of reproduction (!),* plants bequeath to their offspring. The foods of the world, especially the children's foods, are the foods of the children of plants, the foods which unselfish (*sic*) activities store round the cradles of the helpless, so that when the sun wakens them to their new world they may not want. Every plant in the world lives for others. It sets aside something costly, cared for, the highest expression of its nature. The seed is the tithe of love, the tithe which Nature renders to man. When man lives upon seeds he lives upon love." And so on, and so on, *ad nauseam.*

I do not know whether Mr. Drummond means this extraordinary rhapsody to be taken seriously, but to take it seriously is a compliment which few people will pay him.

The new principle, the much-trumpeted discovery which was so noisily heralded by Mr. Drummond, turns out to be nothing more than a childish confusion due to an illegitimate use of one or two words. He is indeed careful, in his more rational moments, to tell us to beware of reading moral contents into lower nature; but he conveniently forgets his own warning as soon as it suits his purpose to do so. If ever there was a word that bore an ethical meaning, it is the word "self-sacrifice"; unless it is used in a purely figurative way, which no competent reasoner would ever think of doing in argument, it can have none but an ethical interpretation; and for Mr. Drummond to talk of the fission of a lowly organised protoplasmic cell—a purely physical process if ever there was one—as an act of self-sacrifice, as a dying to live, is simply to assume all he has to prove, by using the ethical term in a connection that makes its use wholly illegitimate. Altruism *may* have had its genesis in reproduction; but to set out to prove this proposition, and to prove it by saying that altruism comes from reproduction because reproduction = altruism, is really too ingenuous for any one but a theological professor. And he alone could speak of "the perfect forethought of reproduction," and argue that flowers and seeds are love-products because they attract or keep alive other organisms. On the same terms it is love that makes the iron fly to the magnet, and love that prompts the animal with a tape-worm to feed itself in order to keep the parasite alive. It may be a very pretty poetic fancy that it is love that makes the activities of one substance subserve the activities of another; but poetry is not science, and the theological professor who calmly assures us that the evolution theory has been blundering along in the dark until now, and that he has the new light that will make all clear to us, should really be above proving his case by a childish confusion of terms, and a childish belief that metaphor is argument.

The remainder of Mr. Drummond's chapter is an interesting example of how to read evolution backwards, and to imagine you are explaining things by simply stating the mere fact of the existence of the things. He points out once more what every one knows already, that "looking broadly at Nature, one general fact is striking—the more social animals are in overwhelming preponderance over the unsocial. Mr. Darwin's dictum, that 'those communities which included the greatest number of the most sympathetic members would flourish best,' is wholly proved" (p. 305). That is, co-operation has been, among the organisms that practised it, an important factor in the struggle for survival. Mr. Drummond chooses to put it in the theological manner, thus: "But to return to the more direct effects of reproduction. After creating others *there lay before evolution a not less necessary task*—the task of uniting them. . . . Before any higher evolution can take place these units must by some means be brought into relation so as not only to act together, but to react upon each other." And evolution does this by means of sex. If Mr. Drummond's words here mean anything whatever, they mean that evolution, or nature, *invented* sex in order to bring about a higher altruism.

"Now what does all this mean? To say that the sex distinction is necessary to sustain the existence of life in the world is no answer, since it is at least possible that life could have been kept up without it. From the facts of parthenogenesis, illustrated in bees and termites, it is now certain that reproduction can be effected without fertilisation; and the circumstance that fertilisation is nevertheless the rule proves this method of reproduction, though not a necessity, to be in some way beneficial to life. It is important to notice this absence of necessity for sex having been created—the absence of any known necessity—from the merely physiological standpoint. Is it conceivable *that Nature should sometimes do things with an ulterior object*, an ethical one, for instance? .... In those early days when sex was instituted it was a physical universe. Undoubtedly sex then had physiological advantages; but when in a later day the ethical advantages become visible, and rise to such significance that the higher world nearly wholly rests upon them, we are entitled, as viewing the world from that higher level, to have our own suspicions *as to a deeper motive underlying the physical*" (pp. 318, 319).

And again, after mentioning the views of Weismann and others as to the origin of sex, he says:—

"These views may be each true, and probably, in a measure, are; but the fact remains that the later psychical implications of sex are of such transcendent character as to throw all physical considerations into the shade. When we turn to these, their significance is as obvious as in the other case it was obscure. This will appear if we take even the most distinctively biological of these theories—that of Weismann. Sex, to him, is the great source of variation in Nature. ... Now this variety, though not the main object of sex, is precisely what it was *essential for evolution by some means to bring about*. ... Now, *if evolution designed, among other things, to undertake the differentiation of mankind*, it could not have done it more effectively than through the device of sex" (pp. 320, 321).

It is impossible to take very seriously a writer who is capable of penning sentences such as those italicised above; who can talk so unsuspectingly of the designs and intentions of evolution and the ulterior motives of Nature, and imagine all the time that he is conducting a scientific discussion. To say that because sex has something to do with ethics, therefore Nature invented sex in order to make men ethical, is to say that because corks fit bottles, therefore Nature had an eye to bottles when she made the cork-tree. It is really no explanation at all of the genesis of anything to point to the later elements that accompany it. To do this is simply to read backwards instead of forwards. Mr. Drummond, however, absurd as his arguments are, may in this respect be looked upon as sinning in good company; for the profound German specialist whose researches are making such havoc among the older theories of heredity, is very much given to the same style of unmeaning and unprofitable writing. Take the following examples:—

"The power possessed by fungi and mosses of reproducing a new individual from any bit of the plant under favourable conditions has been supposed to contradict my view [of regeneration]. But I do not see what prevents us from regarding this power as an adaptation *for ensuring the existence* of a species surrounded by dangers of all kinds. When the top of a toadstool is knocked off, a new one is formed (Brefeld); and this arrangement is obviously of great use in the preservation of the species. An entire liverwort can be regrown from the smallest fragments of the plant (Vöchting). Why, therefore, should the assumption be improbable that this power *has been acquired in order to ensure the persistence* of a species the existence of which is threatened by every sudden drought?"[1]

". . . sexual reproduction has come into force in organic nature *in order to preserve the variability* which has existed since the time of the primordial beings."[2]

"The tail of a lizard, which is very liable to injury, becomes regenerated *because* (!) it is of great importance to the individual, and if lost its owner is placed at a disadvantage."[3]

These examples are typical of the fallacious form of pseudo-reasoning into which Weismann occasionally falls, and which is simply Mr. Drummond's method from first to last. As one critic has put it, "Weismann, ingenious in experiment and fertile in deduction as he is, has a curiously inverted way

---

[1] *The Germ Plasm*, p. 215.   [2] *Ibid.*, p. 439.   [3] *Ibid.*, p. 122.

of looking at processes of evolution that points to grave defects in him as an all-round reasoner. Reading his first essay, that on *The Duration of Life*—which Professor Karl Pearson has been good enough to admit to be 'fairly sane' in comparison with 'the arithmetico-metaphysical muddle of his theory of amphimixis'—we seem to be looking at everything through the wrong end of the telescope. Death is an adaptation, according to Weismann; and in order to show how death came into the world as one of the conditions of organisms being adapted to their environment—that is, as one of the conditions of life—some very pretty contortions have to be gone through. Mr. Spencer's occasional reading of a purpose into the process of evolution is as nothing compared to Weismann's, who is the Dr. Pangloss of biology; there being no God but adaptation, and Weismann being his prophet. And so, when we read that there could not have been much variety in the world so long as organisms multiplied asexually, and that amphimixis, or sexual reproduction, was introduced *in order to* ensure greater variety of forms, we are not so startled as we might have been, only we begin to ask what are the odds against such a reasoner interpreting the process of evolution in terms of genuine cause and effect. Weismann, indeed, has a curious habit of taking existent things, and then supposing their existence to be due to the fact of their being existent: the preliminary question of what change in the processes of organic and inorganic Nature caused this new factor to come into existence is quietly passed over. The consequence is that his explanations of origins are mainly fictitious, and consist not in showing how new structures have originated, but how they were usefully related to their environment when they had actually come into being. You ask the physiological cause, let us say, of the hollow in the horse's back, and you are invited, in reply, to observe how beautifully this hollow fits the saddle; or you ask what is the chemical structure of cork, and your mentor gravely shows you the adaptation between the cork and the neck of the bottle."[1]

This criticism applies to Mr. Drummond as much as to Professor Weismann; but in the case of the former the illogical method is rendered all the more exasperating by the strong infusion of theological quackery. After all, Mr. Drummond's elaborate and sentimental rhapsodising about the struggle for the life of others, we are just left with the old proposition that altruism is, at all events in part, coeternal with reproduction. All the rest is mere verbose paralogism, and the constant talk about the "intentions" of Nature only serves to deepen the fallacies. If Mr. Drummond were writing on the present commercial supremacy of England he would probably say that if ever England was to be supreme in commerce it was necessary that she should be inhabited by a sturdy race, trained and developed by the struggle with a not too-bountiful Nature, that all parts of the interior should be within easy distance of the sea, that there should be plenteous supplies of coal and iron, that she should be an island somewhat removed from the continent of Europe, and thus escape many of the convulsions and embroilments of continental nations; and so on, and so on. And he would be quite right. The commercial supremacy of England has been due to these things among others. But to show that is not to show how these things came about. Mr. Drummond would say that Nature "meant" England to be supreme, and arranged her coal and iron, and the rivers and the seas, accordingly. To credit Nature with intentions in this manner, even when they are good intentions, and to call it science, is simply to make a monkey jabber through a human mask and call it acting; and Mr. Drummond's vain conviction that he is really writing science when he is indulging in these theological inversions, makes any other comparison than this hopelessly inadequate to the case.

[1] Mr. Ernest Newman in the *Free Review*, pp. 214, 215, December, 1896.

With the two remaining chapters of Mr. Drummond's theological biology we have no practical concern. They are of the same order as those already dealt with, except that they are somewhat more sentimental and somewhat more foolish. Argument against them is impossible, but a few quotations will show at once the drift of the exposition and what it is worth.

The two chapters in question are entitled respectively "The Evolution of a Mother" and "The Evolution of a Father". "The evolution of a mother," he writes, " . . . was the most stupendous task evolution ever undertook (*sic*). . . . Is it too much to say that the one motive (*sic*) of organic Nature was to make mothers? It is at least certain that this was the chief thing she did. . . . In as real a sense as a factory is meant to turn out locomotives or clocks, the machinery of Nature is designed in the last resort to turn out mothers." The note of the professional theologian being heard thus early, we are prepared for the coming strains. Mr. Drummond brings a sentimental tear into the corner of his eye, and proceeds to ring the changes once more upon love. In the lower orders of Nature there were no mothers. "That early world, therefore, for millions and millions of years was a bleak and loveless world. It was a world without children and a world without mothers. It is good to realise how heartless Nature was till these arrived" (p. 246). And when "Nature" did take it into her head to make mothers, it was with an eye to "the ethical effect". "Nature is working not aimlessly, not even mysteriously, but in a specific direction ; . . . somehow the idea of *mothers* is in her mind, and . . . she is trying to draw closer and closer the bonds which are to unite the children of men" (p. 354). And so she brings in certain devices which shall prolong the period of infantile helplessness, and so make the bond between mother and children all the closer and more permanent ; because, as Mr.

Drummond puts it, " Nature is in earnest here if anywhere," and " love had no chance till the human mother came ".

Leaving the mothers, Mr. Drummond proceeds to the fathers; and after telling us that the evolution of a mother was the most stupendous task evolution ever undertook, and that the one motive of organic Nature was to make mothers, he now informs us that "there was still *a crowning task* to accomplish. The world was now beginning to fill with mothers, *but there were no fathers*" (pp. 374, 375). Nature, observing this lamentable defect, immediately girds up her loins, so to speak, and proceeds to make fathers, or rather, to make the uncivilised father a civilised father, to lick him into shape, as it were. As Mr. Drummond puts it: " Now here is a very pretty problem for evolution. She has at once to make good husbands and good fathers out of lawless savages. Unless this problem is solved the higher progress of the world is at an end." Nature, of course, ultimately proves equal to the task, and the fathers are duly made. They then represent righteousness, while the mothers represent love; and so the moral order is at last firmly established.

Criticism is superfluous upon this egregious piece of professional curatese, and it is almost unnecessary to point out that if " Nature," or the " Power behind Nature," is to be credited with having at last made fathers and mothers and a moral order, she or it must also be debited with the errors and breakages upon the way. The human family and the human virtues merely represent the survival of a very profitable variation, the virtues in question being just those that were of a very material advantage in the struggle for existence. Even Mr. Drummond seems aware of this at times. Thus he tells us in one place that one mother leaves children and another does not, because the first has a sympathy which the other does not possess. " On occasion sympathy will be called out in unusual ways. Crises will occur—dangers, famines, sicknesses. At first the mother will be unable to meet these extreme demands—her fund of sympathy is too poor. She cannot take any exceptional trouble, or forget herself, or do anything very heroic. The child, unable to breast the danger alone, dies. It is well that this should be so. It is the severity and righteous justice (!) of Nature—the tragedy of Iván Ivánovitch anticipated by evolution. A mother who has failed in helpfulness must leave no successor to perpetuate her unworthiness in posterity. Somewhere else, however, developing along similar lines, there is another fractionally better mother. When the emergency occurs she rises to the occasion. For one hour she transcends herself. . . . Unselfishness has scored; its child has proved itself fitter to survive than the child of Selfishness" (p. 371). Passing over the monstrous ethic that can speak of the *justice* of "Nature" in killing her own imperfect types, and passing over the absurdity of singing hymns of laudation to the Author of Nature for making the type he wanted and the type he did not want, and then killing the latter to show that he did not want it—what is the upshot of this passage? Simply that unselfishness is, in certain circumstances, a variation tending to ensure survival; that is, it is a favourable variation in the struggle for life.

So with Mr. Drummond's argument about the ultimate triumph of monogamy. "The stress just laid upon the ethical gains of the monogamous state as contrasted with the polygamous of course only emphasises one side of the question, and by the pure naturalist might be ruled out of court. Were the physiologist to go over the same ground he could give a parallel account of the development, and show that on the merely physiological plane the transition to monogamy and the rise of the family was a likely if not an inevitable result. It is at least certain that during those later stages of social evolution in which monogamy has prevailed, the change has been in the best physical interests alike of the parents, the offspring, and of society" (pp. 387, 388). That is, a society adopting these institutions would have an advantage in the struggle for life.

Again, " For a prolonged and protective fatherhood, once introduced into the world, was immediately taken charge of by natural selection. The children who had fathers to fight for them grew up ; those who had not were killed or starved. The lengthening of the period during which father and mother kept together meant double protection for the little ones ; and the more they kept together for the first few days or weeks, and the more the father helped to defend mother and child, the more chance for all three in the end " (pp. 393, 394). Once more, the animals possessing these instincts stood a better chance of survival ; that is, the qualities which Mr. Drummond supposes to be the peculiar characteristic of the "struggle for the life of others" are simply phases of the struggle for life, which remains the one formula that sums up the course of evolution. And to talk of the "intentions of Nature," and to say that Nature meant the loving and sympathetic organisms to survive, is again merely to read evolution backwards, to look at it through the wrong end of the telescope. These factors have survived for the simple reason that they were factors tending to survival ; that given a certain combination of circumstances, no others could have survived ; just as the grub that mimics the leaf it lies on has survived, not because "evolution" had an eye to the survival of this particular grub, but because its fellows who did not mimic the leaf have been interred in the bodies of their enemies. If "Nature" is to be credited with intentions in the case of one survival, merely because it *is* a survival, she must be credited with similar intentions all round ; and put in this manner, the ascription of intentions at all to Nature is seen to be a theological, that is, an unscientific, absurdity.

CHAPTER V.

LEAVING, then, Mr. Drummond's sentimental rhapsodies to the fate that lies in store for all bathos, let us glance at his final chapter, entitled "Involution". The object of this chapter may be most fitly stated in the question he himself poses at the outset: "Working upwards through the clay, the biologist finds what he took to be an organism of the clay leaving his domain and passing into a world above—a world which he had scarcely noticed before, and into which, with such instruments as he employs, he cannot follow it. Working downward through the higher world, the psychologist, the moralist, the sociologist, behold the even more wonderful spectacle of the things they had counted a peculiar possession of the upper kingdom, burying themselves in ever attenuating forms in the clay beneath. What is to be made of this discovery? Once more, Is it a stigmaria or a sigillaria world? Is the biologist to give up his clay or the moralist his higher kingdom? Are mind, morals, men, to be interpreted in terms of roots, or are atoms and cells to be judged by the flowers and fruits of the tree?" (p. 410).

Mr. Drummond proceeds to answer the question thus, in a passage which must be quoted in its entirety:—

"Yet did sigillaria grow out of stigmaria? Did mind, morals, men, evolve out of matter? Surely if one is the tree and the other the root of that tree, and if evolution means the passage of the one into the other, there is no escape from this conclusion—no escape, therefore, from the crassest materialism? If this is really the situation, the lower must then include the higher, and evolution, after all, be a process of the clay? This is a frequent, a natural, and a wholly unreflecting (*sic*) inference from a very common way of stating the evolution theory. It arises from a total misconception of what a root is. Because a thing is seen to have roots, it is assumed that it has grown out of these roots, and must therefore belong to the root order. But neither of these things is true in Nature. Are the stem, branch, leaf, flower, fruit of a tree roots? Do they belong to the root order? They do not. Their whole morphology is different; their whole physiology is different; their reactions upon the world around are different. But it must be allowed that they are at least contained in the root? No single one of them is contained in the root. If not in the root, then in the clay? Neither are they contained in the clay. But they grow out of clay; are they not made out of clay? They do not grow out of clay, and they are not made out of clay. It is astounding sometimes how little those who venture to criticise biological processes seem to know of its (*sic*) simplest facts. Fill a flower-pot with clay and plant in it a seedling. At the end of four years it has become a small tree; it is six feet high; it weighs ten pounds. But the clay in the pot is still there? A moiety of it has gone, but it is not appreciably diminished; it has not, except the moiety, passed into the tree; the tree does not live on clay nor on any force contained in the clay. It cannot have grown out of the seedling, for the seedling contained but a grain for every pound contained in the tree. It cannot have grown from the root, because the root is there now, has lost nothing to the tree, has itself gained from the tree, and at first was no more there than the tree.

" Sigillaria, then, as representing the ethical order, did not grow out of stigmaria as representing the organic or the material order. Trees not only do not evolve out of their roots, but whole classes in the plant world—the sea-weeds, for instance—have no roots at all. If any possible relation exists it is exactly the opposite one—it is the root which evolves from the tree. Trees send down roots in a far truer sense than roots send up trees. Yet neither is the whole truth. The true function of the root is to give stability to the tree, and to afford a medium for conveying into it inorganic matter from without. And this brings us face to face with the real relation. Tree and root—the seed apart—find their explanation not in one another nor in something in themselves, but mainly in something outside themselves. The secret of evolution lies, in short, with the *environment*. In the environment—in that in which things live and move and have their being—is found the secret of their being, and especially of their becoming. And what is that in which things live and move and have their being? It is Nature, the world, the cosmos—and something more, some One more, an Infinite Intelligence and an Eternal Will. Everything that lives, lives in virtue of its correspondences with this environment. Evolution is not to unfold from within; it is to infold from without. Growth is no mere extension from a root, but a taking possession of, or a being possessed by, an ever-widening environment, a continuous process of assimilation of the seen or unseen, a ceaseless redistribution of energies flowing into the evolving organism from the universe around it. The supreme factor in all development is environment. Half the confusions which reign round the process of evolution, and half the objections to it, arise from considering the evolving object as a self-sufficient whole (!). Produce an organism, plant, animal, man, society, which will evolve *in vacuo*, and the right is yours to say that the tree lies in the root, the flower in the bud, the man in the embryo, the social organism in the family of an anthropoid ape. If an organism is to be judged in terms of the immediate environment of its roots, the tree is a clay tree;

but if it is to be judged by stem, leaves, fruit, it is not a clay tree. If the moral or social organism is to be judged in terms of the environment of its roots, the moral and social organism is a material organism; but if it is to be judged in terms of the higher influences which enter into the making of its stem, leaves, fruit, it is not a material organism. Everything that lives, and every part of everything that lives, enters into relation with different parts of the environment and with different things in the environment.; and at every step of its ascent it compasses new ranges of the environment, and is acted upon, and acts, in different ways from those in which it was acted upon, or acted, at the previous stage" (pp. 412-416).

Mr. Drummond, it will be observed, is very anxious to guard against the impression that "the lower includes the higher," that the mind and morals of men have come from the atom. This, coming from the writer who has laid such stress on the continuity of evolution, who has told us that altruism is merely the ethical side of what on the physiological side is simply reproduction, is, to say the least, somewhat extraordinary. But not less extraordinary is the process of reasoning by which Mr. Drummond attempts to show that the lower must be interpreted in terms of the higher, not the higher in terms of the lower. His illustration of the root and tree is the merest trifling. A tree does not grow out of its roots, he says, and does not live on the clay, or on any force contained in the clay. If he means that the final tree is the root plus the clay plus something else, he is merely uttering a truism; if he means that the tree is not potentially contained in the seedling, he is simply evading a very plain logical issue. Without the clay and the air and the rest the seedling no doubt would not grow into the tree; but on the other hand the clay and the air and the rest would not grow into the tree without the seedling. Logically speaking, all these factors are necessary for the production of the tree; but as there is nothing very distinctive about the clay and the air, and as it is the particular piece of matter known as the seedling that gives the key to the future product, we are entitled to say that it is from the seedling that the tree comes. Similarly, though the morbid changes produced in the body by a micro-organism could not be produced without a certain concurrence of circumstances in the tissues, yet since, these circumstances remaining the same in the case of ten different foreign substances, the morbid changes in question follow only upon the introduction of this particular micro-organism, we are justified in saying that they follow upon or grow out of this. And Mr. Drummond himself, up to this stage of his argument, has not hesitated to say that man has grown out of a single cell, although we might answer him, in his own style, by saying that " man cannot have grown out of the cell, for the cell contained but a grain for every pound contained in the man ". In his anxiety to prove his point by means of an analogy, he has unfortunately proved too much.

His remarks on environment are not less confused. To say that most evolutionists have neglected the factor of environment, and to challenge them to produce "an organism . . . which will develop *in vacuo*," is simply to talk blustering nonsense. Evolutionists have always recognised the factor of environment—were bound, indeed, by the very terms of their theory to recognise it, for what does the survival of the fittest mean if not that some organisms are adapted to their environment while others are not? Evolutionists, however, have avoided the error into which Mr. Drummond so unsuspectingly falls, of considering environment as "the supreme factor in all development". Neither organism nor environment is the "supreme factor," because the one is essential to the other —is, indeed, a meaningless term without the other. One might as well argue that when a bullet is shot horizontally from a rifle, the "supreme factor" determining its parabolic course is gravitation, and gravitation alone. The relation between organism and environment is just one phase of the universal law of action and reaction, and the one is no more the "supreme factor" than the other. Losing sight of this fact, indeed, Mr. Drummond loses sight of the cognate fact that his "environment," in the sense in which he uses the word, is a pure abstraction. What is the environment? he asks. "What is that in which things live and move and have their being? It is Nature, the world, the cosmos—and something more, some One more, an Infinite Intelligence and an Eternal Will." The characteristically theological snuffle of the last clause may profitably be ignored, but the earlier part of it is worth observing. The environment of "things" is "Nature, the world, the cosmos". As if "things" were not *themselves* "Nature, the world, the cosmos"! Does Mr. Drummond really think that a tree is a thing distinct from Nature, and that nature forms an environment to it much as a bottle forms an environment to the water contained in it? It is difficult to imagine that the man who undertakes to set us all right on the subject of evolution can be capable of so palpable a fallacy as this; yet capable of it he assuredly is. As a matter of fact there are no organisms *quâ* organisms, and no environment *quâ* environment; everything is in term organism and environment. If it be found convenient to mark off from each other in broad distinction an agriculturist and his cornfield, calling the one the organism and the other the environment, well and good; but we must in that case beware of looking upon the environment as something that "acts" upon the man. It is true that he has to adapt himself to the cornfield; but on the other hand it also has to adapt itself to him. The relation between them is not one of activity on the one side and passivity on the other, but of action and reaction. There cannot, indeed, be action without reaction; there cannot be one part of Nature which acts as "the supreme factor in development," and another part which undergoes development. If the bacteria of consumption enter a man's system, to that extent they may be said to represent part of the environment of the man; but inasmuch as they immediately stimulate the phagocytes to react upon them, these phagocytes become in turn *their* environment. It is, indeed, only by a process of rough-and-ready naming that we can speak of organism and environment as if the one was something that grew and the other something that stimulated it to grow. It is convenient to use our words in this manner, but hardly scientific; and when we come to base an argument upon the words, or between the concrete relations which they are supposed to connotate, we must examine their implications more carefully. It then appears that to look upon either organism or environment as "the supreme factor" is to look upon the three or the four as the supreme factor in the multiplication that is to make twelve; that either term is meaningless without the other; and that the true formula for evolution, as for everything else, is simply action and reaction.

And notice the tangle into which Mr. Drummond has finally got his argument through his anxiety to prove that we must interpret the lower in terms of the higher. "If the moral or social organism is to be judged in terms of the environment of its roots, the moral and social organism is a material organism; but if it is to be judged in terms of the higher influences which enter into the making of its stem, leaves, fruit, it is not a material organism." This means, if it means anything, that the environments of the roots and of the tree, that is, of the "material" world and the "ethical" world, are two quite distinct things. But did not Mr. Drummond define the environment, "that in which things live and move and have their being," as "Nature, the world, the cosmos," and the rest of it? What then has become of this definition when he makes his later distinction between the environment of the roots and the environment of the tree? Does he mean that the cosmos is the environment of some things and not of others? Or does he mean that there was a time when the environment of "things" was not what it is now, *i.e.*, a time when the cosmos was not the cosmos? Does he mean that the social tree is bathed in an environment which was not round the social roots, an environment which, though it is the cosmos itself, has only lately come into being, while the former environment, which was also the cosmos itself, has somehow ceased to be; that is, that the cosmos was one thing in those days and quite another thing now? What are the "higher influences which enter into the making of the stem," etc.? Are not these part and parcel of "Nature, the world, the cosmos"? And if so, were they not in that case the environment of the roots also? Mr. Drummond, indeed, seemingly conscious of his fallacy in a vague sort of way, does try to retrieve his position in the next sentence. "Everything that lives ... enters into relation with different parts of the environment and with different things in the environment," which is quite true; "and at every step of its ascent it compasses new ranges of the environment, and is acted upon and acts in different ways from those in which it was acted upon or acted at the previous stage". Quite so; but then what causes this transformation? Why *should* the organism come into relation with different parts of the environment from age to age? For, as Mr. Drummond goes on to remark, "what is most of all essential to remember is that not only is environment the prime factor in development, but that the environment itself rises with every evolution of any form of life. To regard the environment as a fixed quantity and a fixed quality is, next to ignoring the altruistic factor, the cardinal error of evolutional philosophy" (p. 416). Whether the "some One more, an Infinite Intelligence and an Eternal Will," is also to be regarded as not "a fixed quantity and a fixed quality," whether the Infinite Intelligence is subject to changes of quantity, and so is not Infinite, and whether the Eternal Will is subject to changes of quality, and so is not Eternal, I forbear to ask Mr. Drummond. I would rather ask him what causes the environment to change in the manner he has spoken of. The environment changes and the organism changes with it; but the former is "the supreme factor in development". What then causes *it* to change? Apparently the answer must be, "Itself"; an error which Mr. Drummond would have avoided if he had recognised that there is no such thing as "the environment". "There is no social question," said Gambetta; "there are social questions." Similarly, there is no environment; there are environments. Organisms and environments change because of the constant integration and disintegration of matter and motion, and because the slightest change in one of the factors must immediately lead to a redistribution of energy, that is, to a change in all the other factors. When Mr. Drummond says that the environment must change with "every evolution of any form of life," he is talking science; when he says that "the secret of evolution lies . . . with *the environment,*" and defines the environment as "that in which things live and move and have their being," and this again as "Nature, the world, the cosmos," he is simply confusing himself by using a particular word in a general sense, simply tripping over the hem of his own garment.

The confusion, indeed, becomes worse as the exposition goes on. "As in the animal kingdom," says Mr. Drummond, "the senses open one by one—the eye progressing from the mere discernment of light and darkness to the blurred image of things near, and then to clearer vision of the more remote . . . so in the higher world the moral and spiritual senses rise and quicken till they compass qualities unknown before and impossible to the limited faculties of the earlier life. So man, not by any innate tendency to progress himself, nor by the energies inherent in the protoplasmic cell from which he first set out, but by a continuous feeding and reinforcing of the process from without, attains the higher altitudes, and from the sense-world at the mountain foot ascends with ennobling and ennobled faculties until he greets the sun" (p. 418).

What then, he proceeds to ask, is the environment of the social tree? "It is all the things, and all the persons, and all the influences, and all the forces with which, at each successive stage of progress, it enters into correspondence. And this environment inevitably expands as the social tree expands and extends its correspondences. At the savage stage man compasses one set of relations, at the rude social stage another, at the civilised stage a third, and each has its own reactions. The social, the moral and the religious forces beat upon all social beings in the order in which the capacities for them unfold, and according to the measure in which the capacities themselves are fitted to contain them. And from what ultimate source do they come? There is only one source of everything in the world. They come from the same source as the carbonic acid gas, the oxygen, the nitrogen and the vapour of water, which from the outer world enter into the growing plant. These also visit the plant in the order in which the capacities for them unfold, and according to the measure in which these capacities can contain them."

At this point Mr. Drummond seems to become aware that he is drifting perilously near the rocks of folly. The conception of an environment which contains a bagful of physical and social and moral and religious "forces," and which sprinkles a little, now of one, now of another, upon the earth according to its "capacity," is really too grotesque for criticism. But Mr. Drummond sets himself now to show that "the fact that the higher principles come from the same environment as those of the plant, nevertheless does not imply that they are the same as those which enter into the plant. In the plant they are physical, in man spiritual. If anything is to be implied, it is not that the spiritual energies are physical, but that the physical energies are spiritual. . . . Call it all—matter, energy, tree—a physical production, and have we yet touched its ultimate reality? Are we even quite sure that what we call a physical world is, after all, a physical world? The preponderating view of science (!) at present is that it is not. The very term 'material world,' we are told, is a misnomer; that the world is a spiritual world, merely employing 'matter' for its manifestations" (pp. 419, 420).

Thus, although there is really speaking no physical world, but only a spiritual world, yet there *is* a physical world *and* a spiritual world. In the plant the energy is physical, in man it is spiritual. Yet the spiritual energies are not physical, we learn in the next sentence, but the physical energies are spiritual. So that the energy of the plant, being physical, is after all not physical but spiritual, *i.e.*, it is of the same order as that of man; and yet, once more, the "higher principles" are *not* the same as "those which enter into the plant". Mr. Drummond, indeed, is particularly expert in fallacy of this kind. Twelve years ago he was doing it in the same naked and unashamed way in his *Natural Law in the Spiritual World*. "It will be the splendid task of the theology of the future," he wrote there, "to . . . disclose to a waning scepticism the naturalness of the supernatural" (p. 52). Well might one of his critics say of him then, that "if the author be only allowed rope enough of that description he will anticipate critical justice".[1] To argue against the man who can talk of the naturalness of the supernatural, the spirituality of the physical, and yet constantly treat them as distinct, is indeed almost a superfluity.

We may then profitably leave Mr. Drummond's exposition

---

[1] See the article on "Dogma and Masquerade," by Mr. John M. Robertson, in the *Westminster Review* for July, 1885.

of the function of the environment to go down the primrose path by its own momentum; and we may look for a moment at the concluding stages of his book. He tells us, as we have so often been told before, that "instead of abolishing a creative hand, evolution demands it"; but as he does not choose to deal with the atheistic argument that a "creative hand" is inconceivable, it is not worth while spending any more time upon his rough-and-tumble Theism. But he is very emphatic upon the point that God is accountable for the whole of evolution, not merely for parts of it. " There are reverent minds who ceaselessly scan the fields of Nature and the books of Science in search of gaps—gaps which they will fill up with God. As if God lived in gaps? . . . If God is only to be left to the gaps in our knowledge, where shall we be when those gaps are filled up? And if they are never to be filled up, is God only to be found in the disorders of the world? Those who yield to the temptation to reserve a point here and there for special divine interposition are apt to forget that this virtually excludes God from the rest of the process. If God appears periodically, He disappears periodically. . . . Whether is all-God or occasional-God the nobler theory?" (pp. 426-428). Mr. Drummond proves too much. To posit a God who only does certain things in Nature is to credit him only with the good; to look upon him as being the worker and upholder of everything is to bring upon your head the eternal problem of the character of the God who can permit so much evil to be in the world. Even Mr. Drummond admits that there *has* been evil, although he does not attempt to square accounts between this fact and his theology. " Following their movements upward through the organic kingdom, we watched the results which each [*i.e.* selfishness and unselfishness] achieved—always high, and always waxing higher; and though what we call evil dogged each step with sinister and sometimes staggering malevolence, the balance when struck was always good upon the whole" (p. 430). The last remark is pure assumption; and the "*what we call* evil" is particularly rich, for if we do not know it to be evil we obviously do not know its opposite to be good, and so have no right to credit the Creator with it. But the spectacle of a theologian who thinks it a fair defence of omnipotence to say that it has come out right "upon the whole," *i.e.*, has hit the mark about six times out of ten, is decidedly instructive. And forgetting once more his dictum that matter is really spirit, he tells us that "Love is the final result of evolution. . . . Evolution is not progress in matter. Matter cannot progress. It is a progress in spirit. . . . On the biological side, as we have seen, the evolution of the mammalia means the evolution of mothers; on the sociological side, the evolution of the family; and on the moral side, the evolution of love. How are we to characterise a process which ripened fruits like these? . . . That . . . the perfecting of love is thus not an incident in Nature but everywhere the largest part of her task, begun with the first beginnings of life, and continuously developing quantitatively and qualitatively to the close—all this has been read into Nature by our own imaginings, or it is the revelation of a purpose of benevolence and a God whose name is Love. The sceptic, we are sometimes reminded, has presented crucial difficulties to the theist founded on the doctrine of evolution. Here is a problem which the theist may leave with the sceptic." Problem for the sceptic, forsooth! Because there is love in the world, the world is the work of a God of Love! Then if there is hate in the world, is not the world the work of a God of Hate? This is the "problem" which the theist leaves with the sceptic! There is no problem in it, however, for the sceptic; the problem exists for the theist, is of the theist's own making, and may be profitably left for him to solve, if he can. But until he can, let him refrain from hurrying through the trial of his Deity, and snatching a verdict by the presentation of one half only of the case.

One wearies ultimately of this bog of assumption, fallacy and self-contradiction. But we are compelled to follow Mr. Drummond to the end of his volume, to the stage where the inevitable Christianity is dragged across the pages. "For could but all men see the inner meaning and aspiration of the natural order, should we not find at last the universal religion— a religion congruous with the whole part of man, at one with Nature, and with a working creed which science could accept? The answer is a simple one: we have it already. There exists a religion which has anticipated all these requirements —a religion which has been before the world these eighteen hundred years, whose congruity with Nature and with man stands the test at every point. Up to this time no word has been spoken to reconcile Christianity with evolution, or evolution with Christianity. And why? Because the two are one. What is evolution? A method of creation. What is its object? To make more perfect living beings. What is Christianity? A method of creation. What is its object? To make more perfect living beings. Through what does evolution work? Through love. Through what does Christianity work? Through love. Evolution and Christianity have the same Author, the same end, the same spirit" (pp. 437, 438). . . . "A religion which is love and a Nature which is love can never but be one" (p. 440).

To argue seriously against this amazing piece of fatuity would be simply logical prostitution. One can only point out the sheer dishonesty of asserting Christianity to be a religion of love, in face not only of its bloody history but of the sacred books in which its principles are contained. A page of this volume might be filled with utterances of the Gospel Jesus, some of them vile and scurrilous and intolerant beyond expression, all of them breathing the immemorial spirit of the ignorant sectary, all of them giving the lie to the assertion that the Christian religion is a religion of love. As for the good points in the character of Jesus, they are no more characteristic of him than of any other man. And as for the rest, remarks one writer, " I find from the Gospels that Jesus was a narrow, exclusive Jew, who had no conception of setting aside the law of Moses, and no conception of extending his morality beyond the limits of the elect of the Jewish nation ; he frequently alluded in terms of contempt and hatred to the Gentiles ; he had no idea of reforming the world ; he believed in its approaching destruction, the ' salvation ' of a few elect, and the eternal damnation of the rest ; he was monarchical in principle ; he discouraged honest and necessary toil ; he had ideas on divorce that could not be matched for ignorant brutality even in our day ; he taught non-resistance to evil and indiscriminate charity to the poor ; he was the malevolent foe of honest thinking, proclaiming faith in his own pretensions as the passport to heaven, and damnation for every honest and sensible man who had no faith ; he more than once refused to heal sick persons till they convinced him of their irrational and unquestioning faith in his pretensions; he threatened with awful punishment all who should reject the ravings of his twelve ignorant disciples ; his conception even of heaven was strictly Jewish ; he forbade his disciples, when sending them out to preach the truth that alone could save men from hell, to go into the cities of the Samaritans or the Gentiles ; he lumped together all nations other than the Jews in the one opprobrious term ' Gentiles ' ; he categorically stated more than once that the world would come to an end in that very generation ; he expressly disclaimed the purpose of bringing peace into the world, and expressly proclaimed that he would sow dissension even among men of the same house ; he was delighted to think that the greater portion of mankind should remain ignorant of the very truths that alone could ensure their salvation; he was invariably discourteous and vituperative towards his opponents; all the while preaching to others to love their enemies, his own tone towards his own enemies was one of hatred and abuse; he taught a family ethic that was below even the semi-civilised ethic of our own day; he decried marriage and recommended sexual asceticism; his social and economic teachings are a standing absurdity; he never raised his voice against the slavery of his time, and on one occasion gave his explicit endorsement to it".

We need not follow Mr. Drummond any further in his bogus analogies between Christianity and evolution. His thesis that the "object" of evolution is love is erroneous from whichever side we look at it; and his arguments as to the meaning of evolution, the course of evolution, the method and forces of evolution, and the testimony which all these bear to the goodness of his Deity, have been shown to be not only fallacies, but the most vulgar of fallacies. He has simply taken the oldest and crudest arguments of the professional theologian, and by a little manipulation of them, and a little infusion of the jargon of second-hand science and philosophy, has fitted them into the frame of evolution. His facts are just the facts every one has known for years past; his interpretation of them is either hopelessly fallacious or altogether grotesque; and his philosophy is the sentimental rhetoric of the street-preacher. As one of his critics very pertinently remarked, whatever is true in the book is not new, and whatever is new in it is not true. Let us then leave him in peace, and devote ourselves to the consideration of a more intelligent man.

MR. BALFOUR'S *FOUNDATIONS OF BELIEF.*

CHAPTER I.

WITH Mr. Balfour's book we step upon somewhat different ground. Not that nine-tenths of his ideas are any better, either theoretically or in their practical application, than those of Mr. Kidd or Mr Drummond; but he is at least not so glaringly fallacious as these writers. His arguments have a peculiar quality of their own, an amplitude of raiment and a mincing delicacy of gait that make them appear of better bodily texture than they really are. There can be no question, of course, of the fact that his arguments have a certain acuteness that distinguishes them from the clumsy blunderings of his two fellow-irrationalists; but the acuteness is not so much in the direction of any real grip or thrust of thought, as in that of giving to intrinsically mediocre arguments a factitious appearance of distinction and profundity. All that "sophist" has come to mean among us may safely be applied to Mr. Balfour upon the strength of his literary performances alone, irrespective of his political career; in dealing with doctrines that clash with his inborn and acquired prejudices, his method is eristic pure and simple. He is indeed in many ways an unfortunate type, one that inspires almost more regret for what he might have been than anger at what he is. We may not unprofitably speculate upon what his powers of intellect and emotion might have grown into had he been born and bred in another atmosphere than that of irrational conservatism; had he never been subjected to the temptation of forcing his reason to play second to the social prejudices of his class. He might not, of course, have been very much different from what he is now. All his work gives the one impression of a mind of no ordinary acuteness in certain departments of thought, but for the most part failing in broad synthetic views, and with at times an unreasoning petulance that suggests the word effeminate, and recalls the limp parliamentary figure that the caricaturists have made familiar to us. And along with all this is a tendency to be intellectually destructive rather than constructive—if we may make use for a moment of that somewhat fallacious distinction. How much of this fatal habit of mind is due in the case of Mr. Balfour to innate predisposition, and how much to the intellectual atmosphere in which he has grown up, it is of course impossible to say. It is at any rate certain that the most unpleasant of the many unpleasant features which his character presents, is his constant tendency to cry down the views of other men as being open to this or that objection, when all the time, as may be shown from other of his utterances, his own secret opinions are practically identical with theirs. The upshot of it is that he is in an environment from which he has never had the courage to break loose; an environment that coerces him into maintaining publicly, for political or class purposes of reaction, various opinions which his own reason secretly tells him are fallacious. And the result is that while on a subject such as music, which, controversial though it may be in one way, sets up no dividing lines of class interest, he is acute, illuminative, and suggestive, on a religious subject his utterances have about them a ring of duplicity and insincerity that is fatal to their acceptance among men of any intellectual honesty.

His book on *The Foundations of Belief* is, in a sense, a dilution of his former work, *A Defence of Philosophic Doubt*, to suit the weaker digestion of the general reader, with an added flavouring of theological sentiment. It is, indeed, designed to reach a public to whom the *Defence of Philosophic Doubt*, by reason of its incursions into the mysteries of metaphysics, was practically a sealed book. "It is intended," he says, "for the general body of readers interested in such subjects rather than for the specialist in philosophy. I do not, of course, mean that I have either desired or been able to avoid questions which in essence are strictly philosophical. Such an attempt would have been wholly absurd. But no knowledge either of the history or the technicalities of philosophy is assumed in the reader, nor do I believe that there is any train of thought here suggested which, if he thinks it worth his while, he will have the least difficulty in following." He very considerately, however, recommends the "general reader" to omit one chapter, which merely contains a not very profound criticism of recent English idealism; so that, it would appear, he is shrewdly conscious that many of those whose assent he hopes will run with him to the conclusion of his book will be breathless before they get past the middle of it. For this he would probably not care so long as he can win their assent somehow; and there is surely no safer way of getting the ordinary Christian on your side than by writing a smart book which he is too dense to understand, and telling him at the end of it that you, like himself, are on the side of the angels. You may not be taken very seriously by the philosophers, but you are sure to carry the rank and file with you. The philosophers, indeed, were rather chary in their commendation of Mr. Balfour's book; Mr. Benn, for example, remarking that while those who were not students of philosophy would probably not understand most of it at all, those who were would find nothing in it that had not been said a great many times before. But the fact that the book was incomprehensible by the ordinary run of Christians only made it the more acceptable to them, only made them the more rejoice that Mr. Balfour was on their side. Thus the great chorus of praise came from reviewers, of whom he of the *Methodist Times* may be taken as an example, who could not possibly have understood one quarter of Mr. Balfour's arguments. But after plodding painfully through the book they could at least lay their fingers on the passages in which Mr. Balfour grows sentimental over the incarnation; and though they could not for the life of them see the connection between an attack on the scientific basis of naturalism and a belief in the incarnation, could not see how a sceptical analysis of the ultimate conceptions—or supposed ultimate conceptions—of science was made to prove that nineteen hundred years ago a virgin gave birth to a child—still the fact remained that Mr. Balfour was kneeling with them in the same pew, though how he got there might be a mystery. As Sir Frederick Pollock expressed it in a not unfriendly review of the book : " As for the plain man who wants to be confirmed in his faith, I have no doubt that a certain number of most worthy persons have derived great comfort from being told that Mr. Balfour has written a brilliant book which leaves the wicked men of science and the cobweb-spinning philosophers with never a leg to stand on ".[1]

I have spoken of the feeling with which we rise from the perusal of most of Mr. Balfour's writing—a feeling of the hopeless insincerity of most that he has said. And in order to give a concrete example of what is meant by this, it will be as well before going on to consider *The Foundations of Belief*, to look at the opinions expressed in two earlier productions of his. There is a dual reason for beginning with these two works; they cast a light on what may be called the moral as well as the intellectual construction of Mr. Balfour's mind, and they not only anticipate many of the arguments of the later book, but serve to reveal the devices by which it is attempted to maintain these arguments.

The two productions in question are Mr. Balfour's papers on " The Religion of Humanity " and " A Fragment on Pro-

[1] *Mind*, p. 377, July, 1895.

gress," the former of which was read to the Church Congress at Manchester in 1888, while the latter was Mr. Balfour's Rectorial Address at Glasgow University in 1891. Rarely has a writer turned out two pieces of work of which the one is in such flagrant contradiction to the other; yet Mr. Balfour, with a folly of which one would scarcely believe him capable, has actually printed them side by side in his volume of *Essays and Addresses* (1893). There they stand to-day, casting a very powerful and very searching light upon the tortuous moral processes of their author. In order to understand the reason for the contradiction, it must be remembered that the one address was given to the assembled clergy of the Anglican Church, the other to the students and professors of a university; and in the former case at least the opinions bear the mark of having been specially prepared for the palates of those who were to listen to them. Let us consider this one first.

Ostensibly, the thesis of the paper is the contrast between the emotional and social values of Christianity and positivism; but though he sometimes restricts the latter word to the limited meaning of "followers of Comte," his argument on the whole is not against positivism *per se*, but against rationalism in general. As he himself says : " I rather suppose the word to be used in a wider sense. I take it to mean that general habit or scheme of thought which, on its negative side, refuses all belief in anything beyond phenomena and the laws connecting them, and on the positive side attempts to find in the 'worship of humanity,' or, as some more soberly phrase it, in the 'service of man,' a form of religion unpolluted by any element of the supernatural."[1] Characteristically enough, Mr. Balfour declines to discuss the negative side, or, as rationalists would prefer to call it, the positive side of this creed. He will rather discuss the "religious element in positivism, and its

[1] *Essays and Addresses*, pp. 283, 284.

adequacy to meet the highest needs of beings such as we are, placed in a world such as ours". Accordingly he begins by laying it down that positivism is emotionally inadequate, because it finds no place for the supernatural; and he chooses to state the issue between the rival creeds on the importance of a belief in immortality. "The belief in a future state is one of the most striking—I will not say the most important—differences between positive and supernatural religion. It is one upon which no agreement or compromise is possible. It admits of no gradations, of no less or more. It is true or it is false. And my purpose is to contribute one or two observations towards a *qualitative* estimate of the immediate gain or loss to some of the highest interests of mankind, which would follow upon a substitution of the positivist for the Christian theory on the subject" (p. 288).

Observe the sheer crookedness of the argument to commence with. He is not going to prove to us that it is right and sensible to believe in a future life; he simply invites us to believe irrationally in it because of the "consequences" of such a belief! He may reply that he cannot pronounce the belief to be true, although he has expressly said that it must be either true or false, because experience and reason give him no warrant to pronounce it true; but in that case we may rejoin that if he is content to hold to the belief irrationally, he should not try to justify it to us by reason. At any rate, no one can regard it as the acme of honesty to tell us that although we cannot know a thing to be true or false, we must believe it to be true, or delude ourselves into the belief that we believe it to be true, in order that we may feel more consoled than if we believed it to be false. A philosophy of religion of this kind is mere spiritual dram-drinking.

Mr. Balfour, indeed, is acute enough to remember that there are many people, rationalists to wit, whose lives and opinions give the lie to his thesis that a belief in immortality is more conducive to hopefulness than the absence of such a belief. But after a characteristic piece of vacillation and contradiction, in which it is first of all "freely conceded" that there are "many persons ... to whom the knowledge that there are wrongs to be remedied is a stimulus to remedying them," and then maintained that these "many persons" do not form a class that "is common," we are once again assured that "the faith that what we see is but part, and a small part, of a general scheme which will complete the destiny, not merely of humanity, but (which is a very different thing) of every man, woman and child born into the world, has supplied and may again supply consolation and encouragement, energy and hope". This sounds well, but Mr. Balfour may be left to square it with his statement on the previous page, that "nothing that humanity can enjoy in the future will make up for what it has suffered in the past; for those who will enjoy are not the same as those who have suffered; one set of persons is injured, another set will receive compensation". Evidently the argument is becoming a trifle chaotic.

The thin, sentimental rhetoric dribbles on, through "the love of man" and "the love of God" to the question, Is life worth living? and the cognate question of the ideal ends of action as presented to the positivist and to the Christian. Natural selection will do little to ensure the ultimate perfection of the world, for degeneration is as common a phenomenon in the history of races as progress. "To me, therefore, it seems that the 'positive' view of the world must needs end in a chilling scepticism concerning the final worth of human effort, which can hardly fail to freeze and paralyse the warmest enthusiasm and the most zealous energy" (p. 305). The ideal stimulus to action, presumably, is a belief in a heaven to which you may not go, and a hell to which you are pretty certain to go.

And after using an argument which reappears in the later

Foundations of Belief, namely, that every religion and every philosophy that " insists on regarding man as merely a phenomenon among phenomena, a natural object among other natural objects, is condemned by science to failure as an effective stimulus to high endeavour," he offers up his usual apology. He is conscious that he has really said very little about Christianity itself and its doctrines, that he has merely inquired " which is the religion most fitted, in the face of advancing knowledge, to concentrate in the service of man those high emotions and far-reaching hopes from which the moral law, as a practical system, draws nourishment and strength. That such a method of treatment is essentially incomplete is of course obvious. It arbitrarily isolates, and exclusively deals with, but a small fraction of the question at issue between supernaturalism and naturalism. *It leaves out of account the greatest question of all, namely, the question of comparative proof, and directs attention only to the less august problem of comparative advantage."* Unthinking people may object to this, but Mr. Balfour assures them that when mankind learns to look at these things from the proper standpoint, then " adaptation to the moral wants and aspirations of humanity will not be regarded as wholly alien to the problems over which so many earnest minds are at present disquieting themselves in vain " (p. 312).

This, then, is the argument of the address to the Church Congress: that Christianity may or may not be true, but even if it be false, it is worth believing in, or worth fancying we believe in it, because it is a useful sort of belief to have. With it, a man is enabled to do his duty in life and to have some stimulus for acting for the good of future generations ; while naturalism not only fails to supply any such stimulus, but by its teaching that man is only a phenomenon among phenomena, and that in the evening of the world he will pass out of existence like a tale that is told, it dwarfs the moral sense and paralyses the spiritual energies. Christianity is hope; naturalism is despair. And now for the conclusion. Positivism "cannot penetrate and vivify the inmost life of ordinary humanity. There is in it no nourishment for ordinary human souls, no comfort for ordinary human sorrow, no help for ordinary human weakness. Not less than the crudest irreligion does it leave us men divorced from all communion with God, face to face with the unthinking energies of Nature which gave us birth, and into which, if supernatural religion be indeed a dream, we must after a few fruitless struggles be again resolved" (p. 314).

So much for the address on "The Religion of Humanity". Remembering its thesis and its arguments, let us now turn to the "Fragment on Progress," which, it must be borne in mind, was *not* delivered to a clerical audience. The opening words are: "There is no more interesting characteristic of ordinary social and political speculation than the settled belief that there exists a natural law or tendency governing human affairs by which, on the whole, and in the long run, the general progress of our race is ensured". And Mr. Balfour's concern is to show that there is no logical ground for this belief. He points out the decline of mighty states, and the arrested development of others; he shows that natural selection gives us no warrant for supposing that the movement of evolution is a continuously upward one to perfection; that heredity is no more favourable to our hopes, especially if Weismann's doctrines be true; that if we cannot reckon on improved "organisms," neither can we look forward to the perfection of the race being worked out by means of improved "environments"; that there are limits to our knowledge; that the state can do little for progress; that even supposing the state might be disposed to create a new and better environment, yet the community will probably not have the requisite knowledge for this, nor, if it has the knowledge, will it have the power to turn it to account; that it is "a great delusion" to imagine that "we have only got to reason more and to reason better, in order speedily to perfect the whole machinery by which human felicity is to be secured"; that a state in which the community should consciously make new experiments in sociology would be "in a condition of unstable equilibrium," and would be "in danger of far-reaching changes"; not, of course, that the changes must necessarily be unsuccessful, but they are "beyond our powers of calculation"; that "we are therefore driven to the conclusion that, as our expectations of limitless progress for the race cannot depend upon the blind operation of the laws of heredity, so neither can they depend upon the deliberate action of national governments"; that we cannot estimate the remoter consequences of individual actions, "neither can we tell how they will act and re-act upon one another, nor how they will in the long run affect morality, religion and other fundamental elements of human society".

This is the argument; now note the conclusion. "*The future of the race is thus encompassed with darkness.* No faculty of calculation that we possess, no instrument that we are likely to invent, will enable us to map out its course or penetrate the secret of its destiny. It is easy, no doubt, to find in the clouds which obscure our path what shapes we please; to see in them *the promise of some millennial paradise, or the threat of endless and unmeaning travel through waste and perilous places. But in such visions the wise man will put but little confidence;* content, in a sober and cautious spirit, with a full consciousness of his feeble powers of foresight, and the narrow limits of his activity, to deal as they arise with the problems of his own generation" (pp. 279, 280). And in a postscript dealing with the objection that "the treatment of the subject was unsuited to the occasion, and to the age of many among my audience; that it was calculated to chill youthful enthusiasm and to check youthful enterprise"; after remarking that "much optimistic speculation about the future is quite unworthy the consideration of serious men," he lays it down that "any state is tolerably secure from decay in which the greater private and civic virtues go hand in hand with a desire for knowledge".

Not a word here of the consoling virtues of Christianity. "I am no pessimist," he tells the Church Congress. "The future of the race is encompassed with darkness," he tells the Glasgow students. The practical philosophy of the rectorial address is precisely what has always been held by the majority of rationalists; yet Mr. Balfour tells the Church Congress that this, his own philosophy, is powerless to regenerate humanity. Where there is no motive for maintaining opinions he does not really hold, it turns out that his philosophy of life is not only based on naturalism pure and simple, but is rigidly negative and dispiriting to a degree which few naturalists would share with him. When he is addressing a clerical assembly whose suffrages he wishes to win, he adapts his opinions to his environment; he tells the Congress that naturalism leads only to despair, and that it is negative and dispiriting, where Christianity is positive and consoling. He, the Christian, or the man who wishes to be thought a Christian, slanders an opponent creed to his clerical audience, and tells them that this creed has certain social implications for evil and despair which do not go along with Christianity; while all the time it appears, from the address given three years later in Glasgow, that these opinions which Mr. Balfour is so concerned to denigrate are really his own. According to one address, naturalism is bound to induce "a chilling scepticism concerning the final worth of human effort"; according to another, Mr. Balfour himself, the avowed enemy of naturalism, confesses to having a more than chilling scepticism on the subject, confesses to the belief that "the final worth of human effort" is a thing of which we have absolutely no knowledge whatever; that "no faculty we possess" will "enable us to map out its course, or penetrate the secret of its destiny". It is superfluous to dwell any longer upon this disingenuous tissue of contradictions; the question may alone be put whether the politician who can adapt his opinions to his audience in this manner is merely a defective thinker, or whether his intellectual processes deserve to be characterised in stronger and less complimentary terms. In any case, he is a striking testimony to the moral value of the faith whose cause he champions.

CHAPTER II.

This preliminary dissertation on Mr. Balfour's methods of seeking truth will prepare us for a very similar spectacle when we come to discuss *The Foundations of Belief*. We shall expect to meet with the same urging of trivial objections against the theory Mr. Balfour does not like, the same wilful blindness to the good points of the theory, the same ingenious insistence upon the good side only of Christianity, and the same clinching of a feeble argument with a piece of still more feeble rhetoric. All these things we have in profusion in *The Foundations of Belief*.

Defining naturalism as the belief that we may know phenomena and the laws by which they are connected, but nothing more, he purposes first to examine "certain of its consequences in various departments of human thought and emotion". One recognises at once the note of the address on "The Religion of Humanity". Mr. Balfour is not exactly going to prove to us that naturalism is wrong and supernaturalism is right. He is going to tell us that if we follow our reason wherever it leads us, and believe in naturalism because we honestly think it to be a true explanation of things, certain "consequences" must inevitably follow. The theme is very simple, and candour compels us to say at once that it might be maintained, by a competent and sincere reasoner, in a far more convincing way than Mr. Balfour has been able to maintain it. Critics who have praised the brilliant logical quality of the book, have apparently been blinded by its tenuous rhetoric to the real hollowness of its argument. For Mr. Balfour, in the chapters in which he attempts to show the dreadful consequences of naturalism, gives no shadow of a reason for holding its assertions to be untrue—gives, indeed, a good many reasons for holding them to be quite true, but simply drops into tearful sentiment at the finish, and implores us not to believe in naturalism, not because it is false, but because it is horrid. And as this point can be better brought out in connection with a subject that does not rouse any theological or anti-theological rancour, we will begin with Mr. Balfour's second chapter, "Naturalism and Æsthetic," instead of with his first, "Naturalism and Ethics". As in his first chapter, he says, he considered "the effects which naturalism must tend to produce upon the sentiments associated with morality," so now he will "consider the same question in connection with the sentiments known as æsthetic; and as I assumed that the former class were, like other evolutionary utilities, in the main produced by the normal operation of selection, so I now assume that the latter, being (at least in any developed stage) quite useless for the preservation of the individual or species, must be regarded, upon the naturalistic hypothesis, as mere by-products of the great machinery by which organic life is varied and sustained" (p. 33). His object is "to indicate the consequences which flow from a purely naturalistic treatment of the theory of the beautiful"; and in order to do this, answers must be given to two questions: (1) "What are the causes, historical, psychological and physiological, which enable us to derive æsthetic gratification from some objects, and forbid us to derive it from others?" (2) "Is there any fixed and permanent element in beauty, any unchanging reality which we perceive in or through beautiful objects, and to which normal æsthetic feelings correspond?"

Taking up the first question, in connection with the art of

music, Mr. Balfour contends that naturalism has given us only unsatisfactory and inadequate answers to it. He discards the suggestion that our delight in music has originated in sexual selection, equally with Mr. Spencer's theory of the association between certain emotions and the contraction of the muscles of the chest, abdomen, and vocal chords. With Mr. Balfour's examination—in six pages—of the big question of the causes of our delight in music and the origin of the musical sense, we have here nothing to do; on the principle that any stick will do for the beating of the naturalistic dog, Mr. Balfour may imagine that by stating one or two time-worn objections to the association theory he has upset the whole system of evolutional æsthetic; but if he really does imagine that, it is not worth our while to branch off into a discussion of æsthetics. It is more to our purpose to follow him in his own path. He fancies he has given—always in six pages, be it remembered —" a sufficiently striking example of the unsatisfactory condition of scientific æsthetics"; and he rightly surmises that "no person who is at all in sympathy with the naturalistic view of things would maintain that there anywhere exists an intrinsic and essential quality of beauty, independent of the feelings and the taste of the observer" (p. 42). And taking up his opponent's case in a really generous way, he argues that not only is there no universal standard of beauty, but that beauty is not even approximately "objective" in the sense that it "depends upon the fixed relations between our senses and their material surroundings". Is there any evidence, he asks, on the naturalistic hypothesis, that "beauty is more than the name for a miscellaneous flux of endlessly varying causes, possessing no property in common except that at some place, at some time, and in some person, they have shown themselves able to evoke the kind of feeling which we choose to describe as æsthetic"? There can be only one answer, he replies, to this question. He shows (1) that "the variations of opinion on the subject of beauty are notorious"; (2) that "the ordinary critical estimate of a work of art is the result of a highly complicated set of antecedents," these varying, of course, from age to age and from person to person; (3) that fashion accounts for many æsthetic likings and dislikings which are usually attributed to uniformity of æsthetic "taste"; and so on. Now few æstheticians will agree that Mr. Balfour is stating his case quite fairly, and he certainly is not stating it quite completely. Moreover, to show that men's opinions of the beautiful vary so much is more an argument against intuitionalism than against empiricism; for if there be a permanent, unchanging principle of beauty, it is hard to conceive how this comes to be misunderstood or unperceived by most of us. But Mr. Balfour chooses to regard his arguments as fatal to the discovery of "a theory of æsthetics in harmony with naturalism". It appears, however, as if they were equally opposed to a theory of æsthetics in harmony with intuitionalism; and Mr. Balfour's method of argument here is worth observing. He carefully points out once more that we do not find "permanent relations" in or behind the feeling of beauty; that there is no ground for supposing that there is in Nature "any standard of beauty to which all human tastes tend to conform, any beautiful objects which all normally constituted individuals are moved to admire, any æsthetic judgments which can claim to be universal"; nor, he goes on, "in considering the causes which produce the rise and fall of schools, and all the smaller mutations in the character of æsthetic production, did we perceive more room for the belief that there is somewhere to be found a permanent element in the beautiful. There is no evidence that these changes constitute stages in any process of gradual approximation to an unchanging standard; they are not born of any strivings after some ideal archetype; they do not, like the movements of science, bring us ever nearer to central and immutable truth."

All this time Mr. Balfour has been arguing his opponent's case for him; stating, that is, a theory of things which he himself does not hold. If he thus carefully and elaborately states the reasons for the theory he does not hold, in what detail, and with what rigour of triumphant logic, we may ask, will he not argue out the reasons for the belief he does hold? Alas, Mr. Balfour does not argue his case at all. He adopts the device he found so useful at the Church Congress; he becomes sentimental. The passage—the concluding one of the chapter—must be given in full:—

"And yet the persistent and almost pathetic endeavours of æsthetic theory to show that the beautiful is a necessary and unchanging element in the general scheme of things, if they prove nothing else, may at least convince us that mankind will not easily reconcile themselves to the view which the naturalistic theory of the world would seemingly compel them to accept. We need feel no difficulty, perhaps, in admitting the full consequences of that theory at the lower end of the æsthetic scale, in the region, for instance, of bonnets and wallpapers. We may tolerate it even when it deals with important elements in the highest art, such as the sense of technical excellence, or sympathy with the craftsman's skill. But when we look back on those too rare moments when feelings stirred in us by some beautiful object not only seem wholly to absorb us, but to raise us to the vision of things far above the ken of bodily sense or discursive reason, we cannot acquiesce in any attempt at explanation which confines itself to the bare enumeration of psychological and physiological causes and effects. We cannot willingly assent to a theory which makes a good composer only differ from a good cook in that he deals in more complicated relations, moves in a wider circle of associations, and arouses our feelings through a different sense. However little, therefore, we may be prepared to accept any particular scheme of metaphysical æsthetics—and most of these appear to me to be very absurd—we must believe that somewhere and for some Being there shines an unchanging splendour of beauty, of which in Nature and in Art we see, each of us from our own standpoint, only passing gleams and stray reflections, whose different aspects we cannot now co-ordinate, whose import we cannot fully comprehend, but which at least is something other than the chance play of subjective sensibility or the far-off echo of ancestral lusts" (pp. 64-66).

This is Mr. Balfour's defence of his faith; this is the *à priori* manner in which he smites naturalism hip and thigh. We need not pause to remark on the striking duplicity of his analogies; what is more to the purpose is the logic of this extraordinary passage. There is no reason for holding that the naturalistic view of beauty is wrong; yet we must hold it to be wrong. There is no reason to be alleged in support of the other view; yet we must hold it to be right. We may, indeed, give in to the naturalist so long as he confines himself to the lower regions of life and art; that is, so long as he does not come into collision with our cherished emotions; but when he does come into collision with these we are to protest against his intrusion, on the ground of half a dozen preposterous analogies. If naturalism shows that there is no permanent element in beauty, it must be told of the "persistent and almost pathetic endeavours of æsthetic theory" to show that there is; as if the naturalistic view of the case was not an "æsthetic theory," and as if its endeavours also were not persistent. Mankind will not easily reconcile themselves to the naturalistic view—as if it was not "mankind" that held this view. Most metaphysical theories of æsthetic are very absurd, and though we cannot prove any of these theories to be correct, yet we *must* believe that somewhere and for some Being, etc., etc.

This is Mr. Balfour's mode of what he facetiously calls

argument in the department of æsthetics. Let us now turn back to his treatment of ethics, and observe how he applies the method there. He begins by affirming two propositions: "(1) That, practically, human beings being what they are, no moral code can be effective which does not inspire, in those who are asked to obey it, emotions of reverence; (2) that, practically, the capacity of any code to excite this or any other elevated emotion cannot be wholly independent of the origin from which those who accept that code suppose it to emanate" (p. 13). It will be noticed thus early in which direction the argument is drifting; stress will evidently be laid on the fact, or the supposed fact, that since naturalism asserts that the moral sense is bound up with the general beginning of things and the general course of evolution, it must therefore denude the moral sense of any feeling of emotional reverence with which we have been wont to regard it. "How, on this view," remarks Mr. Balfour, "is the 'beauty of holiness' to retain its lustre in the minds of those who know so much of its pedigree? In despite of theories, mankind—even instructed mankind—may, indeed, long preserve uninjured sentiments which they have learned in their most impressionable years from those they love best; but if, while they are being taught the supremacy of conscience and the austere majesty of duty, they are also to be taught that these sentiments and beliefs are merely samples of the complicated contrivances, many of them mean and many of them disgusting, wrought into the physical or into the social organism by the shaping forces of selection and elimination, assuredly much of the efficacy of these moral lessons will be destroyed, and the contradiction between ethical sentiment and naturalistic theory will remain intrusive and perplexing, a constant stumbling-block to those who endeavour to combine in one harmonious creed the bare explanations of biology and the lofty claims of ethics" (pp. 18, 19). To which it may be sufficient to reply with the question, What then does Mr. Balfour propose to do? To put it briefly, either biology is right or it is wrong. If it is wrong, Mr. Balfour should show us how and why it is wrong, and we will give up our theory. If it is right, what harm can there be in teaching men the truth? If it is right, and the opposing view is wrong, why should we teach people the wrong view and not the right, on the ground that the wrong view will make people more moral? And does Mr. Balfour really think that he is serving the cause of ethics by using arguments like these?

Branching off into a digression on free will, he maintains that determinism is calculated to produce moral impoverishment—no reasons, of course, being given to induce us to believe that determinism is erroneous in theory. And he warns us that "the persistent conflict between that which is thought to be true, and that which is felt to be noble and of good report, not only produces a sense of moral unrest in the individual, but makes it impossible for us to avoid the conclusion that the creed which leads to such results is, somehow, unsuited for 'such beings as we are in such a world as ours'". It is naturalism, apparently, which "leads to such results". There need, of course, be no conflict whatever between what we have always felt to be noble and what we now feel to be true; but if such a conflict should arise, why should we give up the belief which we can verify, in favour of a feeling for which we have only the authority of tradition? To say, as Mr. Balfour says, that "there is thus an incongruity between the sentiments subservient to morality, and the naturalistic account of their origin," is simply to employ the device of the most vulgar religious catchpenny. The question as to what has really been the origin of certain beautiful sentiments is not worth considering in relation to so thoroughly dishonest an argument as this of Mr. Balfour's; nor need we pause to consider whether there is or is not the antagonism which he alleges. The fact remains that in phrasing his proposition so as to suggest the surrender of our knowledge to an old tradition, the wilful blinding of our eyes to facts that are beyond dispute, he is, in the very act of gushing over the cause of morals, committing a profoundly immoral act. And it becomes absurd in addition when we recognise that, under the guise of an acute modern argument against naturalism, he is simply employing one of the oldest and most vulgar of devices. From time immemorial the religious man has told the sceptic that even if the sacred books are not true, they should be taught to the people as true, because ethical conduct has always been dependent upon them. Juvenal complains, in one of his satires, that ever since the decline in the belief in gods, perjury had become more common in Rome. Supposing, for the sake of argument, that the two phenomena are related as cause and effect, did the Roman poet really think that the true remedy was to persuade people to believe in theism in order to terrify the potential perjurer? If the belief in gods is irrational, it is to that extent harmful to society; and to offer no argument in favour of the rationality of the belief, but to uphold it on the ground that the belief may be irrational but will make men good, is to blunder no less morally than intellectually.

Or, to illustrate the position here maintained, let us take another example, drawn this time from the theory of heredity. It has always been the opinion of the mass of men that physical and mental characteristics acquired during the lifetime of a parent were transmitted to his offspring; that if he led a healthy life in body and mind his children would benefit by it, and *vice versâ*. Suppose now a man to be thoroughly convinced by Weismann that this theory is altogether erroneous, to believe that whether he stores his mind with philosophy or pornography his son will be none the worse, and, the previous motive for avoiding disgusting literature being removed, to prefer the reading of pornography. Now to tell this man of the dreadful consequences of his manner of living might be useful; but a conscientious reasoner, if he firmly believed that the man's evil conduct depended on an erroneous view of heredity, would try to upset this before recommending him to reform. That is, if certain new modes of living are found to spring from a new mode of belief, the only sure way of changing the former is to change the latter. In the long run we must adapt our conduct to our knowledge, not our knowledge to our conduct. And so for Mr. Balfour and his colleagues to warn us of the dreadful consequences that will follow upon the spread of naturalistic principles, is really to spend their breath unprofitably. If these principles are wrong they must be shown to be wrong; if they are right, and certain old emotions clash with them, in the long run these emotions must learn to adapt themselves to their new environment.

Most striking of all the examples of Mr. Balfour's insincerity of method is the passage in which he contrasts the creeds of naturalism and supernaturalism. " I offer the following pairs of contrasted propositions, the first members of each pair representing current teaching, the second representing the teaching which ought to be substituted for it if the naturalistic theory be accepted :—

" A. The universe is the creation of reason, and all things work together towards a reasonable end.

" B. So far as we can tell, reason is to be found neither in the beginning of things nor in their end; and though everything is predetermined, nothing is fore-ordained.

" A. Creative reason is interfused with infinite love.

" B. As reason is absent, so also is love. The universal flux is ordered by blind causation alone " (pp. 83, 84). And so on.

Mr. Balfour does not attempt to show that his one set of propositions is right and the other set wrong. As he himself says: "The doctrines embodied in the second member of each of these alternatives may be true, or may at least represent the nearest approach to truth of which we are at present capable. Into this question I do not yet inquire." He has, in fact, an easier method of disposing of the theories that are repugnant to him. He works the artificial lump into his throat, and the sentiment comes forth, broken by sobs: "But if they are to constitute the dogmatic scaffolding by which our educational system is to be supported; if it is to be in harmony with principles like these that the child is to be taught at its mother's knee, and the young man is to build up the ideals of his life, then, unless I greatly mistake, it will be found that the inner discord which exists, and which must gradually declare itself, between the emotions proper to naturalism and those which have actually grown up under the shadow of traditional convictions, will at no distant date most unpleasantly translate itself into practice" (pp. 79, 80). What are the dreadful consequences to which we must thus look forward, Mr. Balfour is considerate enough not to tell us. But it is worth noticing that this tearful outburst of hysteria is induced merely by the name of a system which Mr. Balfour does not like. Let us hope, however, that naturalism may be exposed and defeated, and supernaturalism gain the day. The service to moral conduct will be undoubted; and perhaps the child, when it has left its mother's knee and come to years of discretion, may be able to exhibit the results of its irrational but ethical training, by maintaining at a Church Congress opinions obligingly made to order, and by opportunely blackening the character of men he does not like, for holding a faith which he himself in secret also holds, and which he will expound when there is nothing to be gained by expounding the opposite.

CHAPTER III.

At this point Mr. Balfour seems to become conscious that his polemic against naturalism has not altogether been conducted on the best possible lines. "So far," he writes, "we have been occupied in weighing certain indirect and collateral consequences which seem likely to flow from a particular theory of the world in which we live. The theory itself was taken for granted. No attempt was made to examine its foundations or to test their strength ; no comparison between its different parts was instituted for the purpose of determining how far they really constituted a coherent and intelligible whole. . . . This course is not the most logical ; and it might appear a more fitting procedure to reserve our consideration of the consequences of a system until some conclusion has been arrived at concerning its truth" (p. 89). Mr. Balfour has certainly caught to perfection the theological trick of slandering an antagonistic doctrine instead of confuting it ; and the section of his book which we have just been examining differs in no way from the rant of a Christian-Evidence orator in a park, except in the superior amenity of the tone. Intellectually, the arguments are on the same level. And the rationalist comment upon Mr. Balfour's first section is that it well illustrates the prevailing dishonesty of the controversial school to which Mr. Balfour has chosen to attach himself. A really sincere reasoner would not ask whether a consideration of the consequences—or supposed consequences—of a certain belief ought to come before or after an examination of its truth or falsity; he would simply decline to raise such a question at all, feeling sure that if the belief is true it must ultimately prevail, be the consequences what they may to society.

But Mr. Balfour has a further reason for postponing the discussion of the basis of naturalism to this later stage of his inquiry; "a reason based on the fact that, had I begun these notes with the discussion on which I am about to embark, their whole character would probably have been misunderstood. They would have been regarded as contributions to philosophical discussion of a kind which would only interest the specialist; and the general reader, to whom I desire particularly to appeal, would have abandoned their perusal in disgust. For I cannot deny, either that I am about to ask him to accompany me in a search after first principles; or (which is, perhaps, worse) that the search is destined to be ineffectual. He will not only have to occupy himself with arguments of a remote and abstract kind, and for a moment to disturb the placid depths of ordinary thought with unaccustomed soundings, but the arguments will be to all appearance barren, and the soundings will not find bottom" (p. 90). That is, Mr. Balfour did not talk philosophy because he was afraid his readers would not understand him; but as he wanted the votes of his readers, he made sure of these in the first place by appealing to their unphilosophical fears and prejudices. One hardly knows which to admire the more—the ingenious insincerity of Mr. Balfour's dialectic, or the candour with which he reveals its hollowness.

In this chapter, then, Mr. Balfour is going to examine the philosophic basis of naturalism; and though he doubts the plain man's acquaintance with philosophy, and though he considerately prints a chapter on idealism in small type and begs the plain man not to read it, he seems to anticipate sufficient knowledge of philosophy on the part of the plain man to carry him through the discussion, or at all events to carry him as far as Mr. Balfour wants him to go. Now an examination of the basis of naturalism requires a fairly complete knowledge both of philosophy and of science; and the plain man is as little competent to judge of the matter without a philosophic training as he is to judge of the merits of a single metallic standard of money without a previous training in economics. The general reader, then, is simply wasting his time in endeavouring to master the subject from the superficial treatment given to it in Mr. Balfour's pages; and the specialists in science and philosophy, it need hardly be said, have not yet shown any surprise at the novelty of Mr. Balfour's arguments, or any terror at their logical quality. They do not in fact seem to be very much impressed with arguments which, so far as they have anything in them, have been repeated to weariness before; while some have bluntly warned Mr. Balfour of the danger of a criticism of science without a decent knowledge of science.[1]

I do not propose to examine here in detail Mr. Balfour's attack on the foundations of science. His thesis is that we have really no more rational grounds for believing in the fundamental dicta of science than we have for believing in the fundamental assertions of theology. With the real question of the philosophy of science we are not here concerned, but simply with the bearing of Mr. Balfour's negative polemic upon the positive side of his book—that is, with the extent to which any sceptical attack upon science, be it fifty times as acute as that of Mr. Balfour, can be made to rehabilitate the discredited dogmas of theology.[2] Some attention, however, must be

---

[1] See Mr. Karl Pearson's *Reaction*, p. 12, etc.: "Mr. Balfour will hardly be able to disguise from any scientific reader that his acquaintance with science is of a very limited character".

[2] The purely philosophical aspect of Mr. Balfour's argument will be briefly ealt with in the final chapter, in connection with the criticisms of Mr Spencer, Mr. Huxley and Mr. Pearson.

given to Mr. Balfour's thesis here, and that chiefly with a view to pointing out how frequently Mr. Balfour can contradict himself, and how glibly he can assume without compunction, when it suits his purpose to do so, everything which he disputes the right of the enemy to assume.

At the end of his chapter, after attempting to show that empiricism "fails us," that "as in the case of our judgments about particular matters of fact, so also in the case of these other judgments, whose scope is co-extensive with the whole realm of Nature, we find that any endeavour to formulate a rational justification for them based on experience alone breaks down" (p. 132), and that "a purely empirical theory of things, a philosophy which depends for its premises in the last resort upon the particulars revealed to us in perceptive experience alone, is one that cannot rationally be accepted" (p. 133), he assures us that this criticism merely draws down naturalism, and does not, as some might suppose, drag down science as well. "Science preceded the theory of science, and is independent of it. Science preceded naturalism, and will survive it." Yet in the course of the argument itself he has constantly employed science and naturalism as if the two terms were synonymous; he has spoken (p. 121) of "the great oddity of the creed which science requires us to adopt respecting the world in which we live"; and he has attempted to show, from a consideration of the "primary" and "secondary" qualities of matter, that science practically commits suicide when it attempts to justify its assertion of an external world corresponding to our ideas of it.

This note of inconsistency is maintained throughout. When Mr. Balfour wants to impress the plain man with the metaphysical difficulties in the way of science, he triumphantly challenges the man of science to prove the reality of the world in which he believes; when he wants to discredit the scientific reading of the world, he unhesitatingly assumes the reality of it, and points to the fallacious distinction between the so-called primary and secondary qualities of matter. Thus he argues (1) that according to science our knowledge of the world comes from experience; (2) that the perception of "a green tree about fifty yards off," is an extremely complex series of causes and effects, and that "among these innumerable causes, the thing 'immediately experienced' is but one, and is moreover, one separated from the 'immediate experience' which it modestly assists in producing by a very large number of intermediate causes which are never experienced at all"; that "anything . . . which would distribute similar green rays on the retina of my eyes in the same pattern as that produced by the tree, or anything which would produce a like irritation of the optic nerve or a like modification of the cerebral tissues, would give me an experience in itself quite indistinguishable from my experience of the tree, although it has the unfortunate peculiarity of being wholly incorrect"; that "we can hardly avoid being struck by the incongruity of a scheme of belief whose premises are wholly derived from witnesses admittedly untrustworthy, yet which is unable to supply any criterion, other than the evidence of these witnesses themselves, by which the character of their evidence can in any given case be determined"; that "we need only to consider carefully our perceptions regarded as psychological results, in order to see that, regarded as sources of information, they are not merely occasionally inaccurate, but habitually mendacious," because "nine-tenths of our immediate experiences of objects are visual; and all visual experiences without exception are, according to science, erroneous. As everybody knows, colour is not a property of the thing seen; it is a sensation produced in us by that thing. The thing itself consists of uncoloured particles, which become visible solely in consequence of their power of either producing or reflecting ethereal undulations." So that although Mr. Balfour quarrels with naturalism for saying that all our knowledge comes from experience, and though he holds in a semi-Kantian kind of way that "experience" cannot produce "knowledge," he himself is quite willing to utilise experience in order to damage the scientific citadel. We cannot prove our experiences to be correct, he maintains; yet he uses experience itself to prove that certain experiences are "mendacious," as if a standard of mendacity were possible without a standard of veracity; as if, that is, the sceptic could make use of the supposed falsity of certain experiences to prove that there was no criterion of truth, without thereby tacitly admitting and employing a criterion of truth. Mr. Balfour, in his sceptical mood, would not admit that we were justified in speaking of matter as a real something outside us; but Mr. Balfour, in his anti-scientific mood, is quite willing to fasten upon the distinction between the colour of matter and its substance, laying it down that "colour is not a property of *the thing seen*," but that "*the thing in itself* consists of uncoloured particles".[1]

Mr. Balfour's scepticism, in fact, has come down from so many centuries that it has become rather thin in transit. It may terrify the plain man, and drive him to take shelter under the wing of the politician who can talk so learnedly about matter and space and time and causation; but the student of philosophy is inclined to yawn over it, and the scientist quietly ignores it. It does not matter one whit to scientific men whether there are "things in themselves" or not, or whether the idea of causation can or cannot be acquired

[1] As Mr. Karl Pearson points out, the "primary" qualities of matter are no more "real" than the secondary, if by real be meant something existing independently of our subjective manner of receiving impressions. "The theory of light makes the degree of brightness depend on the energy of vibration; the kinetic theory of pressure would, I presume, also reduce the resistance we term hardness to a motion of the cohering particles; and why the energy measured by one nerve is to be real, and that measured by another 'no part of reality,' I fail to understand" (*Reaction*, p. 29, note).

solely from experience. All that the scientific man does is to deduce from the past a probability as to the future, and the accuracy of his anticipation is in its turn verified by experience. Outside this circle, indeed, we cannot get, and Mr. Balfour is perfectly right on that head; but then we do not want and do not need to get outside the circle. A passage from Mr. Benn, à *propos* of the Greek sceptics, will not be out of place here in reference to Mr. Balfour's attack on naturalism. "Timon would not admit of such a thing as first principles. Every assumption, he says, must rest on some previous assumption, and as this process cannot be continued for ever, there can be no demonstration at all. This became a very favourite weapon with the later sceptics, and, still at the suggestion of Aristotle, they added the further 'trope' of compelling their adversaries to choose between going back *ad infinitum* and reasoning in a circle; in other words, proving the premises by means of the conclusion. Modern science would not feel much appalled by the sceptical dilemma. Its actual first principles are only provisionally assumed as ultimate, and it is impossible for us to tell how much farther their analysis may be pursued; while, again, their validity is guaranteed by the circular process of showing that the consequences deduced from them agree with the facts of experience."[1] Mr. Balfour, indeed, when he endeavours to pit science against the philosophy of science, or *a* philosophy of science, loses sight of the fact that it is not the latter, but *science itself*, with which the assertions of theology come into conflict, and of the fact that there can really be nothing more than a purely provisional philosophy of science so long as the advance of knowledge is continually altering our notions of the universe, and consequently of the terms in which we try to express the leading features of the universe. Will any one allege, for example, that the term matter bore anything like

[1] A. W. Benn, *The Greek Philosophers*, vol. ii., p. 139.

the same significance to the ancient Greek that it does to the modern physicist, or that the ancient and the modern could view the problem of causation from the same standpoint? The question may indeed be raised whether there can ever be a philosophy of science in the sense in which Mr. Balfour uses the phrase. But whether there can or cannot be such a science, it remains undoubted that we cannot construct it yet, nor would it, if constructed, in any way alter our position towards the dogmas of theology. Mr. Balfour, indeed, would have been better occupied in building his own theological house than in casting stones at the temple of science. Even if he had proved his point about the basis of naturalism, that would not give the slightest support to the basis of theology. To prove Darwinism wrong would not prove Genesis to be right, though some theologians appear to think it would; and any amount of cannonading at the foundations of science will not make us swallow the fundamental proposition of theology, "There is a God," without some positive argument in its favour. If the argument is strong enough to prove it, well and good; if it is not, we cannot look upon it as proved because a piece of ancient scepticism riddles another piece of ancient metaphysic.

To linger longer over the arguments of Mr. Balfour would be a work of supererogation. The metaphysician who is capable of writing that "the plain lesson taught by personal observation is not the regularity, but the irregularity of Nature," without perceiving that the so-called irregularities of Nature are accounted for by science as much as the regularities, seems singularly ill-fitted to lead an attack upon the foundations of science. And when he tells us in one breath that "as for the general mass of mankind, so far are they from finding, either in their personal experiences or elsewhere, any sufficient reason for accepting in its perfected form the principle of universal causation, that, as a matter of fact, this doctrine has been steadily ignored by them up to the present hour," and in the next that " we bring to the interpretation of our sense-perception the principle of causation ready made," we may admire the dexterity by which the phrasing of the first proposition is calculated to hide its contradiction with the second, but we recognise the hand of the unscientific metaphysician, who ignores anthropology in his psychological investigations, and attempts to construct mental science *in vacuo*. And, characteristically enough, Mr. Balfour concludes his chapter with self-contradiction. "Who would pay the slightest attention to naturalism if it did not force itself into the retinue of science, assume her livery, and claim, as a kind of poor relation, in some sort to represent her authority and to speak with her voice? Of itself it is nothing. It neither ministers to the needs of mankind, nor does it satisfy their reason. And if, in spite of this, its influence has increased, is increasing, and as yet shows no signs of diminution; if more and more the educated and the half-educated are acquiescing in its pretensions, and, however reluctantly, submitting to its domination, this is, at least in part, because they have not learned to distinguish between the practical and inevitable claims which experience has on their allegiance, and the speculative but quite illusory title by which the empirical school have endeavoured to associate naturalism and science in a kind of joint supremacy over the thoughts and consciences of mankind" (pp. 135, 136).

From which it appears that in spite of all the unkind things Mr. Balfour has said about experience, its "practical and inevitable claims upon our allegiance" are undisputed; that although science becomes so painfully entangled when it tries to explain itself, it must still be looked upon as giving us a substantially correct reading of the world; that science is all right, but naturalism is merely an impostor; that "in itself it is nothing," neither ministering to the needs of mankind nor satisfying their reason; that although it cannot satisfy our reason, the educated and the half-educated are taking more kindly to it every day,[1] and although it cannot minister to our needs, " its influence has increased, is increasing, and as yet shows no signs of diminution ". It is difficult to know exactly what Mr. Balfour means to imply by this farrago of self-contradiction; but it may safely be said that no ordinarily educated person could be deluded into accepting his conclusions on the strength of such arguments, and that if the plain man is seduced into accepting them, that estimable being is really so painfully stupid that the only place for him is on the side of the angels.

[1] The uneducated presumably drifting into Mr. Balfour's camp.

CHAPTER IV.

WE need not pause to consider in detail Mr. Balfour's chapter on "Philosophy and Rationalism," in which he lays it down that "naturalism . . . is nothing more than the result of rationalising methods applied with pitiless consistency to the whole circuit of belief," and protests against "the assumption that consistency is a necessity of the intellectual life to be purchased, if need be, at famine prices" (pp. 172, 173). Consistency, if we may judge from *The Foundations of Belief* and the *Essays and Addresses*, is certainly not a virtue for which Mr. Balfour would feel impelled to make any great sacrifice; though it is rather difficult to understand why, after disparaging it in this way, he should tell us, half a dozen lines farther on, that "it is impossible to regard any theory which lacks self-consistency as either satisfactory or final". "But principles going far beyond admissions like these are required to compel us to acquiesce in rationalising methods and naturalistic results to the destruction of every form of belief with which they do not happen to agree. Before such terms of surrender are accepted, at least the victorious system must show, not merely that its various parts are consistent with each other, but that the whole is authenticated by reason" (p. 174). So that while Mr. Balfour is willing enough to discredit reason in favour of authority when reason makes onslaught upon the pretensions of theology, he is equally willing to make every use of reason when he thinks he can in that manner attack the methods and results of rationalism. This, to be sure, can scarcely be looked upon as a practical use of the canon of consistency; though Mr. Balfour's theoretical regard for consistency in relation to rationalism would logically end in purchasing the commodity at famine prices after all.

Before coming to the constructive portion of his book, however, Mr. Balfour first wishes to remove some stumbling-blocks from the path of theology, and to warn his friends of the danger of trying to give a rational demonstration of the truth of their faith. With that fatal aptitude of his for finding better reasons against his own creed than he can find for it, he points out that there are many difficulties in the way both of natural and of revealed religion, and that while the former can only be deduced by reason from the observed facts of Nature, the latter can only be proved by reason from certain facts of history. " Now it must be conceded that if this general train of reasoning be assumed to cover the whole ground of ' Christian Evidences,' then, whether it be conclusive or inconclusive, it does at least attain the desideratum of connecting science on the one hand, religion—'natural' and 'revealed'—on the other, into one single scheme of inter-connected propositions. But it attains it by making theology in form a mere annex or appendix to science; a mere footnote to history; a series of conclusions inferred from data which have been arrived at by precisely the same methods as those which enable us to pronounce upon the probability of any other events in the past history of man or of the world in which he lives. We are no longer dealing with a creed whose real premises lie deep in the nature of things. It is no question of metaphysical speculation, moral intuition, or mystical ecstasy with which we are concerned. We are asked to believe the universe to have been designed by a Deity for the same sort of reason that we believe Canterbury Cathedral to have been designed by an architect, and to believe in the events narrated in the Gospels for the same sort of reason that we believe in the murder of Thomas à Becket" (p. 178).

To many, indeed, it would appear that if natural theology could give us proofs of the existence of a Deity as strong as the proofs that Canterbury Cathedral was designed by an architect, or if revealed religion could really convince us of the historical truth of the events narrated in the Gospels, the whole victory would be won for them. The rationalist who claims to regulate his beliefs according to the evidence for them would certainly believe, for example, in the story of the immaculate conception if the balance of proof were in its favour. But he declines to believe in it because immaculate conceptions in general have never been observed in the human race, because those who allege this particular conception to have occurred can give no evidence whatever in favour of it, because the documents in which the story is told are not authenticated by historical criticism, because virgin births were so common in the religions of antiquity, and for many other equally cogent reasons. Let the Christian show all these reasons to be wrong or insufficient, and give us in addition strong positive proof that the event really did occur, and we will believe in the virgin birth of Jesus as firmly as we believe that Socrates drank the poison. If religion is strong enough to meet its critics on this ground, by all means let it do so. But the adherents of religion know too well that, tried by any test of reason, their creed crumbles wherever it is touched. And accordingly, as Mr. Balfour puts it, "more than this is desirable—more than this is, indeed, necessary. For however good arguments of this sort are, or may be made, they are not equal by themselves to the task of upsetting so massive an obstacle as developed naturalism;" of upsetting, that is, a creed which of itself is nothing, as Mr. Balfour himself has assured us; a creed which neither ministers to the needs of mankind nor satisfies their reason. "They have not, as it were, sufficient intrinsic energy to effect so great a change. They may not be ill directed, but they lack momentum. They may not be technically defective, but they are assuredly practically inadequate" (p. 179). In other and less sophistical words, since theology cannot prove its assertions by an appeal to reason, a verdict must be snatched by less open and more disingenuous means.

For Mr. Balfour himself goes on to show that a naturalistic philosopher, trained in science, in anthropology, and in the history of religions, will easily pick holes in the threadbare logic by which the natural religionist tries to demonstrate the existence of a First Cause, and will run amuck through the historical evidences of Christianity, considered as a supernaturally revealed religion. "Thus, slightly modifying Hume, might the disciple of naturalism reply. And as against the rationalising theologian, is not his answer conclusive? The former has borrowed the premises, the methods, and all the positive conclusions of naturalism. He advances on the same strategic principles and from the same base of operations. And though he professes by these means to have overrun a whole continent of alien conclusions with which naturalism will have nothing to do, can he permanently retain it? Is it not certain that the huge expanse of his theology, attached by so slender a tie to the main system of which it is intended to be a dependency, will sooner or later have to be abandoned; and that the weak and artificial connection which has been so ingeniously contrived will snap at the first strain to which it shall be subjected by the forces either of criticism or sentiment?" (p. 182). That is, if theology cannot be reinstated by showing its own assertions to be true, or the assertions of its opponents to be false, it can at least be smuggled into favour again by other methods. What these other methods are Mr. Balfour will show us in the third part of his book—"Some Causes of Belief".

"No mere inferences of the ordinary pattern, based upon experience," he admits, "will enable us to break out of the naturalistic prison-house." Nor is it the wisest thing simply to set up "side by side with the creed of natural science another and supplementary set of beliefs, which may minister to needs and aspirations which science cannot meet, and may speak amid silences which science is powerless to break. . . . To thousands of persons this patchwork scheme of belief, though it may be in a form less sharply defined, has, in substance, commended itself; and if and in so far as it really meets their needs I have nothing to say against it, and can hold out small hope of bettering it" (p. 187); though, of course, he has a great deal to say against naturalism, which "really meets the needs" of a great many people. This method of running two creeds at the same time, however, has "obvious inconveniences. There are many persons, and they are increasing in number, who find it difficult or impossible to acquiesce in this unconsidered division of the 'whole' of knowledge into two or more unconnected fragments. Naturalism may be practically unsatisfactory.[1] But at least the positive teaching of naturalism has secured general assent;[2] and it shocks their philosophic instinct for unity to be asked to patch and plaster this accepted creed with a number of heterogeneous propositions drawn from an entirely different source, and on behalf of which no such common agreement can be claimed. What such persons ask for, and rightly, is a philosophy, a scheme of knowledge which shall give rational unity to an adequate

---

[1] That is, of course, to Mr. Balfour.

[2] Mr. Balfour should have said "the positive teaching of *science* has secured general assent". His unconscious use of the word "naturalism" in this place shows how insincere was his former attempt to dissociate naturalism from science, and how hollow his pretence of only attacking the former while agreeing with the conclusions of the latter.

(*sic*) creed." This unity, Mr. Balfour confesses, he is not able to supply; and accordingly "we must either pursue the rationalising and naturalistic method already criticised, and compel the desired unification of belief by the summary rejection of everything which does not fit into some convenient niche in the scheme of things developed by empirical methods out of sense-perception; or if . . . we reject this method, we must turn for assistance towards a new quarter, and apply ourselves to the problem by the aid of some more comprehensive, or at least more manageable, principle" (p. 188).

To this end Mr. Balfour begins with the reflections of an imaginary observer from another planet, who should view our thoughts and beliefs from the outside, and with the object not so much of discovering their truth or falsity as of investigating the manner in which they have come into being. After observing that there were two great orders of belief—those that were founded upon immediate sense-perception, and those that sprang from memories of the past or anticipations of the future—he "would soon find out that there were other influences besides reasoning required to supplement the relatively simple physiological and psychological causes which originate the immediate beliefs of perception, memory, and expectation. These immediate beliefs belong to man as an individual. They involve no commerce between mind and mind. They might equally exist, and would equally be necessary, if each man stood face to face with material Nature in friendless isolation. But they neither provide, nor by any merely logical extension can be made to provide, the apparatus of beliefs which we find actually connected with the higher scientific social and spiritual life of the race. These also are, without doubt, the product of antecedent causes—causes many in number and most diverse in character. They presuppose, to begin with, the beliefs of perception, memory, and expectation in their elementary shape; and they also imply the existence of an organism fitted for their hospitable reception by ages of ancestral preparation. But these conditions, though necessary, are clearly not enough; the appropriate environment has also to be provided." (pp. 192, 193).

In this environment the main group of causes is "perhaps best described by the term authority". And Mr. Balfour first sets himself to show that the current sense of antagonism between the rival pretensions of authority and reason is due to a wrong idea of the function of reason in the production of belief. "Suppose for a moment," he says, "a community of which each member should deliberately set himself to the task of throwing off so far as possible all prejudices due to education; where each should consider it his duty critically to examine the grounds whereon rest every positive enactment and every moral precept which he has been accustomed to obey; to dissect all the great loyalties which make social life possible, and all the minor conventions which help to make it easy; and to weigh out with scrupulous precision the exact degree of assent which in each particular case the results of this process might seem to justify. To say that such a community, if it acted upon the opinions thus arrived at, would stand but a poor chance in the struggle for existence is to say far too little. It could never even begin to be; and if by a miracle it was created, it would without doubt immediately resolve itself into its constituent elements" (p. 196).

Observe the sublime inconsequence of the sophistry to begin with. Mr. Balfour hopes to show that theological propositions ought to be believed although they cannot be proved to be true, by showing that reason does not have conscious jurisdiction over *the whole* of our beliefs! We must not judge by reason the propositions, "There is a God," or, "Eighteen centuries ago a Jewish Virgin gave birth to a child," because any community that tried to be consciously rational in *every* thought and action of its daily life would immediately perish! In other words, because we cannot by an effort of the mind acquire control over such an automatic movement as that of the heart, so as to regulate each beat of it, we must also give up our right to judge that fire will burn our fingers if we thrust them into it. With Mr. Balfour's demonstration that nine-tenths of the convictions on which we momentarily act are not the product of individual reasoning we have no particular quarrel, except in so far as he attempts to prejudice the case by a sophistical use of the term authority. In the main, no one would ever think of disputing the proposition that Mr. Balfour so triumphantly enunciates; but the truth of that proposition does not invalidate the use of reason where we *can* use it. Sooner or later we must justify our beliefs, and they can be justified in no other way than by a process of reasoning. The whole point, however, is worth further and more minute consideration, this being probably the most sophistical chapter in Mr. Balfour's book.

The argument proceeds very much on the lines already laid down. The case of morality is taken as an illustration of the fact that it would be impossible for any society to examine critically, in all their details, the moral maxims upon which conduct was based. The whole of the population having engaged in this pleasing occupation, Mr. Balfour conceives it to be " highly probable that the conclusions at which on this point they would arrive would be of a purely negative character. The ethical systems competing for acceptance would, by their very numbers and variety, suggest suspicions as to their character and origin. Here, would our students explain, is a clear presumption to be found on the very face of these moralisings that they were contrived, not in the interests of truth, but in the interests of traditional dogma. How else explain the fact that, while there is no great difference of opinion as to what things are right or wrong, there is no semblance of agreement as to why they are right or why they are wrong?" (p. 198). . . . "Now whence, it would be asked, this curious mixture of agreement and disagreement? How account for the strange variety exhibited in the premises of these various systems, and the not less strange uniformity exhibited in their conclusions? Why does not as great a divergence manifest itself in the results arrived at as we undoubtedly find in the methods employed? . . . Plainly but one plausible method of solving the difficulty exists. The conclusions were, in every case, determined before the argument began ; the goal was, in every case, settled before the travellers set out. There is here no surrender of belief to the inward guidance of unfettered reason. Rather is reason coerced to a foreordained issue by the external operation of prejudice and education or by the rougher machinery of social ostracism and legal penalty " (p. 199). The conclusion being, of course, that reason is a force far inferior in power to authority. "But, in truth, it were a vain task to try to work out in further detail the results of an experiment which, human nature being what it is, can never be seriously attempted. That it can never be seriously attempted is not, be it observed, because it is of so dangerous a character that the community in its wisdom would refuse to embark upon it. This would be a frail protection, indeed. Not the danger of the adventure, but its impossibility, is our security. To reject all convictions which are not the products of free speculative investigation is, fortunately, an exercise of which humanity is, in the strictest sense, incapable. Some societies and some individuals may show more inclination to indulge in it than others. But in no condition of society and in no individual will the inclination be more than very partially satisfied. Always and everywhere our imaginary observer, contemplating from some external coign of vantage the course of human history, would note the immense, the inevitable, and on the whole the beneficent part which authority plays in the production of belief" (p. 200).

So that it appears we are safe after all. After the dreadful warnings of the fate likely to overtake any community that goes in for reason pure and simple, it is consoling to learn that it is quite impossible for any community to be so foolish. Just as Mr. Kidd tells us in one breath that if we are rational we will check progress, and in the next breath that progress is an organic law "from which there is simply no escape," so Mr. Balfour is anxious to warn us against the evils of being rational in everything, all the while that he is assuring us that we *cannot* be rational in everything. And as no one has ever asserted that we could, as no one with the slightest knowledge of psychology would ever think of disputing so old and threadbare a proposition as this, Mr. Balfour's elaborate demonstration is something of a futility. It is only interesting so far as it relates to what follows. Mr. Balfour is considerate enough to allow that some societies and some individuals show more inclination to indulge in the bad habit of reasoning about their beliefs than others; but he is not obliging enough to tell us how far we ought to examine the speculative bases of our beliefs, and how far we ought to refrain. Perhaps an outsider may be permitted to supply the deficiency. It seems wrong for any one to question the bases of those beliefs of theology which Mr. Balfour has so disinterestedly taken under his exiguous wing; here we ought to be content to rest upon authority. Thus the rationalist is inclined to point out that the Christian scheme of theology depends upon the truth of some highly disputable assertions, as that (1) there is a God who took the Jews for his chosen people, and who inspired the books of the Old and the New Testaments; (2) man was originally created perfect, and afterwards fell; (3) this brought the curse of sin upon all his descendants; (4) God sent his Son to remove this curse and redeem the world ; (5) this Son was born of a certain Virgin at a certain time and in a certain place ; (6) before being crucified he gave utterance to a body of teaching the acceptance of which is essential to salvation ; and so on. If the rationalist is inclined to indulge, as Mr. Balfour puts it, in the exercise of examining the truth or falsity of all these statements, he is politely referred to authority. But when Mr. Balfour is concerned to discredit the religious systems of other nations, or the philosophical system of an opponent, he is perfectly willing to examine with any amount of rigour the speculative bases of these systems. More especially in the department of science is he willing to use all the sceptical and negative weapons which reason has at her command, in order to arouse doubts concerning a number of common-sense beliefs about the material world which are the offshoot of "authority" if anything is. So that his phrase about "the immense, the inevitable, *and on the whole the beneficent part* which authority plays in the production of belief," must only be taken to apply, at all events as far as the third adjective is concerned, to the beliefs to which Mr. Balfour is so anxious to afford a prop. To admit, however, that authority only "on the whole" plays a beneficent part, is to admit that its influence is occasionally harmful. On these occasions recourse must presumably be had to reason ; and, this being so, Mr. Balfour, if he had been really concerned to teach the public anything about the relative importance of reason and authority, instead of merely to throw dust in their eyes, would have attempted to mark out, in a scientific manner, the spheres of the two forces. This, of course, he has not attempted to do. All he has done is to beat the drum ecclesiastic to the tune of an ancient psychological truism, and to fall into two or three characteristic pieces of self-contradiction. And in any case he finally confutes himself, as does Mr. Kidd, by the mere publication of his own book. Either authority can be trusted to keep our beliefs right or it cannot. If it cannot, then we must have recourse to reason. If it can, what in the name of common sense is the use of such minor things as Mr. Balfour and his book? And if Mr. Balfour answers that his book may aid the formation of right beliefs, the rejoinder is that if it accomplishes any such purpose it does so by virtue of its reasoning, and Mr. Balfour's thesis about authority comes once more to the ground. And, finally, if a critical examination into the basis of what Mr. Balfour thinks our wrong opinions as to reason is legitimate on his part, it is surely legitimate on the part of rationalists to examine critically what they conceive to be the wrong opinions of the intuitionalist as to the bases of religion and morality. Once more we recognise the old theological sharping in the spin of the coin.

CHAPTER V.

"WE have now considered beliefs, or certain important classes of them," says Mr. Balfour, "under three aspects. We have considered them from the point of view of their practical necessity; from that of their philosophic proof; and from that of their scientific origin." Of the first section of his book we have to say that a carefully and deliberately induced attack of hysteria is no argument against the truth of doctrines which Mr. Balfour does not like; of the second, that his sceptical criticism of the foundations of science is quite unable to damage science in any way, or in any way to rehabilitate specific dogmas of religion; and of the third, that while Mr. Balfour's use of the word "authority" is altogether illegitimate, carrying misleading connotations as it does, no rationalist would dispute the main truth of what Mr. Balfour has said about the function of reason in daily life, all that he has said being, indeed, a mere commonplace of psychology, that has no practical bearing upon the struggle between religion and science. We now come to the fourth section of the book, "Suggestions towards a Provisional Philosophy," in which Mr. Balfour offers to abandon the club for the spade; in other words, to leave off strewing the metaphysical ground with the brains of other men, and give us something of the fruit of his own.

At the outset a becoming sense of modesty steals over him. He has already, with the noble sob of emotion in his throat, protested against the claims of naturalism—this creed "which is not even consistent with itself"—to force all our beliefs into harmony with its premises and conclusions. That was something not to be tolerated. But Mr. Balfour, coming to construct his own positive philosophy, gets a chill sense that the task is not so easy as it formerly looked. Accordingly we are reminded that his philosophy cannot possibly cover all the ground, and be complete and consistent throughout; this, be it remembered, after the petulant feminine snap at science and naturalism for not being consistent. "It is evident, of course, that this general view, if we are fortunate enough to reach it, will not be of the nature of a complete or adequate philosophy. The unification of all belief into an ordered whole, compacted into one coherent structure under the stress of reason, is an ideal which we can never abandon; but it is also one which, in the present condition of our knowledge, perhaps even of our faculties, we seem incapable of attaining. For the moment we must content ourselves with something less than this. The best system we can hope to construct will suffer from gaps and rents, from loose ends and ragged edges. It does not, however, follow from this that it will be without a high degree of value; and, whether valuable or worthless, it may at least represent the best within our reach" (pp. 233, 234). Which is really a very handsome testimonial to naturalism, could Mr. Balfour but see it.

"By the best," he goes on, "I, of course, mean best in relation to reflective reason. If we have to submit, as I think we must, to an incomplete rationalisation of belief, this ought not to be because in a fit of intellectual despair we are driven to treat reason as an illusion; nor yet because we have deliberately resolved to transfer our allegiance to irrational or non-rational inclination; but because reason itself assures us that such a course is, at the lowest, the least irrational one open to us. . . . Now, the first and most elementary principle which ought to guide us in framing any provisional scheme of unification, is to decline to draw any distinction between different classes of belief where no relevant distinction can as a matter of fact be discovered. To pursue the opposite course would be gratuitously to irrationalise (to coin a convenient word) our scheme from the very start; to destroy, by a quite arbitrary treatment, any hope of its symmetrical and healthy development. And yet, if there be any value in the criticisms contained in the second part of these notes, this is precisely the mistake into which the advocates of naturalism have invariably blundered. Without any preliminary analysis, nay, without any apparent suspicion that a preliminary analysis was necessary or desirable, they have chosen to assume that scientific beliefs stand not only on a different, but upon a much more solid, platform than any others; that scientific standards supply the sole test of truth, and scientific methods the sole instruments of discovery" (pp. 234, 235).

The drift of the argument is already becoming apparent. Mr. Balfour is going to show us that when we distinguish between the relative certitude of a "belief" of science and a "belief" of religion, we are "drawing a distinction between different classes of belief where no relevant distinction can as a matter of fact be discovered"; that is, he will argue that scientific beliefs being no more capable of fundamental justification by reason than religious beliefs, we have no right to assert the former to be more true, on rational grounds, than the latter; but that since we *do* believe very confidently in the former, there must be some other ground of belief, say faith or intuition; and this being so, religious beliefs, which indubitably are not capable of rational defence, and which do certainly repose on faith or intuition, are at all events no worse off than the beliefs of science. These are the lines upon which Mr. Balfour's argument is going to run.

Now the first remark that will spring to the lips of every scientific reader upon meeting with this argument, will be that Mr. Balfour is making an ingenious but wholly unwarrantable analogy between the psychological process, unjustifiable by reason, let us say, by which we believe that there is an external world, and the process by which we believe that there is a Deity; and he will point out that while the second belief is peculiar to a few people, the second belief is universal, so universal that even the sceptical philosopher who denies the existence of an external world has to begin by tacitly affirming it. The first belief is, in fact, universal and inevitable; the second, being neither universal nor inevitable, as is shown by the fact that some men hold it while others do not, is apparently the product of various special mental and physical and social forces. The two classes of belief thus stand on different planes, the one being held by human beings *quâ* human beings, the second only by human beings who have followed a certain peculiar line of mental development.

This being the most obvious criticism upon Mr. Balfour's argument, the reader who knows anything of Mr. Balfour's method of attack is not surprised to find in the next few pages an anticipation of this criticism, and an attempt to minimise its value. Not the least striking characteristic of Mr. Balfour is, indeed, this very uncandid air of candour which he can assume at times, an air of meeting criticism half way and disarming it by concessions or by threats. The method is not without its dialectical value. You have only to put forward a proposition which you inwardly feel to be untenable, and then, before your opponent has time to pass the criticism which you know is coming, to state the criticism yourself in a peculiarly mild form, and with an air of having tried it carefully and found it wanting. Thus Mr. Balfour: "I will not repeat the arguments which have led me to the conviction that such pretensions[1] have no foundation in

---

[1] *I.e.*, the pretensions "that scientific standards supply the sole test of truth, and scientific methods the sole instruments of discovery".

reason. The reader is already in possession of some of the arguments which are, as it seems to me, fatal to such claims, and it is not necessary here to repeat them. What is more to our present purpose is to find out whether, in the absence of philosophic proof, judgments about the phenomenal and more particularly about the material world possess any other characteristics which, in our attempt at a provisional unification of knowledge, forbid us to place them on a level with other classes of belief. That there are differences of some sort no one, I imagine, will attempt to deny. But are they of a kind which require us either to give any special precedence to science or to exclude other beliefs altogether from our general scheme?

"One peculiarity there is which seems at first sight effectually to distinguish certain scientific beliefs from any which belong, say, to ethics or theology; a peculiarity which may, perhaps, be best expressed by the word 'inevitableness'. Everybody has and everybody is obliged to have some convictions about the world in which he lives—convictions which in their narrow and particular form (as what I have before called beliefs of perception, memory, and expectation) guide us all, children, savages, and philosophers alike, in the ordinary conduct of day-to-day existence; which, when generalised and extended, supply us with some of the leading presuppositions on which the whole fabric of science appears logically to depend. No convictions quite answering to this description can, I think, be found either in ethics, æsthetics, or theology. . . . Certainly there is nothing in either of these great departments of thought quite corresponding to our habitual judgments about the things we see and handle; judgments which, with reason or without it, all mankind are practically compelled to entertain.

"Compare, for example, the central truth of theology— 'There is a God'—with one of the fundamental presuppositions of science (itself a generalised statement of what is given in ordinary judgments of perception)—' There is an independent material world'. I am myself disposed to doubt whether so good a case can be made out for accepting the second of these propositions as can be made out for accepting the first.[1] But while it has been found by many not only possible but easy to doubt the existence of God, doubts as to the independent existence of matter have assuredly been confined to the rarest moments of subjective reflection, and have dissolved like summer mists at the first touch of what we are pleased to call reality" (pp. 235-237).

Thus the poison; now for the antidote. Mr. Balfour has been constrained to admit that, while the belief in an independent material world is one which all men hold, which no man, indeed, can escape, the belief in the existence of a God has nothing of this "inevitableness". Accordingly, Mr. Balfour will try to make out that this quality of inevitableness is of very small account, and that the beliefs of theology have a "worthier" quality derived from their connection with our "higher" nature. In the same way, it will be remembered, he stated the naturalistic case in ethics and æsthetics with some amount of care and accuracy, and then tried to sweep the arguments away with a flood of very feminine-rhetoric. Even so will he now proceed to get rid of the unpleasant criticism he has had to state against himself.

"Now, what are we to make of this fact? In the opinion of many persons, perhaps of most, it affords a conclusive ground for elevating science to a different plane of certitude from that on which other systems of belief must be content to dwell. The evidence of the senses, as we loosely describe these judgments of perception, is for such persons the best of all evidence; it is inevitable, so it is true; seeing, as the pro-

---

[1] This delightful sentence, with its air of conscious profundity and of invincible logic held in reserve, is, of course, simply intended to bluff the plain man and the religious reviewer.

verb has it, is indeed believing. This somewhat crude view, however, is not one which we can accept. The coercion exercised in the production of these beliefs is not, as has been already shown, a rational coercion. Even while we submit to it we may judge it, and in the very act of believing we may be conscious that the strength of our belief is far in excess of anything which mere reason can justify" (pp. 237, 238). And he further remarks that while a race that would doubt the existence of an external world, "and require all its metaphysical difficulties to be solved before reposing full belief in some such material surroundings as those which we habitually postulate," would quickly be eliminated by natural selection, and that heredity may, therefore, have had much to do with the inevitableness of our belief in a real world ; on the other hand, "no such process would come to the assistance of other faiths, however true, which were the growth of higher and later stages of civilised development".

"We are now in a position," he goes on, "to answer the question put a few pages back. What, I then asked, if any, is the import, from our present point of view, of the universality and inevitableness which unquestionably attach to certain judgments about the world of phenomena, and to these judgments alone? The answer must (*sic*) be that these peculiarities have no import. They exist, but they are irrelevant. Faith or assurance, which, if not in excess of reason, is at least independent of it, seems to be a necessity in every great department of knowledge which touches on action ; and which great department is there which does not? The analysis of sense-experience teaches us that we require it in our ordinary dealings with the material world. The most cursory examination into the springs of moral action shows that it is an indispensable supplement to ethical speculation. . . . The comparative value, however, of these faiths is not to be measured either by their intensity or by the degree of their diffusion. It is true that all men, whatever their speculative opinions, enjoy a practical assurance with regard to what they see and touch. It is also true that few men have an assurance equally strong about matters of which their senses tell them nothing immediately; and that many men have on such subjects no assurance at all. But as this is precisely what we should expect if, in the progress of evolution, the need for other faiths had arisen under conditions very different from those which produced our innate and long-descended confidence in sense-perception, how can we regard it as a distinction in favour of the latter? We can scarcely reckon universality and necessity as badges of pre-eminence, at the same moment that we recognise them as marks of the elementary and primitive character of the beliefs to which they give their all-powerful, but none the less irrational, sanction. The time has passed for believing that the farther we go back towards the 'state of nature,' the nearer we get to virtue and to truth" (pp. 241, 242).

This is surely sophistry at its very thinnest. Mr. Balfour's protest against the argument that the belief in a real world is universal and inevitable, while the belief in a God is neither universal nor inevitable, turns out to be supported by nothing stronger than the old theistic trick of labelling some feelings "higher" and others "lower"—the higher feelings being, of course, the theist's own, the lower those of his opponents. It is true, says Mr. Balfour, that every one has an unshakeable belief in the existence of an independent material world. But then this belief is of the lowest order, being held by philosophers and savages alike. As we progress in civilisation, other "needs" arise, which have to be satisfied by other beliefs. Among these we may class the belief in the existence of God; and the fact that only certain people hold that belief is due to the fact that man has to attain to a certain stage of culture before the need for the belief makes itself felt. This is very charming and very ingenious, but hardly convincing. Mr. Balfour knows perfectly well that the "need" for belief in a deity is something totally different in nature from the "need" for belief in an external world. He knows that the two psychological problems are so opposed in nature that to apply the unqualified word "need" to both of them is simply to try to win a verdict by a dexterous ambiguity of terms; that while our reasons for believing in a real world are ultimately unanalysable, and the belief itself quite beyond our control, the belief in any proposition of theology is a product of a number of influences —social, physical, mental and moral—a belief that can be induced or destroyed; that so far from the belief in a deity being characteristic of high mental or social development, it is infinitely more characteristic of the grossest barbarism, all modern forms of theism being simply defecations of the primitive form; that, on the other hand, in every community that has existed, there have been some men who denied the validity of the belief of the majority; and that in our own civilisation great intellectual or moral development is not, to say the least, usually found to go along with unquestioning faith in the existence of God. Mr. Balfour knows all this; yet he is not above arguing that the superstition of the vulgar many is of a "higher" nature than the rationalism of the enlightened few. No rationalist alleges that "the farther we go back towards the 'state of nature' the nearer we get to virtue and to truth"; no rationalist would make so absurd a contrast between one set of beliefs and another, as if *all* beliefs were not part of Nature. But the rationalist does at least claim that he should not be bowed out of court by a self-constituted judge who undertakes to give his own garbled version of the case. Mr. Balfour complains that the adherents of naturalism "require us arbitrarily to narrow down the impulses which we may follow to the almost animal instincts lying at the root of our judgments about material phenomena ". I leave it to the reader to say whether the vile religious trick of blackening an opponent doctrine by the use of words of mean connotation—such as this phrase about the "animal instincts"—is not in itself vulgar and animal in the lowest degree. He is solicitous that we should " frame for ourselves some wider scheme which, though it be founded in the last resort upon our needs, shall at least take account of other needs than those we share with our brute progenitors". Why talk of brute progenitors and animal instincts, except to rouse an animal prejudice against the feared and hated criticism of religion? Does Mr. Balfour seriously think that to call a universal and inevitable belief in a real world an " animal instinct " is to give any strength to beliefs that have not this universality and inevitableness? Does he seriously think that any rational man will accept his cool assumption that a theistic belief is part of our " higher " nature, and that those who do not possess this belief are, in some unspecified respects, nearer our brute progenitors than the theist? It may be so; but we shall at least decline to accept a dictum supported by no better argument than the upturned white of a sanctimonious eye, and the Pharisaic beat upon the breast. Nor is Mr. Balfour any happier, or any less disingenuous, when he proceeds to remark that " the most famous masters of speculation " are evidences of the fact for which he is contending. " Though they have not, it may be, succeeded in supplying us with a satisfactory explanation of the universe, at least the universe which they have sought to explain has been something more than a mere collection of hypostatised sense-perceptions, packed side by side in space, and following each other with blind uniformity in time. All the great architects of systems have striven to provide accommodation within their schemes for ideas of wider sweep and richer content; and whether they desired to support, to modify, or to oppose the popular theology of their day, they have at least given hospitable welcome to some of its most important conceptions." And he proceeds to cite Leibnitz, Kant, Hegel and Spinoza in support of his contention; laying it down that "facts like these furnish fresh confirmation of a truth reached before by another method. The naturalistic creed, which merely systematises and expands the ordinary judgments of sense-perception, we found by direct examination to be quite inadequate. We now note that its inadequacy has been commonly assumed by men whose speculative genius is admitted, who have seldom been content to allow that the world of which they had to give an account could be narrowed down to the naturalistic pattern" (pp. 243, 245).

Disingenuousness surely could not farther go. Mr. Balfour's words mean, if they mean anything, that men of the highest genius and noblest soul have condemned naturalism as being insufficient for the higher nature of mankind. And to prove this he drags out the names of three or four dead metaphysicians, of whom the very latest lived at least a generation before the naturalism which Mr. Balfour is attacking had grown to anything like strength and consistency! And what are we to think of the implication of Mr. Balfour's words—the implication that the adherents of naturalism have been men neither of supreme intellectual genius nor capable of feeling the highest emotions of life? To argue with him on the former point would be to follow his own childish line; but on the second point I am compelled to say that Mr. Balfour's mean suggestion is simply on a level with the whole character of his book. Surely even the religious advocate has learned by this time the folly and immorality of striving to make out that naturalism in any way tends to moral or emotional debasement. It is to be regretted that Mr. Balfour's acquaintance with and admiration for Spinoza has brought him so little of that philosopher's integrity of mind and serenity of disposition; while even from Mr. Spencer, the philosopher who has the misfortune to be a naturalist, he might have learned that there are better methods of argument than the stab in the dark at the moral characters of opponents, and that he who wishes to prove the moral superiority of his own creed is in some way bound to afford personal evidence of that superiority, and not to imitate the most disreputable tactics of the vulgarest Christian Evidence lecturer.

At this point Mr. Balfour begins to ward off some of the blows of criticism, more especially those directed against his disparagement of reason. "Is not, it will be asked, the whole method followed throughout the course of these notes intrinsically unsound? Is it not substantially identical with the attempt, not made now for the first time, to rest superstition upon scepticism, and to frame our creed, not in accordance with the rules of logic, but with the promptings of desire? It begins (may it not be said?) by discrediting reason; and having thus guaranteed its results against inconvenient criticism, it proceeds to make the needs of man the measure of 'objective' reality, to erect his convenience into the touchstone of eternal truth, and to mete out the universe on a plan authenticated only by his wishes." Against this criticism Mr. Balfour urges that his object has *not* been to discredit reason, because "if one consequence of this investigation has been to diminish the importance commonly attributed to reason among the causes by which belief is produced, it is by the action of reason itself that this result has been brought about" (p. 246), which is a particularly neat piece of self-confutation. Say what Mr. Balfour will, his object so far *has* been to discredit reason, and his attempt to recover ground here simply makes his position worse. If by reason he was able to show that our beliefs about the functions of reason and authority were wrong, then so far from "diminishing the importance commonly attributed to reason," he was but heightening it; and in thus claiming the right of reason to exercise final supervision over all beliefs, he was simply making the recognised claim of rationalism. And when he writes that, "if another consequence has been that doubts have been expressed as to the theoretic validity of certain universally accepted beliefs, this is because the right of reason to deal with every province of knowledge, untrammelled by arbitrary restrictions or customary immunities, has been assumed and acted upon," he makes his confusion still worse confounded. What has now become of the claims of authority upon our beliefs? If authority is not held to cover "universally accepted beliefs," what *can* it be held to cover? And if even universally accepted beliefs are not to be exempt from criticism under the protection of authority, what is this protection worth to beliefs that are not universally accepted? And if it is reason that discriminates between these beliefs, telling us which to retain and which to reject, what has become of Mr. Balfour's own assertion that the *rôle* played by reasoning in human affairs is one of "comparative pettiness"; that not only is it "authority rather than reason which lays deep the foundations of social life," but that "it is authority rather than reason which cements its superstructure"? The illogical see-saw is to be accounted for by no other hypothesis than that Mr. Balfour has been perforce no more successful than any man can be in using reason to discredit reason, and that he has been even more unsuccessful than he need have been, by attempting to rehabilitate the claims of reason for one specific purpose after disparaging them for another.

His new-found zeal for reason is, of course, due to the fact that at this stage an argument for theism can be extracted from the rational nature of man—not a particularly new argument, and not a particularly strong one. "Is it true," he continues, "to say that, in the absence of reason, we have contentedly accepted mere desire for our guide? No doubt the theory here advocated requires us to take account, not merely of premises and their conclusions, but of needs and their satisfaction. But this is only asking us to do explicitly and on system what on the naturalistic theory is done unconsciously and at random. By the very constitution of our being we seem practically driven to assume a real world in correspondence with our ordinary judgments of perception. A harmony of some kind between our inner selves and the universe of which we form a part is thus the tacit postulate at the root of every belief we entertain about 'phenomena'; and all that I now contend for is that a like harmony should provisionally be assumed between that universe and other elements in our nature which are of a later, of a more uncertain, but of no ignobler growth. Whether this correspondence is best described as that which obtains between a 'need' and its 'satisfaction' may be open to question. But, at all events, let it be understood that if the relation so described is, on the one side, something different from that between a premise and its conclusion, so, on the other, it is intended to be equally remote from that between a desire and its fulfilment. That it has not the logical validity of the first I have already admitted, or rather asserted. That it has not the casual, wavering, and purely 'subjective' character of the second is not less true. For the correspondence postulated is not between the fleeting fancies of the individual and the immutable verities of an unseen world, but between those characteristics of our nature which we recognise as that in us which, though not necessarily the strongest, is the highest ; which, though not always the most universal, is nevertheless the best" (pp. 247, 248).

What the last chaotic sentence may mean it is difficult to say, but the argument as a whole is this : we cannot prove our belief in an external world to be true, yet we are all practically *compelled* to believe in it ; similarly, the necessity of the higher parts of our nature to believe in certain super-rational things is sufficient proof of their existence. And as this is really the central doctrine of the book, the piece of constructive philosophy which Mr. Balfour puts forward as supplying the deficiencies of naturalism, it will be well to look at it more closely. To bring it into better relief, I may quote from a very eulogistic article on Mr. Balfour by Professor Seth, in which he points out the similarity between this argument and one of Kant's:—

"Its true nature will be best shown by the concrete examples of its use, and we shall then be better able to form a judgment as to its legitimacy. It is first applied in the intellectual sphere to demonstrate the implications or presuppositions of the scientific view itself, or of the mere fact that we know. Mr. Balfour had already pointed out, in dealing with our belief in the uniformity of Nature, that this belief cannot be *proved* by the facts, seeing that it is a postulate impliedin the very idea of investigating facts. In these constructive chapters he amplifies the thought in a remarkably fresh and striking way. After dealing instructively with some of the usual arguments for theism, he proceeds to push the question a stage farther back. But 'something may also be inferred *from the mere fact that we know*, a fact which, like every other, has to be accounted for'. And after some luminous pages in which he presses home the fundamental inconsequence of naturalism in requiring us to 'accept a system as rational, one of whose doctrines is that the system itself is the product of causes which have no tendency to truth rather than falsehood or to falsehood rather than truth,' he concludes: 'I do not believe that any escape from these perplexities is possible, unless we are prepared to bring to the study of the world the presupposition that it was the work of a rational Being who made *it* intelligible, and at the same time made *us*, in however feeble a fashion, able to understand it' (p. 301). Theism is thus a 'presupposition,' 'not only tolerated, but actually required by science' (p. 321). It is 'forced upon us by the single assumption that science is not an illusion'. As he put it before, we are 'driven in mere self-defence' to the belief in a Supreme Reason directing the apparently non-rational forces of Nature; we 'must' believe in Supreme Reason 'if we are to believe in anything'. But this admission, if once made, cannot stand alone. If we 'postulate a rational God in the interests of science, we can scarcely decline to postulate a moral God in the interests of morality'. And in the light of this presupposition the whole process by which the ethical code and the moral sentiments have been slowly developed appears in a different setting, as 'an instrument for carrying out a divine purpose,' as a divine education of the human race. Such, without following them into details, are the important conclusions which Mr. Balfour reaches by the method of argument he follows. When they are thus stated summarily, and detached from some of the discussions which accompany them, the philosophical student can hardly fail to remark the striking resemblance of Mr. Balfour's mode of argument to the transcendental method of Kant, and the affinity of his conclusions to those of Kant's idealistic successors. . . . The argument itself is in substance identical with that which Kant patiently dug from the *débris* of rationalism, and built into a system so palpably artificial in its details and so cumbrously pedantic in its terminology, that the philosophical world has been engaged ever since in quarrelling over its interpretation. When we penetrate beneath the portentous phrases to the comparatively humble truth which they labour to express, Kant's 'objective unity of apperception,' as the supreme condition of the possibility of experience, is simply the assertion that the idea of 'a nature' or a rational system is not a conclusion from particular facts, but is involved as a postulate or presupposition in there being any experience of facts at all. And when, at the close of his investigation, he emphasises the adaptation of phenomena to our faculty of cognition as proof of a harmony between sense and understanding, that is to say, ultimately a harmony between the world and the mind; when he argues that this adaptation justifies us in treating reality as everywhere rationalisable, and therefore *as if* it were the product of a Supreme Reason; this, in more scholastic form, and with Kant's well-known reservation as to the merely regulative character of the ideas of reason, is neither more nor less than the argument *from the mere fact that we know*."[1]

We may pass over for the present, with a bare mention of it, the absurdity of speaking of a " Supreme Reason directing the apparently non-rational forces of Nature ". For either this Supreme Reason directs all the forces of Nature or only some of them; if the latter, it can scarcely be regarded as supreme, and if the former, then among the "forces of Nature" which it directs is the force prompting the atheist to deny its very existence. This fundamental absurdity, which is common to all systems of theism, need not be dwelt upon in any greater detail at present. It is more to the purpose here to point out that Mr. Balfour's argument from needs to their satisfaction is, for the reasons already given, quite illegitimate for the purposes for which he makes use of it. Even Professor Seth is constrained to remark that the words are at least unfortunate, in that they carry an emotional significance into a discussion from which emotion ought to be absent; and he prefers some such word as " postulate " to the word " need," as " expressing admirably both this element of intellectual necessity in the argument and, at the same time, the subjective element, which is undoubtedly also present ". But the whole argument has been developed on the strength of the word "needs," and it is a little too disingenuous to throw it over when the victory has apparently been won, to admit its imperfections now, and to employ the safer word " postulate ". For Mr. Balfour's talk about that in us which is *the highest and best* is certainly

[1] " Mr. Balfour and his Critics," in *Contemporary Review*, August, 1896.

intended to carry with it an emotional certificate ; and the whole strength of the argument, such as it is, lies in the illegitimate significance that is given to these words. Nothing, indeed, as has already been pointed out, could well be more philosophically invalid than to argue that the "need" to believe in an independent material world and the "need" to believe in a rational author of that world are in the same category.

Nor is Mr. Balfour any happier in the attempt to ground his belief in a supreme reason upon " the mere fact that we know ". Professor Seth is historically right in pointing out that the argument is just Kant's argument from the " possibility of experience " put into simple and lucid language. Perilous, however, is the descent into transcendentalism ; easy as the descent into Avernus, and the return as difficult. All the more perilous to the reputation of the transcendentalist is the gift of writing plain English, for once the argument is understood it supplies its own confutation. I venture the opinion that Kant would not have bulked so largely in the eyes of the philosophic world had it not been for his abominable obscurity of style and the awkwardness of his terminology, which have made a very simple philosophical idea appear much more profound than it really was. To speak paradoxically, to get to the centre of Kant's position is to get beyond it ; to understand him is to see the simple and fundamental fallacy of his position. The defect of all transcendentalism, as has been more than once pointed out, is the necessarily futile attempt to carry the head in the teeth. Kant's question, " How is knowledge possible ? " is seen to be absurd when we realise that the answer, if it can be given at all, can only be given in terms of knowledge, and that we are thus as far as ever from "accounting" for our knowledge of objects. His division of our perceptive cognition into the two factors of sense and understanding, the former being the faculty through which objects are "given" to us, the latter the faculty by which they are "thought," was not, as he imagined, an *explanation* of how we are able to cognise objects, but just an arbitrary separation of two elements in the cognition of what we already know. "Knowledge" we certainly cannot get behind for the purpose of explaining it, since every attempt to explain it involves the employment of it. And Mr. Balfour's version of Kant is no more logical than Kant's own position. When Mr. Balfour writes that "something may also be inferred *from the mere fact that we know*, a fact which, like every other, has to be accounted for," we can only ask him *how* he can account for the fact that we know except in terms of knowledge. His thesis has been that the old design-argument has undoubtedly broken down. "In a famous answer to that argument it has been pointed out that the inference from the adaptation of means to ends, which rightly convinces us in the case of manufactured articles that they are not the result of chance, but are produced by intelligent contrivance, can scarcely be legitimately applied to the case of the universe as a whole. An induction which may be perfectly valid within the circle of phenomena, may be quite meaningless when it is employed to account for the circle itself. You cannot infer a God from the existence of the world as you infer an architect from the existence of a house, or a mechanic from the existence of a watch" (p. 294). A vacillating passage follows, in which Mr. Balfour, while obviously unable to answer this objection, will not say so outright, but rather recommends theologians not to employ the design-argument; then he lays it down that instead of arguing from "the world as known," more can be achieved by arguing "from the mere fact that we know".

Now, independently of the objection that we cannot possibly "account" for the fact that we know, there is the further objection that *from* the fact that we know, we cannot legitimately infer the existence of a Supreme Reason as the creator of things. And this for two reasons; in the first place, because the fact that we have reason no more proves that we are created by reason—whatever that may mean—than the fact "that there is pepper in the broth proves that there is pepper in the cook"; and in the second place, because the transcendental argument as to the "rationality" of Nature is itself hollow at its very foundations. Kant had argued that if there were not a harmony between objects and our mode of cognising them there would be no knowledge of them possible at all. Objects make impressions upon our capacity for sense-affection, and these impressions are then sorted out by the categories of the mind, which thus reduce the blind rush of sense-impressions to order and coherence. "Notions without sensuous intuitions are empty; sensuous intuitions without notions are blind." It is by means of the categories that the mind is able to "think" objects, that is, to mould the mere blind sense-impressions into orderly and connected knowledge; these categories not being the product of sensuous intuition, but lying *a priori* in the mind. From the fact that these correspond in their activities with the sense-impressions given by objects, knowledge alone is "possible," according to Kant; and, as Professor Seth has expressed it in the passage I have already quoted, "he emphasises the adaptation of phenomena to our faculty of cognition as proof of a harmony between sense and understanding, that is to say, ultimately a harmony between the world and the mind"; and he argues "that this adaptation justifies us in treating reality as everywhere rationalisable, and therefore *as if* it were the product of a Supreme Reason".

The attempt to find out *why* we can cognise objects is, however, a mere pursuit of the will-o'-the-wisp. To discover *that* our cognitions correspond to objects is not to discover *why* there is this correspondence; and the arbitrary division of our cognitions into the two elements of sense and understanding, with phenomena outside waiting to be "known," is merely a convenient form of statement of possible stages in our knowledge, not of the reason for it. To give a reason for our knowledge, to explain how experience is possible, is, indeed, a radical impossibility ; and instead of trying to account for knowledge we have just to accept the fact that we have it. This, however, does not help out any attempt to found the universe upon theism. We do not know *because* there is a harmony between the world and our understanding, *because* the world is rational, or rationalisable. The very term "because" is wholly illegitimate. To speak of the world as being rationalisable, *i.e.*, one in Nature with the structure of our own minds and our modes of cognition, is to assume that we have some knowledge of the world *as apart from these modes of cognition*. When Professor Seth, for example, puts it that Kant "emphasises the adaptation of phenomena to our faculty of cognition as proof of a harmony between sense and understanding," the question immediately arises—What do we know or can we know of these phenomena apart from our faculty of cognition ? To know them at all is to know them in terms of this faculty ; nor can we know them in any other way. We cannot get behind our own mental processes, because these very processes have to be employed in any such attempt ; we cannot look at them at one moment, and at another at Nature without them ; our knowledge of Nature is just obtained *through* these mental processes. Any endeavour, therefore, to make out that Nature is a rational system because it harmonises with the rational processes of our own minds, loses sight of the fact that we do not and cannot know anything of Nature apart from those very processes with which it is supposed to harmonise. So that "the mree fact that we know" cannot be pressed into the service of theology in any way, it being as absurd to deduce a rational author of the universe from the fact that we have reason, as it would be to make the supposed author of the universe coloured or heavy because we and Nature have colour and weight. The theist interposes, of course, with the objection that since reason is the highest part of us, it is not illegitimate to regard the creator of us as being the Supreme Reason. Such terms as highest and lowest, however, are purely relative to ourselves, and have no meaning except within what Mr. Balfour would call the circle of phenomena. To extend its application to an eternal and infinite existence that is supposed to exist without this circle is as illegitimate as any other of his modes of logical procedure.

CHAPTER VI.

OUR discussion of the ultimate bearings of Mr. Balfour's argument from needs to their satisfaction upon his argument from a rationalisable Nature to a supreme reason, has made us anticipate the later stages of his book; and it will now be well to return to the point at which we left Mr. Balfour arguing that the qualities of universality and inevitableness confer no precedence upon the beliefs of sense-perception, and that while his philosophy " admits judgments of sense-perception to be the most inevitable," it "denies them to be the most worthy " (p. 249). Following upon this, he analyses the relation between beliefs and the formulas that express them, and finds that between the two there is a constant action and reaction, which is "the most salient, and in some respects the most interesting, fact in the history of thought. Called into being, for the most part, to justify, or at least to organise, pre-existing beliefs, they can seldom perform their office without modifying part, at least, of their material. While they give precision to what would otherwise be indeterminate, and a relative permanence to what would otherwise be in a state of flux, they do so at the cost of some occasional violence to the beliefs with which they deal. Some of these are distorted to make them fit into their predestined niches, others, more refractory, are destroyed or ignored. . . . But this reaction of formulas on the beliefs which they co-ordinate or explain is but the first stage in the process we are describing. The next is the change, perhaps even the destruction, of the formula itself by the victorious forces that it has previously had in check. The plastic body of belief, or some portion of it, under the growing stress of external and internal influences, breaks through—it may be with destructive violence—the barriers by which it was at one time controlled. A new theory has to be formed, a new arrangement of knowledge has to be accepted, and under changed conditions the same cycle of not unfruitful changes begins again " (pp. 253, 254).

There is, however, an important difference between science and theology in this respect. In theology, "as elsewhere, theories arise, have their day, and fall; but there, far more than elsewhere, do these theories in their fall endanger other interests than their own. More than one reason may be given for this difference. To begin with, in science the beliefs of sense-perception, which, as I have implied, are commonly vigorous enough to resist the warping effect of theory, even when the latter is in its full strength, are not imperilled by its decay. They provide a solid nucleus of unalterable conviction which survives uninjured through all the mutations of intellectual fashion. We do not require the assistance of hypotheses to sustain our faith in what we see and hear. Speaking broadly, that faith is unalterable and self-sufficient. Theology is less happily situated. There it often happens that when a theory decays, the beliefs to which it refers are infected by a contagious weakness. The explanation and the thing explained are mutually dependent. They are animated as it were with a common life, and there is always a danger lest they should be overtaken by a common destruction " (pp. 255, 256).

He proceeds to illustrate this by two examples. In science, the older belief that heat was a form of matter has now given way to the belief that it is a mode of motion, without thereby shaking any one's conviction that certain objects have the quality of producing in us the sensation of warmth.

In theology, on the other hand, the Christian theology of Reconciliation with God has been so dependent upon the explanations that have been given of it, that with the demonstration of the futility of these explanations the belief itself is inclined to pass away. With all this, however, we have no quarrel. It is only when Mr. Balfour comes to his conclusion that we are compelled to part company with him. Being hard put to it to find a reason for clinging to a religious belief after the formula that expressed it has been damaged by criticism, he finally lays it down that "the precedent set . . . by science is the one which ought to be followed by theology". If a belief is only held as an inference from a certain chain of reasoning and observation, anything that weakens this chain must of course weaken the belief proportionately. "If, for instance, we believe that there is hydrogen in the sun, solely because that conclusion is forced upon us by certain arguments based upon spectroscopic observations, then, if these arguments should ever be discredited, the belief in solar hydrogen would, as a necessary consequence, be shaken or destroyed. *But in cases where the belief is rather the occasion of an hypothesis than a conclusion from it, the destruction of the hypothesis may be a reason for devising a new one, but is certainly no reason for abandoning the belief.*[1] Nor in science do we ever take any other view. We do not, for example, step over a precipice because we are dissatisfied with all the attempts to account for gravitation. In theology, however, experience does sometimes lean too timidly on theory, and when in the course of time theory decays, it drags down experience in its fall. How many persons are there, for example, who, because they dislike the theories of Atonement propounded, say, by Anselm, or by Grotius, or the versions of these which have imbedded themselves in the devotional literature of Western Europe, feel bound 'in

[1] Italics mine.

reason' to give up the doctrine itself? Because they cannot compress within the rigid limits of some semi-legal formula a mystery, which, unless it were too vast for our full intellectual comprehension, would surely be too narrow for our spiritual needs, the mystery itself is to be rejected! Because they cannot contrive to their satisfaction a system of theological jurisprudence which shall include Redemption as a leading case, Redemption is no longer to be counted among the consolations of mankind!" (pp. 258, 259).

That is, in plainer language, when you have what you think good reasons for a belief, the belief must be held to be damaged by anything that damages the reasons; but when you have admittedly bad reasons for your belief, and choose to put these reasons forward, you can meet any attack upon the belief by coolly saying that the reasons have nothing whatever to do with it. If a dying consumptive, for example, feeling stronger for the moment, believes that his health is permanently restored, and frames a hypothesis in harmony with this belief to account for his momentary return of strength, then if the doctor proves to him that this latter can be accounted for in another way, and that his hypothesis is therefore valueless, the grounds of the consumptive's "belief" must be held to be still undamaged! Here "the belief is rather the occasion of the hypothesis than a conclusion from it". According to Mr. Balfour, then, "the destruction of the hypothesis may be a reason for devising a new one, but is certainly no reason for abandoning the belief". He forgets, or would wish it to appear that he did not know, that beliefs which do not seem to have sprung from reason have in reality been generated by rational processes of some kind. The theist's belief in the existence of God, even if he cannot formulate the several stages by which the belief has progressed, is none the less the product of rational processes—vague and perhaps subconscious, it may be, but none the less proceeding by inference and suggestion. Now the framing of an hypothesis to account for such a belief is simply bringing the subconscious reasons into the light of day, and making them conscious; and any criticism that proves that here and there an illegitimate inference has been made, must be held to damage the truth of the belief to some extent. To affirm, in the face of this, that the hypothesis, as Mr. Balfour calls it, may be shaken, and the belief still be left standing, is pure nonsense. A man puts forward a hypothesis in order to show the congruity of a belief with other beliefs of his mind, and in order to produce in the reader the same belief for which the hypothesis was framed. If Anselm propounds a theory of the Atonement, for example, it is because there are some who do not believe in the Atonement at all, while others believe in it, but for reasons different from those of Anselm; and the prelate's object is to bring opponents round to his point of view. Either the theory is supposed to follow in its demonstration the course of facts and inferences which have produced the belief, and which, thus stated, may be supposed to produce the same belief in other men, or it does not. If it does not, what is the object of the theory? and if it does, what is then its relation to the belief? Either the belief must be held to stand or fall with the theory, or it must not. If yes, Mr. Balfour's point is seen to be absurd; if not, what in the name of reason is the object of giving out the theory at all? Whichever way the argument is looked at it is preposterous, while its conclusion is simply lamentable, with its jejune rhetoric about redemption as a consolation to mankind. If Mr. Balfour has meant all along merely that those who find "consolation"—blessed word!—in a certain belief should continue to cherish the belief even after it has been proved absurd, he should have said so. We are all pretty well accustomed to *that* argument by this time; and since there is very little more in Mr. Balfour's argument about beliefs and formulas than this plea of the "consolation" it gives certain sentimental people to believe incredible things, he might well have spared us the wire-drawn sophistry of the rest of the chapter.

Nor need we spend too much time over his next two chapters on "Beliefs, Formulas, and Realities," and "Ultimate Scientific Ideas" respectively. Here he argues that there is never any very precise relation on the one hand between language and belief, on the other hand between belief and reality. Thus though we may all believe that Julius Cæsar was murdered at Rome in the first century B.C., this proposition does not "mean the same thing in the mouths of all who use it". It does not, for example, rouse the same mental states in the schoolboy and in the philosophic historian; "while any alteration in our views on the nature of death or on the nature of man must necessarily alter the import of a proposition which asserts of a particular man that he suffered a particular kind of death" (p. 264). This exquisite piece of futile subtlety may prepare us for what is to follow, and may also serve to justify some of the criticisms that have been passed upon Mr. Balfour as a man and as a writer. There is perhaps no chapter in the whole of *The Foundations of Belief* which so well illustrates the thin, feminine, shrewish, acidulous nature of Mr. Balfour's mind—the mind, as one critic has put it, of "an amateur fond of casuistry and delicate points, but hypersensitive in touch, and in tone rather feeble, valetudinarian. . . . One may be justified in reading *Philosophic Doubt* in order to make a study of Mr. Balfour; one would hardly be justified, or at any rate rewarded, in reading it to study philosophy. We do not mean to assert that it is false, for this is hardly the place to discuss it; but we can assert that it is weak, meagre, nay, attenuated to a very distressing degree."[1] Another critic has said, á

[1] Arthur Lynch, *Human Documents*, pp. 91, 92.

propos of Mr. Balfour's article on "Cobden and the Manchester School," what one feels impelled to say of *The Foundations of Belief* as a whole, and of these chapters in particular, that "one realises on the literary side what it is in Mr. Balfour that set his Irish antagonists calling him an old maid. The thin, shrewish criticism, the sidelong, pin-pricking attack, partially relieved by the touches of broad estimate which come to a party leader of good judgment—everything but the generalisation suggests a soprano voice and a soprano temper. Cobden was a man ; and whenever Mr. Balfour is set against a true man, even if he have at times the intellectual advantage, it is never a masculine advantage, and his advantage always tends to turn into a disadvantage by reason of his halfness, his niggling, his lack of the *mâle tristesse* which vouches for character and personality."[1] One finishes the chapter on " Beliefs, Formulas, and Realities" with a sigh of regret that any man should waste his time in an elaborate exposition of a theory which, so far as it has any truth in it, is already known to every one, and of which the only new feature is the preposterous attempt to press it into the service of discredited theological beliefs.

Thus no one would dispute his propositions that the ordinary relations between language and belief and between belief and reality are not precise in all their details. No one would refuse to admit that, "outside the relations of abstract propositions . . . neither in our knowledge of ourselves, nor in our knowledge of each other, nor in our knowledge of the material world, nor in our knowledge of God, is there any belief which is more than an approximation, any method which is free from flaw, any result not tainted with error". The only point which the rationalist is concerned to dispute is the assumption that this in any way helps out the dogmas of religion. The rationalist asserts, for example, that there is no

[1] John M. Robertson, "Mr. Balfour, a Study," *Free Review*, July, 1894.

reason whatever for believing that the immaculate conception ever happened, or that the picture of the Gospel Jesus is the picture of any one character, or that the miracles alleged to have been performed by him ever were performed. To reply to this that *none* of our beliefs touch reality at all points is ludicrously beside the question. If all beliefs, even our fundamental beliefs as to matter and motion, must be looked upon as offering only a partial correspondence to reality, nothing can be extracted from this proposition to help out an individual belief in a case of conflict of opinion. Since no belief corresponds precisely to reality, all beliefs are in this respect on a par; and the only question remaining is, what, within this circle, are the relative credentials of this belief and that? We may not know what matter is in its "reality," and we may not know what colour is in its "reality," but that does not stand in the way of our belief that coal was black ten thousand years ago just as it is black now. Our reasons for this belief can be given as against reasons for the opposite belief, and it is a question, not of whether our beliefs as to "coal" and "blackness" correspond to what Mr. Balfour calls "reality," but simply of which belief is the better justified, taking "coal" and "blackness" to signify what our opponent and ourselves are quite agreed they shall signify. Similarly, we may say that, since the acceptance of the Christian religion depends upon the beliefs that a certain Jew was born of a virgin; that he was divinely sent, even if he were not divine himself; that he performed certain miracles and gave certain moral precepts; that he was crucified; that he died, rose again the third day, and ascended into heaven—all this must be shown to be true merely in the sense in which the term "true" is always used; that is, the Christian must prove to our satisfaction that it is more reasonable to believe that these things happened than that they did not happen, just as it is more reasonable to believe that Plato wrote the Socratic dialogues than that he did not; and any hair-splitting about the correspondence between beliefs and realities is mere trifling.

For Mr. Balfour's argument finally, be it noted, falls back once more on sentiment instead of on demonstration. He warns us against assuming that our beliefs are true because they are our beliefs, and our opponents' beliefs wrong because they are the reverse of ours; and he lays it down that, "however profound may be our ignorance of our ignorance, at least we should realise that to describe (when using language strictly) any scheme of belief as wholly false which has even imperfectly met the needs of mankind, is the height of arrogance; and that to claim for any beliefs which we happen to approve that they are wholly true, is the height of absurdity" (p. 270). The implicit, if not explicit, contention is that, since Christianity "meets the needs of mankind," we must not be too severe upon its shortcomings in the matter of rational proof. The argument, however, unfortunately, cuts both ways. If Christianity "meets the needs of mankind," so does the rationalism which attacks it, for if rationalism did not "meet the needs" of those who maintained that creed, it could never have been born. So that the rationalist is as much justified in his critical examination of the basis of Christianity as Mr. Balfour in his examination of the basis of naturalism. To that extent, then, the two systems of belief are on a par, neither having any sentimental claim to precedence over the other; and the argument as to "meeting the needs of mankind" ceases to be one of the bulwarks of religion. As for describing any scheme of belief as "wholly false," the rationalist no more does that than Mr. Balfour. Atheism and theism come into conflict, not because the atheist affirms that the theist ought to have full knowledge of the reality of God, while he himself need have only a partial knowledge of the reality of the universe of objects, but because the proofs for the existence of God fail in the same way as the proofs for the existence of a four-sided triangle. All that the atheist does is to point out to the theist that the term "God," when defined to mean a Supreme Reason or a First Cause, is as meaningless as the term four-sided triangle or square circle. If the atheist is wrong, he can be shown to be wrong by confuting his reasoning, and the relation of our beliefs to realities has simply nothing to do with the argument. Once more it comes down, as every theistic argument must do, to the "illative sense" or to vague sentiment about "the needs of mankind". And once more, if these beliefs that are said to meet the needs of mankind do really perform that office, whence comes it that Mr. Balfour's book has to point out the fact to persons *whose needs are not met by these beliefs?* And if by his book he succeeds in inducing any one to adopt these beliefs, it is because he has persuaded them by his reasoning, because he has shown them that it is more reasonable to hold these beliefs than to reject them; that is, he has simply won his victory by using the weapons which he has all along been forbidding the rationalist to use. His argument, again, that we ought not to be surprised "that we do not adequately comprehend God, seeing that we can give no very satisfactory account of 'a thing,'" is invalid in that it confuses what is within the circle of phenomena with what is supposed to lie without it; that is, though we can hardly say what "a thing" is, this does not affect our judgments about *things* and about the relative credibility of men's assertions about things. These must be tried before the bar of such reason as we all possess, on the grounds of their conformity with such knowledge as we all possess. Now the belief in a God does not stand on the same plane as the belief in "a thing". The latter belief is irreducible and unanalysable; the former is not. The belief in a God is merely, from the rationalistic point of view, an error in inference. The theist and the atheist are equally ignorant of the foundations of our belief in a real world; but having agreed to this, and each sharing the belief, they are, henceforth, within the same circle. Any further beliefs must be judged by their conformity with reason; and the atheist's contention is simply that the theist's belief in a God is either an emotional product, due to physique, environment and other influences, or else an illegitimately conducted series of inferences from the processes of Nature. So that it will not do for the theist to attempt to found his belief in a God upon the same fundamental psychical process as that upon which the atheist and the theist alike found their belief in a real world. The theist is really upon much safer ground when he plays his favourite card of sentiment. Thus Mr. Balfour concludes his chapter with the remark that Mr. Spencer "has not seen that, if this simple-minded creed[1] be once abandoned, there is no convenient halting-place till we have swung round to a theory of things which is its precise opposite; a theory which, though it shrinks on its speculative side from no severity of critical analysis, yet on its practical side finds the source of its constructive energy in the deepest needs of man, and thus recognises, alike in science, in ethics, in beauty, in religion, the halting expression of a reality beyond our reach, the half-seen vision of transcendent truth" (p. 289). Whether Mr. Balfour's creed is so impregnable to critical attack may perhaps be doubted; but when he says that *his* creed finds its source "in the deepest needs of man," we may point out the unconscious vanity of supposing *his* needs to be the deepest, but we shall have as much difficulty in getting him to look at the matter from our standpoint as we have in inducing him to look at it from others'. So that, if the theist really wishes to purchase immunity from the atheist, let him give up his attempts at demonstration and retire into the fastnesses of emotion, whither no one will care to follow him up because it is not worth any one's while to do so.

[1] *I.e.*, that form of agnosticism which Mr. Spencer "explicitly repudiates by his theory, if not by his practice".

CHAPTER VII.

WE have now reached the final stages of Mr. Balfour's book. He has always been at his best, in politics as in philosophy, in sceptical criticism of the efforts of other men, and always at his worst in the moments when he has attempted some constructive work of his own. The remaining chapters of *The Foundations of Belief* have only such interest as attaches to the endeavours of a very clever man to find reasons for believing in very stupid dogmas. I will not yet go so far as to say, with some of his critics, that Mr. Balfour does not believe in the religion he has taken upon himself to defend. That is putting it somewhat crudely; and I prefer to say, for my part, that if I could find no better reasons for believing in Christianity than those which Mr. Balfour brings forward, I should either believe through faith pure and simple or not believe at all.

His argument for the existence of God, " drawn from the mere fact that we know," has already been examined; and here we need only glance at one of the corollaries of the argument. Mr. Balfour contends that " on the naturalistic hypothesis, the whole premises of knowledge are clearly due to the blind operation of material causes, and in the last resort to these alone. On that hypothesis we no more possess free reason than we possess free will. . . . These conclusions are . . . absolutely ruinous to knowledge. For they require us to accept a system as rational, one of whose doctrines is that the system itself is the product of causes which have no tendency to truth rather than falsehood, or to falsehood rather than truth. . . . Consider the following propositions, selected from the naturalistic creed or deduced from it :—

"(1) My beliefs, in so far as they are the result of reasoning at all, are founded on premises produced in the last resort by the 'collision of atoms'.

"(2) Atoms, having no prejudices in favour of truth, are as likely to turn out wrong premises as right ones; nay, more likely, inasmuch as truth is single and error manifold.

"(3) My premises, therefore, in the first place, and my conclusions in the second, are certainly untrustworthy, and probably false. Their falsity, moreover, is of a kind which cannot be remedied ; since any attempt to correct it must start from premises not suffering under the same defect. But no such premises exist.

"(4) Therefore, again, my opinion about the original causes which produced my premises, as it is an inference from them, partakes of their weakness; so that I cannot either securely doubt my own certainties or be certain about my own doubts" (pp. 276, 7, 8, 9).

"This is scepticism, indeed," remarks Mr. Balfour; and he proceeds to express his opinion that no "escape from these perplexities is possible, unless we are prepared to bring to the study of the world the presupposition that it was the work of a rational Being, who made *it* intelligible, and at the same time made *us*, in however feeble a fashion, able to understand it. This conception does not solve all difficulties; far from it. But, at least, it is not on the face of it incoherent. It does not attempt the impossible task of extracting reason from unreason ; nor does it require us to accept among scientific conclusions any which effectually shatter the credibility of scientific premises" (pp. 301, 302).

It is at all events gratifying to see Mr. Balfour admit that his theory of a Supreme Reason is not without its difficulties. And as for his philosophic fright at the consequences of naturalism upon the theory of knowledge, we may make some return for his temporary aberration into candour by assuring him that he has been scared merely by his own shadow. I have already argued that Mr. Balfour's proof of the existence of God fails in that it attempts an impossible feat—the knowledge of Nature apart from our manner of cognising it. His sceptical attack upon the naturalistic theory of knowledge fails from precisely the same error. Right and wrong, truth and error, are relative terms valid only within the circle of phenomena as we know it. To assert that "atoms, having no prejudices in favour of truth, are as likely to turn out wrong premises as right ones," is to assume that "truth" and "error" mean something which they can never mean, and to lose sight of the fact that had this earth been peopled by a race of different physical and mental conformation from ours, and therefore having different conceptions of the world of objects, truth and error, though not meaning to them what they mean to us, would still be words which they would be compelled to use, as signifying opposing elements in their cognitions. The atoms, it is true, *might* at the commencement have taken another course, and so produced a different physical and mental world ; but with all this our conception of truth and error has nothing to do. The words have no meaning for us except as discriminating between different orders of that experience which is the only experience we can know.

Mr. Balfour, however, would not any more than another man deny the truth of the scientific theory of the development of the universe from the primæval fire-mist. He would accept the scientific doctrine here as elsewhere, only quarrelling with the naturalistic deductions from it. Observe, however, to what lengths the acceptance of the scientific doctrine itself carries him. All the while that he is arguing that this theory can give us no criterion of truth, he is himself employing such a criterion; for the sceptical attack which he is making implies the possession of some such criterion, even if it be only a negative one. He cannot, that is to say, assert that atoms are as likely to turn out wrong premises as right ones without admitting *that this very argument of his, being ultimately the product of atoms, comes under the same condemnation;* or if he chooses to affirm that he is capable of pronouncing his opponents' doctrine to be wrong—*i.e.*, of judging between truth and error—he cannot consistently urge against naturalism that such a creed provides no criterion of truth and error. The dilemma in which he imagines he has put naturalism, however, arises, he might reply, not from the scientific hypothesis itself, but from the naturalistic philosophy that is based upon it; *i.e.*, from the philosophy that asserts that we may know phenomena and the laws by which they are connected, but nothing more. To this I would answer that the naturalistic theory of knowledge is the only one which can possibly be true if the scientific theory of the origin of the universe be accepted. At no point in the line of development from atom to atom, from the primæval nebula to our thoughts to-day, can Mr. Balfour insert a new agency, a new nonmaterial factor in the production of thought. He can only dissent from the naturalistic theory by placing that new factor at the very beginning, and styling it the Supreme Reason. From this four results follow. In the first place, Mr. Balfour's escape from the dreadful doctrines of naturalism depends wholly upon his proof of the existence of this Supreme Reason, and that proof, as we have seen, is feeble in the extreme; in the second place, reason being merely the term for a phenomenon among other phenomena, found under certain circumstances and under no others, Mr. Balfour has no right to extend its application to that which is supposed to lie outside the circle of phenomena—the very phrase " Supreme

Reason" being, indeed, a contradiction in terms; in the third place, every argument that tells against the inherent tendency of atoms to truth rather than falsehood has equal weight, even if we assume the existence of a Supreme Reason, for the veracity of this reason has in turn to be proved: such proof can only be afforded by reasoning from what we know of truth and error in our own experience to what we might assume of the relation to truth and error of the Author of experience: Mr. Balfour's own argument thus cutting its own throat, for (*a*) we can only assume the validity of this reasoning by assuming the validity of our ordinary experiential reasoning about truth and error; and (*b*) the argument from truth in experience to a God of truth assumes exactly what it has to prove, for it is quite possible that he may be wilfully deluding us all the time as to what truth really is; so that (*c*) Mr. Balfour proves the truth of his experience from the fact that there is a Supreme Reason, and proves the fact that there is a Supreme Reason from the fact that there is truth in his experience—thus tracing the vicious circle he accused the naturalist of tracing; and in the fourth place, if there be a Supreme Reason dominating things, he has been foolish enough to start atoms with no tendency to truth rather than falsehood, though from the fact that he is *Supreme* Reason there ought to be no tendency to falsehood; while if, as Mr. Balfour says, he is not only Supreme Reason but Moral Reason, he is altogether accountable for the train of circumstances that culminates in wrong beliefs, and therefore directly answerable for the fact of the naturalist denying that there is a Supreme Reason.

Mr. Balfour's attempt to reconcile religion and science in this way breaks down, then, I imagine, at every point. He is candid enough to admit the many difficulties which every form of theism has to overcome; and when he alleges that "naturalism has to face these difficulties] in a yet more embarrassing form," it is necessary to remind him once more that whether these difficulties do or do not confront naturalism, it is not with this, but with science itself that the dogmas of religion come into conflict.

Let us, however, assume that Mr. Balfour's attack upon naturalism has been as successful as he imagines it to have been; and let us follow him in his defence of some of the main dogmas of religion in general and of Christianity in particular. He deals incidentally, for example, with the question of evil, admitting that "from the world as presented to us by science we might conjecture a God of power and a God of reason, but we could never infer a God who was wholly loving and wholly just. So that what religion proclaims aloud to be His most essential attributes are precisely those respecting which the oracles of science are doubtful or dumb" (p. 306). A great problem, indeed, to settle which, if Mr. Balfour were capable of it, would go a long way towards reconciling religion and science. Observe now how Mr. Balfour deals with it. "The question therefore seems, though not, I think, quite correctly, to be one which is wholly, as it were, within the frontiers of theology, and which theologians may, therefore, be left to deal with as best they may, undisturbed by any arguments supplied by science. If this be not in theory strictly true, it is in practice but little wide of the mark. The facts which raise the problem in its acutest form belong indeed to that portion of the experience of life which is the common property of science and theology; but theology is much more deeply concerned in them than science can ever be, and has long faced the unsolved problem which they present. The weight which it has thus borne for all these centuries is not likely now to crush it; and, paradoxical though it seems, it is yet surely true that what is a theological stumbling-block may also be a religious aid; and that it is in part the thought of 'all creation groaning and travailing in pain together, waiting for redemption,' which creates in man the deepest need for faith in the love of God" (pp. 306, 307).

This is indeed charming dialectic. The theologian puts forward for acceptance a theory of the world which includes a moral God. Against this theory it is urged that the most ordinary facts of life negate such a conception; to which the theologian replies that this is *his* problem, and that it must be left to him! He will deal with it as best he may, "undisturbed by any arguments supplied by science"! Most of us, I apprehend, would find little difficulty in dealing with any problem, undisturbed by any arguments supplied by our opponents; though I am prepared to admit cheerfully that the theologian is particularly expert in this kind of thing. It is consoling, too, to learn that theology has been " facing " the problem for all these centuries; though considering how little it has been able to make of the problem it ought to have been stared out of countenance by this time. Finally, though theology cannot solve the problem, we are recommended to believe the original proposition about the love of God, the disputing of which made the " problem "; that is, at the same time that theology " faces " the problem she assures us that there is no problem at all. This is Mr. Balfour's first essay in the reconciliation of religion and science. It is at any rate not very promising for what is to follow; and the most that can be said for his future arguments is that if they are no more convincing than this they are at least equally amusing. One finds it, indeed, somewhat difficult to realise that the Mr. Balfour who makes this pitiable exhibition of incompetency is the Mr. Balfour who flourished his claymore so valiantly in the face of naturalism, and called in the sight of heaven for proofs, for logic, for consistency.

After having made light of the difficulty presented by the existence of evil, he proceeds to deal in a somewhat similar manner with the question of miracles. And, first of all, he takes up the point of the clash between the belief in miracles and the belief in the uniformity of Nature. The result of his analysis is the discovery that " if we would use language with perfect accuracy, we ought, it would seem, either to say that the same cause would always be followed by precisely the same effect, if it recurred—which it never does, *or* that, in certain regions of Nature, though only in certain regions, we can detect subordinate uniformities of repetition which, though not exact, enable us, without sensible insecurity or error, to anticipate the future or reconstruct the past " (p. 311). What immediately follows upon this passage is best left alone, out of consideration for Mr. Balfour's reputation for some degree of acuteness, for one expects something more from him than the puerilities of the average park evangelist. He continues, however, in this strain. The real "difficulties connected with theological miracles lie elsewhere. Two qualities seem to be of their essence: they must be wonders, and they must be wonders due to the special action of Divine power; and each of these qualities raises a special problem of its own. That raised by the first is a question of evidence. What amount of evidence, if any, is sufficient to render a miracle credible? And on this . . . I may, perhaps, content myself with pointing out that, if by evidence is meant, as it usually is, historical testimony, that is not a fixed quantity, the same for every reasonable man, no matter what may be his other opinions. It varies —and must necessarily vary—with the general views, the 'psychological climate' which he brings to its consideration. It is possible to get twelve plain men to agree on the evidence which requires them to bring in a verdict of guilty or not guilty, because they start with a common stock of presuppositions in the light of which the evidence submitted to them may, without preliminary discussion, be interpreted. But when, as in the case of theological miracles, there is no such common stock, any agreement on a verdict can scarcely be looked for.

One of the jury may hold the naturalistic view of the world. To him, of course, the occurrence of a miracle involves the abandonment of the whole philosophy in terms of which he is accustomed to interpret the universe. . . . Another may believe in 'verbal inspiration'. To him . . . every miracle, whatever its character . . . is to be accepted with equal confidence, provided it be narrated in the works of inspired authors. . . . A third of our supposed jurymen may reject both naturalism and verbal inspiration. . . . Every event, therefore, whether wonderful or not, a belief in whose occurrence is involved in that religion, every event by whose disproof the religion would be seriously impoverished or altogether destroyed, has behind it the whole combined strength of the system to which it belongs" (pp. 313, 314).

What, the reader asks, is to come out of all this wonderful subtlety? Alas, this is all that results from it : " Many other varieties of 'psychological climate' might be described ; but what I have said is, perhaps, enough to show how absurd it is to expect any unanimity as to the value of historical evidence until some better agreement has been arrived at respecting the presuppositions in the light of which alone such evidence can be estimated. *I pass, therefore, to the difficulty raised by the second . . . attribute of theological miracles* "[1] (p. 315).

This is indeed a short and easy method with rationalists. Difference of opinion about any matter is usually held to justify an examination of the truth or the falsehood of the matter ; but it will be news to most people that we are exempted from giving evidence for our assertions to one who disagrees with us, simply *because* he disagrees with us. It is quite true that to men of different religious or philosophical creeds the question of miracles will appear in different lights. But what if one cause of this difference is the different way in which the historical evidence for miracles has struck them ? I cease to

---

[1] Italics mine.

believe, let us say, in the Gospel miracles because the evidence for them is insufficient, and I appeal to Mr. Balfour to show cause why I should go back to my old belief; and all that Mr. Balfour does is to tell me that *because* I believe the historical evidence to be insufficient, *therefore* he will not tell me wherein he holds it to be sufficient. The naturalistic view will of course make belief in miracles impossible; but in the first place, if the Christian looks upon the historical evidence for them as perfectly good, he is bound to share his superior knowledge with the naturalist; and in the second place, the affording of adequate historical support to the miracles would go far to shake the naturalist's belief in thoroughgoing naturalism. Mr. Balfour, then, must not blame us if we decline to be seduced by such obvious sophistry as this, and if we are unkind enough to say that he does not give us historical evidence for the miracles, not because he thinks us too besotted to appreciate it, but simply because he has it not to give.

Nor will I do more than mention the further points that every religionist in the world might use Mr. Balfour's argument in defence of the miracles of *his* religion; and that if the "psychological climate" of the rationalist is a bar to his sympathetic comprehension of this question, the "psychological climate" of the Christian hinders him from appreciating the beauties of naturalism as well as those of another religion. Let us pass on at once to the second part of Mr. Balfour's defence. Miracles are due "to the 'special action of God'". "But this, be it observed," he goes on, "is, from a religious point of view, no peculiarity of miracles. Few schemes of thought which have any religious flavour about them at all wholly exclude the idea of what I will venture to call the 'preferential exercise of divine power,' whatever differences of opinion may exist as to the manner in which it is manifested." For his own part, Mr. Balfour thinks that all these various opinions are equally open to one form of attack, namely: "How can the Divine Being who is the Ground and Source of everything that is, who sustains all, directs all, produces all, be connected more closely with one part of that which He has created than with another?" (p. 317).

To this Mr. Balfour replies that ethics as well as theology must have a hand in dealing with this problem. "Once assume a God, and we shall be obliged, sooner or later, to introduce harmony into our system by making obedience to His will coincident with the established rules of conduct. . . . But if this process of adjustment is to be done consistently with the maintenance of any eternal and absolute distinction between right and wrong, then must His will be a 'good will,' and we must suppose Him to look with favour upon some parts of this mixed world of good and evil, and with disfavour upon others." Even the man of science ought to take this view; "for the doctrine of evolution has in this respect made a change in his position which, curiously enough, brings it closer to that occupied in this matter by theology and ethics than it was in the days when 'special creation' was the fashionable view. I am not contending, be it observed, that evolution strengthens the evidence for theism. My point rather is, that if the existence of God be assumed, evolution does, to a certain extent, harmonise with that belief in His 'preferential action' which religion and morality alike require us to attribute to Him."

That is, though God is the author of everything that happens, he is the author of some things more than others—whatever that may mean. Mr. Balfour's remarks on evolution apparently mean that if I throw two men into the water, and then pick A out and leave B to drown, I perform a "preferential action" with regard to A alone. My action is indeed preferential as regards him, but that is only from the positive standpoint; negatively, my preferential action really covers B also. Similarly, if the positive choosing of certain individuals to carry on the work of evolution indicates a preferential action on the part of the Deity, for which he is to receive some moral credit, he must also receive the moral discredit involved in the negative half of his preferential action—the suffering inflicted on those whom he has rejected. To argue as Mr. Balfour argues here is not exactly the best way to defend the moral character of his Deity. This, however, is a side issue. The main question is, what has Mr. Balfour done for miracles? The upshot of it all is, that *once assume the existence of God*, and miracles follow as a matter of course. No doubt! but miracles have always been put forward *as a proof of the existence of God*, and it is a little late in the day to attempt to bolster up the Deity by his miracles, and the miracles again by their Deity. One does not wade through *The Foundations of Belief* merely to be regaled with the Christian Evidences of two generations ago. For how are we left in the end by Mr. Balfour as to the question of miracles? The rationalist makes two main objections: (1) that there is no historical evidence for the Gospel miracles, to which it is replied that he is not a fit and proper person to receive this evidence; (2) that what we know of Nature negatives the assumption that it is ever interfered with by a supernatural being, to which it is replied that we have only to believe that this supernatural being exists, and we will have no difficulty in further believing that he *does* interfere with Nature. And it is worth observing how unconsciously Mr. Balfour has slid away from his own first position. He began with miracles, and theological, *i.e.* Gospel, miracles at that; he ends with "preferential action" as shown in evolution! Is evolution, then, to be looked upon as a miracle in Mr. Balfour's meaning of the term? And if so, what is the point of similarity between this and such a miracle as turning water into wine? To define one's terms and to keep to one's definitions in a long and abstruse argument is a matter in which any man may be pardoned for failing ; but to blunder so blissfully as this in three or four pages is hardly what one expected from the latest self-constituted defender of the faith, who has all along been inviting the world to observe how severe he could be upon the shortcomings of naturalism. I venture to assert that no naturalistic philosopher, in his worst moments of aberration, reasoned so badly as Mr. Balfour has been doing in relation to the questions of evil and of miracles ; for which the reason may be either that the naturalists have had a better case to begin with, or they have confined their approval to doctrines in which they altogether believed.

CHAPTER VIII.

HAVING proved, to his own satisfaction, that science requires theism as its foundation, and that we can only surmount the difficulty of the origin of knowledge from non-rational forces by postulating a Supreme Reason, Mr. Balfour proceeds to deal with the question of inspiration. He begins with a characteristic piece of confusion. There are some, he says, who profess to be able to dispense with revelation, and to be able by the use of the unassisted reason to discover a satisfactory *natural* religion. "But, for my own part," says Mr. Balfour, "I object altogether to the theory underlying this distinction. I do not believe that, strictly speaking, there is any such thing as 'unassisted reason'. And I am sure that if there be, the conclusions of 'natural religion' are not among its products. The attentive reader does not require to be told that, according to the views here advocated, every idea involved in such a proposition as that 'There is a moral Creator and Ruler of the world' (which I may assume, for purposes of illustration, to constitute the substance of natural religion) is due to a complex of causes, of which human reason was not the most important; and that this natural religion never would have been heard of, much less have been received with approval, had it not been for that traditional religion of which it vainly supposes itself to be independent" (pp. 327, 328).

Mr. Balfour's distinction between rational and irrational beliefs is, as I have already pointed out, thoroughly unscientific.

But in any case, no matter whether we call the belief in a God rational or non-rational, it is quite plain that Mr. Balfour has become very badly confused over "traditional" and "natural" religion. He apparently imagines that the former has always preceded the latter. How then came the former into being? If "revealed" religion, as expounded in certain documents inspired by God, preceded "natural" religion, how were those who received the revelation to know that it came from God? Before, in fact, there can be any belief that the sacred books have been inspired by God, there must already be the belief in God; and this belief is "natural" religion—*i.e.*, it has been induced by analogical reasoning from the facts of life. To suppose, as Mr. Balfour seems to do, that "traditional" religion precedes "natural" religion, is to suppose that at some time or other the traditional religion fell from heaven and penetrated in a moment the heads of a certain number of individuals without being assimilated by their reason.

This, however, is a very trifling point, and is only of interest as exhibiting the straits to which Mr. Balfour has now become reduced. As his argument proceeds he merely sinks deeper into the bog of fallacy and self-contradiction. He is too acute to believe that the Christian books are "inspired," in the sense in which that word has always been used by Christians; yet, since he is engaged in propping up the Christian faith, he has to say something in defence of the theory of inspiration. Hence his inevitable confusion. He begins by admitting that it is somewhat arbitrary to draw a line anywhere, and say "here unassisted human knowledge ends," or "here revelation begins". "It would, no doubt," he remarks, "be inaccurate to say that inspiration is that, seen from its Divine side, which we call discovery when seen from the human side. But it is not, I think, inaccurate to say that every addition to knowledge, whether in the individual or the community, whether scientific, ethical, or theological, is due to a co-operation between the human soul which assimilates and the Divine power which inspires" (p. 329). On these terms every utterance is inspired, the atheist's equally with the theist's; and once more we have the ridiculous spectacle of a Deity assisting men to acquire a knowledge of the universe, which is bound to end in their denying his very existence. Here, however, Mr. Balfour becomes more cautious. "But because this view involves a use of the term 'inspiration' which, ignoring all minor distinctions, extends it to every case in which the production of belief is due to the 'preferential action' of Divine power, it does not, of course, follow that minor distinctions do not exist." This saving clause is, of course, meant to keep the way clear for Christianity at a later stage. Everything is inspired, but some things are more inspired than others; and the most inspired books in the world are those bound together in the Bible. You must not ask for evidence of this. If you do, you will be frowned upon with a remark about the weakness of unassisted human reason in the production of belief; and you must be content with the surmise that a Christian knows his sacred books to be the most inspired of all simply because they are *his* sacred books.

The pendulum, however, swings back once more. Mr. Balfour protests against the assumption that some literatures are inspired while others are not. "Inspiration . . . is limited to no age, to no country, to no people. . . . Wherever an approach has been made to truth, wherever any individual soul has assimilated some old discovery, or has forced the secret of a new one, there is its co-operation to be discovered." Then the theologian repents of his audacity and draws back again: "Now, that there may be, or rather plainly are, many modes in which belief is assisted by Divine co-operation I have already admitted. That the word 'inspiration' may, with advantage, be confined to one or more of these I do not desire to deny;" that is, some beliefs are inspired and some are not, though Mr. Balfour has told us only a moment ago that "*every* addition to knowledge" involves the assistance of God. His theory is that "though the beliefs which [the Divine element] assists in producing differ infinitely from one another in their nearness to absolute truth, the fact is not disguised, nor the honour due to the most spiritually perfect utterances in aught imperilled, by recognising in all some marks of Divine intervention" (p. 332). So that while God inspires all beliefs, he inspires some to be right and some to be wrong—which is an entirely novel use of the word "inspiration". Mr. Balfour, for example, is inspired to right belief on the subject of the existence of God and the divinity of Jesus, Mr. Spencer to wrong belief—which is one more side-light upon the wisdom and the grace of God. And further, since of two "inspired" beliefs one is "infinitely" nearer the truth than the other, and since this difference is due to the difference in the amount of God's "co-operation," why does Mr. Balfour try to get the spiritually blind man to see with *his* eyes, that is, attempt to diminish the distance which God has placed between them, and so attempt to alter the arrangement which God himself has made? Evidently, if Mr. Balfour thinks his final chapter is going to bring any one into the religious camp, he must have more faith in the power of reason than he has been willing to admit, and must have views on the relation of his reasoning to the "co-operation" of God which are, to say the least, somewhat uncomplimentary to his Creator.

"But in the second place," he continues, "it may be objected that inspiration thus broadly conceived is incapable of providing mankind with any satisfactory criterion of religious truth. Since its co-operation can be traced in so much that is imperfect, the mere fact of its co-operation cannot in any particular case be a protection even against gross error. If, therefore, we seek in it not merely a Divinely ordered cause of belief, but also a Divinely ordered ground for believing, there must be some means of marking off those examples of its operation which rightfully command our full intellectual allegiance, from those which are no more than evidences of an influence towards the truth working out its purpose slowly through the ages.

"This is beyond dispute. Nothing that I have said about inspiration in general as a source of belief affects in any way the character of certain instances of inspiration as an authority for belief. Nor was it intended to do so; for the problem, or group of problems, which would thus have been raised *is altogether beside the main course of my argument. They belong not to an introduction to theology, but to theology itself.* . . . It is always possible to ask whence these claimants to authority derive their credentials, what titles the organisation or the individual possesses to our obedience, whether the records are authentic, and what is their precise import. And the mere fact that such questions may be put, and that they can neither be thrust aside as irrelevant nor be answered without elaborate critical and historical discussion, *shows clearly enough that we have no business with them here*" (pp. 333, 334).

"Audacity" is all too weak a term to describe a passage of this kind. Mr. Balfour, through having taken it upon himself to defend a broken cause, becomes entangled in a mass of hopeless absurdities and contradictions from which the only conclusion that appears to emerge is that every literature is "inspired". Challenged then to show cause why we should regard the Christian books as worthy of any more admiration and credence than a hundred other sacred literatures, Mr. Balfour calmly tells that "we have no business" with these questions here! If he has no business with the question of the authenticity of the Christian books, he should have had no business with the prior question of inspiration as a whole which makes the question of authenticity inevitable. But Mr. Balfour has no concern with the truth of this or that opinion; he is concerned solely to utter a few ineptitudes about the Christian religion, to drag a few weaklings into his camp after having stupefied them with irrelevant sophistry, and to slink away with an air of injured dignity as soon as the enemy begins to range himself in battle array. His display at this point is one more confirmation of the fact that Mr. Balfour is only interesting when engaged in snatching immaterial points from his opponents, and that he is a hopeless failure from the ethical no less than from the logical standpoint when he comes to the justification of his own positions.

So far he has done very little for Christianity. He has evaded the problem of evil and the question of the authenticity and inspiration of the Christian records, and he has handled the question of miracles in a manner bordering on the burlesque. His final effort is to raise some point by which the superiority of the Christian scheme can finally be established. " What I have so far tried to establish," he writes, " is this— that the great body of our beliefs, scientific, ethical, theological, form a more coherent and satisfactory whole if we consider them in a theistic setting than if we consider them in a naturalistic one. The further question, therefore, inevitably suggests itself, Whether we can carry the process a step further and say that they are more coherent and satisfactory if considered in a Christian setting than in a merely theistic one? The answer often given is in the negative. It is always assumed by those who do not accept the doctrine of the incarnation, and it is not uncommonly conceded by those who do, that it constitutes an additional burden upon faith, a new stumbling-block to reason. And many who are prepared to accommodate their beliefs to the requirements of (so-called) ' natural religion,' shrink from the difficulties and perplexities in which this central mystery of revealed religion threatens to involve them" (pp. 334, 335). To the objection that it is impossible to understand how the incarnation could have occurred, he replies that "if we cannot devise formulæ which shall elucidate the familiar mystery of our daily existence, we need neither be surprised nor embarrassed if the unique mystery of the Christian faith refuses to lend itself to inductive treatment," which is playing sophistry very low indeed. Mr. Balfour's argument might be used by any religionist in favour of the dogmas of his own religion; nor is it even a particularly ingenious device to urge that we cannot understand the incarnation because it is a "mystery". That argument again might be employed in defence of such a doctrine as the transmigration of souls, or any of the dogmas of theosophy. We decline to believe in the incarnation, however, for the plain and simple reason that there is no evidence to justify belief in it. Mr. Balfour's vapouring about "the familiar mystery of our daily existence" will not succeed in deluding even the plain man for whom it is intended. To make us believe in the incarnation four things are necessary: (1) It must be shown that it is *a priori* possible for a virgin to give birth to a child; (2) it must be shown that the Christian virgin-birth is on a different footing from the virgin-births of other ancient religions; (3) it must be shown that the Gospels are worthy of credence as historical records; (4) it must be shown that Jesus was not man but God. Convince the rationalist upon these four points, and he will believe in the incarnation with the utmost willingness; and the first thing to do is to convince him of the historical credibility of the Gospels.

Conscious of this, and conscious that he can produce no such conviction, Mr. Balfour makes a characteristic attempt to minimise the importance of the historical criticism of the sacred books, arguing, in effect, that the unbeliever is incompetent to appreciate the worth of the evidence for their credibility. He remarks that "various destructive schools of New Testament criticism" have dealt with this question. "Starting from a philosophy which forbade them to accept much of the substance of the Gospel narrative, they very properly set to work to devise a variety of hypotheses which would account for the fact that the narrative, with all its peculiarities, was nevertheless there. . . . But it is a great, though common, error to describe these learned efforts as examples of the unbiassed application of historic methods to historic documents. It would be more correct to say that they are endeavours, by the unstinted employment of an elaborate critical apparatus, to force the testimony of existing records into conformity with theories on the truth or falsity of which it is for philosophy, not history, to pronounce. What view I take of the particular philosophy to which these critics make appeal the reader already knows; and our immediate concern is not again to discuss the presuppositions with which other people have approached the consideration of New Testament history, but to arrive at some conclusion about our own" (p. 338).

That is, a naturalist is not competent to examine the historic evidences for Christianity *because* he does not believe in Christianity, while a Christian presumably is competent *because* he does believe in it. This is certainly a novel way of regarding the question, and if it is not particularly illuminative it is at least amusing. To take it seriously, or, indeed, to suppose that Mr. Balfour wishes us to take it seriously, is of course impossible. Had Mr. Balfour, however, been contented with the humorous treatment of the subject there would not have been much reason to find fault with him. But when he gives the uninstructed reader to understand that the critical attack on the historical basis of Christianity has mostly come from those who embraced the naturalistic creed, he is simply guilty of downright misrepresentation. He knows as well as any one that most of the critical assault in this direction has come from men who were theists, and more sincere in their theism than Mr. Balfour can be said to be in his; and that so far from rationalists blinding themselves to the historical evidence for the Gospels simply because they *are* rationalists, thousands of Christians have been started upon the road to rationalism by their belief in the credibility of the Gospels having been unable to withstand so simple a process as the mere comparison of one with the other.

Unable, then, to give the slightest reason for believing in the incarnation, Mr. Balfour is compelled to play his sole remaining card. "In what mood of expectation ought our provisional philosophy to induce us to consider the extant historic evidence for the Christian story? The reply must, I think, depend, as I shall show in a moment, upon the view we take of the ethical import of Christianity; while its ethical import, again, must depend on the degree to which it ministers to our ethical needs" (p. 339). Surely by this time Mr. Balfour might have learned that nothing is to be gained by the argument from "needs". If it proves anything, it proves *all* beliefs which the believer may choose to base upon a "need"; and it too blandly assumes that the "higher" needs are those of Mr. Balfour and his religious associates. To discuss such a point as this would simply be an unwarrantable waste of time and space; nor need we give the slightest consideration to Mr. Balfour's argument that we ought to believe in the incarnation because of the fact that there is evil in the world, it being a consolation to think that if we suffer God also came upon earth to suffer. We have relegated this kind of inanity to the pulpit, and have no particular desire to come across it at the end of a lengthy pseudo-philosophical treatise. And when, upon the final page of his book, Mr. Balfour remarks that "how far I have succeeded in showing that the least incomplete unification open to us must include the fundamental elements of theology, and of Christian theology,

I leave it for others to determine," one feels impelled to reply indirectly to his question by saying, with one of his critics, that "an interesting moment would be made if any one should ever ask Mr. Balfour, point blank: 'This religion which you defend, do you really believe it?' Of course he would either say Yes, or protest against the question. Either way, the situation would be memorably dramatic." If I do not ask that question here, it is perhaps because I should despair of getting a straightforward answer to it.

So much, then, for Mr. Balfour's *Foun ations of Belief*. He has sought to demonstrate that there are, if anything, superior reasons for believing in Christianity than in naturalism; and we have seen that while his attack on science—conducted under the guise of an attack on naturalism—failed to discredit science in any way, his own positive reasons for belief in the Christian scheme have been nothing short of ludicrous. It only remains to glance at one thesis of his book that has been designedly omitted from our consideration until now. In the course of his protest against the "consequences" of the naturalistic theory upon the moral life, he had to meet the objection that there are "a great many excellent people who hold, in more or less purity, the naturalistic creed, but who, nevertheless, offer prominent examples of that habit of mind with which, as I have been endeavouring to show, the naturalistic creed is essentially inconsistent" (p. 82). To this Mr. Balfour replies that the moral life of such men is purely parasitic; "it is sheltered by convictions which belong not to them, but to the society of which they form a part; it is nourished by processes in which they take no share. And when those convictions decay and those processes come to an end, the alien life which they have maintained can scarce be expected to outlast them." This argument is also employed by Mr. Kidd to meet a similar objection, though he characteristically uses it in the most illogical manner, making half a dozen self-stultifications to Mr. Balfour's one.[1] Into the merits of the argument itself it is scarcely worth while to enter. That moral ideas and moral actions are to a large extent predetermined by the existent constitution of society is what no one will think of disputing; but it is mere unscientific blundering to assume that our ethical code has been created for us by Christianity. Ethical conduct is simply the resultant of a thousand forces, among which a particular set of religious dogmas is but one; nor is it the fact either that we owe our moral code to Christianity, or that the ethical system of any society ever remains constant. It is perpetually changing as new influences become prominent and older ones recede into the background. The ethical constitution of a society depends finally as little upon the religious beliefs of a portion of the individuals composing it as the physical constitution of an individual depends upon the colour of his hair. The religion itself, indeed, so far from being the cause of the ethical code, becomes itself, in time, modified so as to harmonise with this; that is, in an age when the general body of social forces makes for humanism rather than for barbarism, the more barbaric elements in the religion tend to become glossed over or ignored. The relation between a religious system and an ethical code is, in fact, like all other relations, one of action and reaction; the religious beliefs of some men may have an influence upon their conduct, while, on the other hand, a thousand silent social forces are gradually altering men's attitude with respect to these beliefs. Apart from theoretical considerations of this kind, however, the absurdity of Mr. Balfour's position is best seen by an appeal to actual experience. Does he really think that the virtue of Mr. Spencer, for example, bears the same relation to the virtue of Mr. Balfour as a parasite to its host? Is it Christians or rationalists who fill our gaols? Is it Christians or rationalists who keep all Europe in the constant dread of

[1] See *Social Evolution*, pp. 256-258.

war? Is it Christians or rationalists who make a mere difference of belief the excuse for a merciless persecution of the weak by the strong? Mr. Balfour and Mr. Kidd cannot be so ignorant of history as not to be aware that the lead in almost every humanistic movement has been taken by men who claimed to have no belief in Christianity, and that the great body of Christians have as a rule, in these cases, been ranged on the side of oppression and reaction. Are then the parasites better than the host? Are we to understand that, while the Christian creed alone can be looked to as a stimulus to moral conduct, it has practically no effect upon the great majority of those who believe in it, while those who do not believe in it exhibit the virtues that are supposed to be its characteristic product? Such a conclusion is, indeed, absurd, yet it is one that logically follows upon the thesis that the virtue of the rationalist is the product, not of rationalism, but of Christianity. No sensible rationalist, indeed, would urge that rationalism or any other creed is *per se* certain to produce moral conduct. He knows that conduct is a complex of many forces, inner and outer, among which creeds and systems are but one; and in adopting his creed simply because he believes it to be true, he has done all that duty requires of him. But it is not beside the question to ask those who insist upon the dependence of ethical conduct upon the Christian system to give us personal evidence of the consequences of their faith, to show us in their own lives that the fruit of the tree is indeed so beautiful as they would have the rationalist believe. Tried by such a test, Christianity fails ignominiously; it fails in the case of Mr. Balfour himself. It is not for the man against whom the insinuation of insincerity has been whispered by reviewer after reviewer to talk of the ethical virtues that flow from the acceptance of Christianity; it is not for the man who made so mean an opposition to the admission of Mr. Bradlaugh into Parliament to speak of the moral desolation that follows in the wake of atheism. Tried by any standard of perfection, the Christian Mr. Balfour comes out but indifferently in a comparison with the moral qualities of the great atheist, who, at least, was no opportunist, either in religion or in politics, and who would have scorned to pander to the multitude by finding irrational reasons for their irrational beliefs. If it is from the fruit that we are to judge the tree, well and good; but in that case let us be spared the sophistical argument that a good Christian is a good man because he is a Christian, while a good atheist is a good man because he is surrounded by a few thousand Christians, whose creed, though he does not believe in it, yet keeps him from the paths of vice, while they who do believe in it are not restrained by it from the commission of any sin which they find it to their interest to commit.

CONCLUSION.

WE have now passed under review the three books that made so great a sensation when they appeared. The object of this final chapter is to give the gist of some of the more important criticisms that have been passed upon Mr. Balfour's work, for we may now part company for ever, so far as the present volume is concerned, with Mr. Kidd and Mr. Drummond. Mr. Balfour's book, however, called forth a great number of criticisms, among which were a few by men of ability and eminence. It was interesting to the rationalist to note the pleasure, not unmixed with perplexity, of the bulk of the Christians who reviewed *The Foundations of Belief*, and who, while congratulating themselves upon the acquisition of so redoubtable a champion, were obviously uncertain in a great many cases of how the champion had gone about his business. When a popular lady novelist, for example, reviewed the book in the columns of a popular weekly paper, one felt a strong desire, after reading the review, to submit to the writer a few questions with the object of discovering how much she had really understood and remembered of Mr. Balfour's arguments after she had closed the book. Interesting, too, was the attitude of some of the Roman Catholic reviewers, who, glad as they were to have an ally in Mr. Balfour, were unable to think very much of his positive arguments for the existence of the Deity and the truth of the Incarnation. Apart from all the rest, however, stood the three criticisms of Mr.

Spencer,[1] Mr. Huxley,[2] and Mr. Karl Pearson,[3] with a *résumé* of which this final chapter will be mainly concerned.

Mr. Spencer, who was reluctantly drawn into the fray by the sense that if he did not answer Mr. Balfour the conclusion would be drawn that Mr. Balfour's criticism was unanswerable, confines himself mainly to that portion of *The Foundations of Belief* which attacks his own agnosticism. Introductorily, however, he points out the futility of Mr. Balfour's argument from needs to their satisfaction, showing that this argument indirectly begs the question, in that the existence of "a Ruling Power such as that which the current creed asserts" has to be assumed. "In the absence of the assumption that things have been by some agency prearranged for men's benefit, there seems no reason to expect the order of the universe to be one which provides for men's mental 'needs and aspirations'; and that the truth of a theory may be judged by the degree in which it conforms to such expectation." Mr. Balfour's argument, indeed, as has already been shown in the present volume, proves the truth of all religions if it proves the truth of any, because each religion satisfies the needs of its own adherents. "Doubtless," says Mr. Spencer, "the needs and satisfactions which Mr. Balfour has in view are of a higher order than those" of the American Indian or the Hindoo; "but that does not alter the issue. The question is whether the comforting character of a belief is an adequate reason for entertaining it; and the answer to this question is not to be determined by the quality of the comfort looked for, as high or low. The truth is that Mr. Balfour's view . . . is a more refined form of that primitive view which regards things as all arranged for human benefit—the sun to rule the day,

---

[1] "Mr. Balfour's Dialectics," *Fortnightly Review*, June, 1895.

[2] "Mr. Balfour's Attack on Agnosticism," *Nineteenth Century*, March, 1895.

[3] *Reaction! A Criticism of Mr. Balfour's Attack on Rationalism.* London: Wm. Reeves.

the moon to rule the night, animals and plants provided for food, and the seasons beneficently adjusted to men's welfare." This anthropocentric view must give way, in the mind of any one who looks at things without foregone conclusions, to the view " not that the surrounding world has been arranged to fit the physical nature of man, but that, conversely, the physical nature of man has been moulded to fit the surrounding world; and that, by implication, the theory of things, justified by the evidence, may not be one which satisfies men's moral needs and yields them emotional satisfactions, but, conversely, is most likely one to which they have to mould their mental wants as well as they can. The opposite assumption, tacitly made by Mr. Balfour, obviously tends to vitiate his general argument."

Mr. Spencer's remark that " to ask whether science is substantially true is much like asking whether the sun gives light," was thought to be met by Mr. Balfour's question: " But then, on Mr. Spencer's principle, *does* the sun give light?" To this Mr. Spencer replies that in the first place, after Mr. Balfour's sceptical arguments about a real world, it is from his own principles, if from any one's, that it would follow that the proposition, " The sun gives light," cannot be proved to be true; and in the second place, Mr. Balfour's scepticism and logical rigour become extremely yielding when it is a question of bringing in his own theology. " We cannot," he says, " for example, form, I will not say any adequate, but even any tolerable, idea of the mode in which God is related to, and acts on, the world of phenomena. That He created it, that He sustains it, we are driven to believe. How He created it, how He sustains it, it is impossible for us to imagine." To which Mr. Spencer replies that Mr. Balfour has no right to press home the difficulty as to the ultimate incognisability of the material world, yet coolly evade the cognate difficulty as to the incomprehensibility of the supposed Creator of the world. "And why," he asks, "if it must continue 'impossible for us to imagine' the mode of operation of the cause behind 'the ordered system of phenomena,' may it not continue 'impossible for us to imagine' the nature of that cause? If we are obliged to assume the cause to be a 'rational Author,' since otherwise our knowledge of 'the ordered system of phenomena is inexplicable,' why must we not assume a certain mode of action by which 'He created' and 'sustains' 'the ordered system of phenomena,' since otherwise the creation and sustentation of it are inexplicable? To me it seems an indefensible belief that while for one part of the mystery of things we must assign an explanation, all other parts may be left without explanation. If the constitution of matter defies all attempts to understand it, if it is impossible to understand in what way feeling is connected with nervous change, if wherever we analyse our knowledge to the bottom we come down to unanalysable components which elude the grasp of thought, what ground is there for the belief that of one part of the mystery, and that the deepest part, we must and can reach an explanation? Surely there is a strange incongruity in holding that we have here a certainty while denying to be certain that the sun gives light."

Mr. Spencer gives also a passing notice to Mr. Balfour's argument as to the relative claims of reason and authority, pointing out in the first place the fallacy of imagining that it is possible to go completely behind reason; "for if any other ruler is raised to the throne, in part or for a time, it is by reason that this is done;" and showing in the second place that while, from the beginning of history, the authority of science has been growing daily greater, the authority of religion has been growing daily less; for not only are its positive statements being discredited by increased knowledge of the world and of history, but it has conspicuously failed to regulate moral conduct as it claims to do. So that if there is anything whatever in Mr. Balfour's contention that we should follow authority, it is plainly the authority of science that we should follow, and not the authority of religion.

Finally Mr. Spencer deals with Mr. Balfour's direct attack upon his fundamental position. After describing Mr. Spencer as holding that "beyond what we think we know, and in closest relationship with it, lies an infinite field which we do not know and which with our present faculties we can never know, yet which cannot be ignored without making what we do know unintelligible and meaningless," Mr. Balfour proceeds thus :—

"But he has failed to see whither such speculations must inevitably lead him. He has failed to see that if the certitudes of science lose themselves in depths of unfathomable mystery, it may well be that out of these same depths there should emerge the certitudes of religion; and that if the dependence of the 'knowable' upon the 'unknowable' embarrasses us not in the one case, no reason can be assigned why it should embarrass us in the other.

"Mr. Spencer, in short, has avoided the error of dividing all reality into a perceivable which concerns us, and an unperceivable which, if it exists at all, concerns us not. Agnosticism so understood he explicitly repudiates by his theory, if not by his practice. But he has not seen that, if this simple-minded creed be once abandoned, there is no convenient halting-place till we have swung round to a theory of things which is its precise opposite; a theory which, though it shrinks on its speculative side from no severity of critical analysis, yet on its practical side finds the source of its constructive energy in the deepest needs of man, and thus recognises, alike in science, in ethics, in beauty, in religion, the halting expression of a reality beyond our reach, the half-seen vision of transcendent truth" (pp. 288, 289).

Dialectic of this kind, says Mr. Spencer, is merely the

spearing of an effigy which is alleged to be the reality. He has never denied, either directly or indirectly, that "out of the depths of unfathomable mystery there *may* emerge the certitudes of religion," for "the conclusion that by the nature of our intelligence we are for ever debarred from forming any conception of the reality which lies behind appearance has the inevitable corollary that we can assign no limits to the possibilities within it". But he objects to Mr. Balfour's assumption that there not only *may*, but actually *do*, emerge the certitudes of religion. Mr. Balfour, in fact, is here simply dealing with pseud-ideas; the terms of his proposition have no real meaning. "If the thought of a 'rational Author' has emerged out of the 'depths of unfathomable mystery,' it must, if it is distinguishable from the mere blank form of a thought, have some definable characters; and unless Mr. Balfour considers himself and men who have similar thoughts to be fundamentally different from men in general, we must say that thoughts having like characters have emerged into human consciousness at large." When, however, we examine the various conceptions that men have entertained of God, we find scarcely two of them alike; and this difference holds not only between those who worship different gods, but between believers, like Christians, who are supposed to worship the same God; while many men, of course, have no conception of God whatever. Now, says Mr. Spencer, if the conception of a "rational Author" of the universe has "emerged into human consciousness" from the depths of unfathomable mystery, "there arises in the first place the question: How came there to have so emerged the different conceptions which men have entertained from early days when God was said to have appeared to various persons, down to our late days when theophany is nonsense? Then, seeing that many of these conceptions are in direct antagonism, there arises the question : How are we to decide which must be rejected? And once more, if out of all of them one only has truly emerged, in what manner shall we identify it? To all which unanswerable inquiries add one more. Assuming that the conception of a 'rational Author' as existing in Mr. Balfour and those who are on the same high plane of thought, is the only true one, then, if possession of this conception is to be shown, it is requisite that there should be specified some mentally-representable traits which constitute it. And if the asserted traits are unrepresentable—if being, as they must be, abstractions of human attributes existing unlocalised and multiplied by infinity, they are unthinkable — then the assertion of their existence becomes nothing but the blank form of a thought—expresses a pseud-idea."

Further, the word " emerges " implies " some medium out of which some existence previously concealed gradually appears, at first vaguely and at last distinctly. Can Mr. Balfour say that, apart from any impressions given to him in the course of education and subsequent culture, such a representable emergence has taken place in him? If so, one implication is that his mind differs, not in elevation only, but in nature from certain minds which have been so placed as to prevent communication of theological ideas from without ; for it has been shown that among deaf mutes who have received no religious instruction, no idea of God exists. Hence, in the absence of proof to the contrary, we must say that that high conception of a Deity which exists in the minds of Mr. Balfour and others has had a historical origin." That is, the original savage idea of a God with human attributes has become successively refined into the modern theist's idea of a God who is merely " pure intelligence ". Thus the process of emergence has been the exact opposite of that implied by Mr. Balfour. So far from the modern idea of God being a progress " from the imperceptible, through the vague, to the distinct," it has been a progress " from the distinct, through the more and more vague, to the imperceptible, or rather to the scarcely conceivable, or literally inconceivable"; Mr. Balfour's whole passage, in fact, being found devoid of meaning when subjected to analysis.

Mr. Spencer, it will be seen, has not gone over Mr. Balfour's book as a whole, contenting himself with exposing the futility of its argument only on a point that concerns his own philosophy. Mr. Huxley's article also was less complete than one could wish. He begins by comparing the present condition of the intellectual world to that of "the second century of the existence of Imperial Rome". Then there was, on the one hand, the decay of the old religion and the spread of theosophies and revivalisms, while on the other hand, the more educated classes were either professed stoics or deeply tinged with stoicism. Out of the clash of these rival opinions came the future history of Europe. The Roman Empire has vanished, "and in all this time, the struggle for mastery between the scientific spirit, temporarily incarnate in Greek philosophy, and the spirits of post-prophetic Judaism and of that prophetic Judaism, already coloured by Hellenism, which bore the name of Christianity, has gone on; until now, Judaism stands substantially where it did, while the simple Christian faith of the second century has been overlaid and transmuted by Hellenic speculation into the huge and complex dogmatic fabric of ecclesiastical Christianity. Finally, the scientific spirit, freed from all its early wrappings, stands in independence of and for the most part in antagonism to its ancient rivals. Its cosmology, its anthropology are incompatible with theirs; its ethics are independent of theirs." "This," says Mr. Huxley, "is, in broad outline, the state of affairs amongst us, and the future of our civilisation as certainly depends on the result of the contest between science and ecclesiasticism which is now a-foot as the present state of things is the outcome of the former strife."

Accordingly he welcomes Mr. Balfour's book as an indication that our leading men have become aware of the importance of this contest, and are endeavouring to unite the scattered ends of our knowledge into one organic whole. Civilisation cannot long endure while there is so serious an antagonism in the world of thought as that between "naturalism" and what Mr. Balfour calls "current teaching"— this latter being styled by Mr. Huxley "Demômism". While commending Mr. Balfour's purpose, however, he cannot in the same degree commend his performance. And first of all he falls foul of the passages in which Mr. Balfour gives his own summary of the teaching of naturalism, remarking incidentally that Athanasius was not likely "to give a definition of Arianism which would be quite satisfactory to Arius," and still less likely "to draw up a catechism which would prove acceptable to the congregation of the Goths who, unhappily, professed that heresy". He implies, indeed, what so many others have said, that "Naturalism, as defined and catechetically represented" by Mr. Balfour, is a body of doctrine which nobody holds; and that "if 'Naturalistic' teaching and teachers are as devoid of real existence as Hippogriffs and Chimæras, the champion of Demômism is doing battle with the air". Accordingly, Mr. Huxley claims the right to use the term agnosticism where Mr. Balfour uses the term naturalism.

He begins by pointing out that the germs of modern agnosticism were found by him in Hamilton and Mansel. Hamilton, however, perversely forgot his own doctrine as to the relativity of our knowledge and the incognisability of reality, when he wrote that "the Divinity, in a certain sense, is revealed; in a certain sense is concealed; He is at once known and unknown". To write thus was simply "to confuse the necessities of thought with the obligations of things, and hypostatising nescience, [to] pretend, under the guise of faith, to the possession of knowledge". Mr. Huxley, though inclined at one time to follow Hamilton in his rhetorical evasion of his own conclusions, soon outgrew this state of mind, and settled into agnosticism pure and simple. He proceeds to remark that "if our philosopher had contented himself with pointing out the indubitable fact that the limitation of human knowledge to the relative and the finite affords as little foundation for denial as for affirmation concerning that which lies beyond our cognisance; if, by way of counterposie to the proposition that it is 'blasphemy to think that God is as we can think him to be,' he had added that it is preposterous to assert that there is no God, because he cannot be such as we can think him to be, I fancy he would have taken up a position of unassailable security, and might have done something to let the wind out of the bladder of dogmatic atheism".[1]

---

[1] It is impossible, of course, for a pugnacious atheist to let this pass without comment. The atheist simply "denies" the existence of God in the way in which Mr. Huxley himself would deny it; that is, he merely says that the existence of a God is seen to be an impossibility as soon as the word "God" is defined. Mr. Huxley, for example, would have held that a first cause was unthinkable; then he would have denied that there existed anything corresponding to the theist's idea of a first cause; that is, he would to that extent have "denied" the existence of the theist's God. Similarly, if he held, as he certainly would have done, that an Infinite Intelligence is unthinkable, he would to *that* extent have denied the existence of the theist's God; and so on with all the qualities that are predicated of the Deity. Mr. Huxley would have no hesitation in saying that a four-sided triangle or a square circle does not exist; he would not content himself with the remark that these things "lie beyond our cognisance". They are, in fact, unthinkable, just as a Deity is unthinkable; and the atheist who "denies" the existence of something which the theist calls Infinite Intelligence or First Cause is simply in the position of the agnostic who denies the existence of four-sided triangles. The idea of triangle excludes the idea of four-sidedness; similarly, the idea of intelligence excludes the idea of infinity. The idea of circle excludes the idea of squareness; similarly, the idea of cause excludes the idea of a First Cause. The one set of propositions does not any more than the other lie outside the circle of our cognitions; they are both merely phrases which cannot be translated into ideas. And if the agnostic "denies" the existence of four-sided triangles, he ought in the same sense to "deny" the existence of a God. It is in this sense, and this sense alone, that the atheist denies any such existence. When Mr. Huxley writes that "it is preposterous to assert that there is no God because he cannot be such as we

Mr. Huxley's purpose in thus harking back to Hamilton's agnosticism is to show that Mr. Balfour's definition of naturalism would apply equally well to doctrines held not only by Hamilton and modern agnostics, but by Kant, Hume, Berkeley, and Locke. Mr. Balfour has, in fact, in his anxiety to place the detested system of his opponents in the worst possible light, given to naturalism both too wide and too narrow a definition: too wide in that it includes philosophers whom no one would regard as naturalists, and too narrow in that it attempts to limit "natural science" to a very small portion of its legitimate territory. When Mr. Balfour, for example, speaks of naturalism as having concern solely with "that world which is revealed to us through perception," he must mean by "perception" nothing more than "perception through the senses"; and apparently he thus hopes to limit what he calls natural science to the sciences of astronomy, physics, chemistry, geology, mineralogy, and botany. Now, as Mr. Huxley proceeds to show, Mr. Balfour has no

---

think him to be," he is simply meaningless. The whole sentence implies that we have some conception answering to the term "God," whereas the agnostic himself, in his polemic against the theist, proves that every quality which the theist attributes to his deity is either unthinkable or a contradiction in terms. The atheist does not, any more than the agnostic, claim grounds for "denial concerning that which lies beyond our cognisance". He simply says that what lies beyond our cognisance is the unknowable, and not a collection of hypostatised abstractions which men choose to label "God," and which might as well be labelled X or Abracadabra. This does not lie beyond our cognisance, but is merely a confused attempt to mould contradictory conceptions, drawn *from within the circle of our cognisance*, into a consistent whole. So far as agnosticism, by refusing the atheist's right to "deny" the existence of something like Infinite Intelligence, which can no more exist than a four-sided triangle, claims that it is distinct from atheism, it is simply falling a victim to its own confusion; while in so far as, by its own arguments, it shows (1) that the qualities attributed to the Deity are unthinkable, and (2) that every form of theism is only a badly-reasoned attempt to "account" for what can never be accounted for, it is itself atheism pure and simple; and there is no real need to call an old creed by a new name. Mr. Huxley, in fact, always misunderstood atheism as much as Mr. Spencer did in his *First Principles;* but he might at least have understood the implications of his own agnosticism.

right so to frame a definition of natural science as to exclude zoology and physiology; while physiology leads on inevitably into psychology, and so to the whole phenomena of consciousness. And the conclusion is that not only is the "natural science" of Mr. Balfour "unlike anything known to men of science," but "the view of 'Naturalism' founded on it, and the conceptions of empiricism and agnosticism, which are counted among the forms of Naturalism, are equally nonexistent". Mr. Balfour's statement of his opponent's system is, in fact, either hopelessly inaccurate or a mere travesty.

Here, unfortunately, Mr. Huxley's criticism ends. Before the second part of his article could be written he had passed away from this world, to "join the choir invisible". What he was prevented from doing, however, has been done by Mr. Karl Pearson, whose criticism of *The Foundations of Belief* was at once the completest and most telling of all.

Mr. Pearson rightly calls attention to the fact that reaction in religious matters is likely to go hand in hand with reaction in political matters; and that "the nation has yet to learn—may the lesson be not too bitter!—that an aptitude for defending Genesis or for demonstrating the truth of the Incarnation is not the best test of the intellectual fibre needed in a really great statesman". He points out the ambiguity of Mr. Balfour's terms, and the way in which that ingenuous gentleman takes full advantage of the double meanings of his words. "The same word is used in many different senses, often in nearly contiguous paragraphs; different words are used for the same permutation of ideas, although either their scientific or popular sense, or both senses, connote something very distinct from that of Mr. Balfour's usage. Subtle distinctions which are none the less vital and real are slurred over at one point, in order to be emphasised at a second after the desired antinomy has been displayed. A parade is made of philosophic terminology, which is neither used in its technical sense nor in any consistent sense which can be drawn from the context." Thus Mr. Balfour has employed such words as epistemology, knowledge, the knowable, beliefs, science, and cause, without defining them, and has so been able to interpret any of them to suit his dialectical purpose at the moment. Further, when he attempts to carry certain doctrines through the fire of criticism by calling them "higher," and the opposite doctrines "lower," he forgets that these terms are purely relative, and that there is no standard, external to our own prepossessions and prejudices, by which individuals can compare their needs with those of other individuals.

Mr. Pearson then proceeds to show that Mr. Balfour, while professing to treat naturalism, science, and rationalism as distinct, has in reality treated them as if they were identical; and he further inquires, "Are the foundations of science really what Mr. Balfour states them to be? Mr. Balfour," he continues, "will hardly be able to disguise from any scientific reader that his acquaintance with science is of a very limited character. No man even superficially acquainted with the modern physics of the ether, would still speak of ether as 'a substance which behaves as if it were an elastic solid'; nor would even a dabbler in biology, after recent publications, slip glibly over from the formation of habits to their inheritance without a sign of hesitation." And while Mr. Balfour's scientific equipment is so slender, he makes the error of criticising something which he labels "Naturalism," without dealing face-to-face with any particular thinker who could be held answerable for this particular creed: the only scientist to whom Mr. Balfour refers in this connection—and that only in name—being Professor Huxley. And the scientific creed which Mr. Balfour wishes to fasten on to naturalism is nothing more nor less than "the long-exploded materialism of Moleschott and Büchner," which "was never adopted by any physicist of repute."[1] Whether we agree or not with Mr. Pearson as to this, there is no doubt of the trenchant nature of his criticism of Mr. Balfour's attempt to place the "certitudes" of religion and the "certitudes" of science upon the same footing. "We are quite prepared," he remarks, "to follow Mr. Balfour and admit that 'There is a God' and 'There is a material world built up of molecules' are equally unproven statements, but the comparison between science and theology ends here, for while theology is based upon a belief in the former proposition, science in no way depends upon the truth or falsehood of the latter proposition. The validity of scientific conclusions remains untouched, if behind the veil of sense-impressions, which for the Naturalist limits the field of human knowledge, be postulated *Dinge an sich*, mediate or immediate deities, mind-stuff, the unknowable, permanent possibilities of sensation, or a complex of molecules 'endowed with force'." And Mr. Balfour, in asserting that "the whole

---

[1] I am compelled to express a passing dissidence from this "hard saying" of Mr. Pearson, who has yet to convince a great many people that the materialism of Büchner *has* been long exploded. Certainly his own *Grammar of Science*, to which many rationalists are, of course, highly indebted for a clarification of their ideas on many subjects connected with physical science, has not been quite so successful as he imagines in demolishing the materialism usually associated with the names of Büchner and Bradlaugh. Beyond a passing reference, however, this is not the place to enter into the controversy between Mr. Pearson and the materialists. I can only say, for my own part, that the criticism of his position in the second volume of the recent *Life of Bradlaugh* puts very accurately and very completely what a great many of us thought when we read a certain section of the *Grammar of Science*. Mr. Pearson has not done justice to materialism; and I may be excused for drawing attention to the conspicuous bad taste of one of his *Fortnightly Review* articles, in which he spoke of "the pages of abuse to which I am treated in the second volume of Bonner's *Life of Bradlaugh*". I think Mr. Pearson would have some difficulty in pointing out the "abuse"; for his critic simply dealt quite scientifically with Mr. Pearson's misunderstanding of materialism, and the bearing of this upon his own doctrine. So trenchant a polemist as Mr. Pearson, who has never spared an opponent, who has always given full rein to his tongue and his pen, and whose own language has at times seemed, even to rationalists, unnecessarily strong, might have known better than to pass by an unanswerable criticism with the remark that it was "abuse". To call it that was simply to make an exhibition of bad temper and worse taste.

of science has been developed in the belief that its conclusions applied to an independent material universe," overlooks the fact that " large portions of the so-called exact sciences, which for many centuries monopolised the attention of men of science, not only deal with conceptual notions—ideas and not phenomena—but were at an early period of their development recognised by their devotees to be conceptual"; while "at least a moiety of the scientific work and a moiety of the scientific workers of to-day fall respectively into the categories of admittedly conceptual reasoning and admittedly conceptual reasoners ".

Science is, in fact, as Mr. Pearson goes on to show, not concerned to *explain* things but to *describe* them. It does not deal with " things-in-themselves," but merely with concepts drawn from experience; and its mission is only to provide, by means of these concepts, a short-hand summary of our experiences, which serves at once to make portable our knowledge of the past, and to enable us to apply this to anticipations of the future. Thus Mr. Balfour's criticism of science is really quite beside the mark. Science, although it says nothing of " the ultimate reality of things "—because it is not in any way concerned with " ultimate reality "—is yet justified by the practical results of our reasoning on conceptual limits. Similarly, Mr. Balfour's argument about experience and the law of causation is seen to be invalid when we realise that the law of causation is, like any other formula of science, " *a conceptual limit*, and is not a something amid the unknowable *Dinge an sich*"; while the argument that the law of causation is given to us *a priori* is rightly dealt with from the point of view of anthropology and of comparative psychology, instead of from that of abstract metaphysics. " That like causes are followed by like effects is only a gradually learnt truth, and the conceptual limit which we term 'the law of causation' is only reached after prolonged experience and some intellectual exercise." With the fall of Mr. Balfour's thesis of the nature of science there comes to the ground also his attempt to find "reasons for belief" in the leading assertions of theology. As Mr. Pearson puts it: "In theology we assert something and believe something not of ideas, but of an independent, supersensuous existence behind sense-impression. In science we assert something of a conceptual world, and believe something of its relation to the dependent and sensuous."

In an acute passage Mr. Pearson shows the absurdity of Mr. Balfour arguing in one part of his book that reason is of very small account, compared with authority, habit, or instinct, and in another part proving the existence of the Deity from the fact that man has reason, and thinking so highly of reason as to make it the chief attribute of his Deity. Even so might "a canine theologian . . . instinctively realise that 'physiological co-ordination' must be the chief attribute of the unknowable; although the dog would be merely yelping his feelings, and the man would be reasoning on his 'deepest needs'". And Mr. Balfour's argument "that it would be impossible to reason about things, if they had not a rational basis," is dealt with by a *reductio ad absurdum*, in this manner :—

"Let us pause for a moment to apply this type of argument all round. Because the clock keeps time with the stars, there must be clockwork at the back of the universe ; because the loom sends the shuttle flying through the maze of warp, the raw wool itself must be the product of loom and shuttle ; because the chaos of rubble comes out of the stone-sorting machine, cleaned, sized, and sorted, there must be such a machine ultimately creating rubble ; because 'physiological co-ordination' enables brute nature to guide itself through the phenomenal world, instinct and reflex action must have created brute and universe ; because we can digest a whole round of vegetable and animal matters, organic life must be the product of a Transcendental Stomach; because human hands have learnt the art of delicate design in wood and metal, forest and lode are undoubtedly specimens of a Supernatural Engraver's skill; because futilities can be multiplied indefinitely, the material for them as well as the minds which rejoice in them must alike be the creation of a Gigantic Trifler. Not one of these statements seems a whit more ridiculous from the standpoint of logic than the argument of Mr. Balfour with which we have prefaced them."

So again with the argument as to the origin of our ethical faculties. Mr. Balfour, it will be remembered, contended that it was insufficient to trace reason back to non-rational origins; we must suppose that behind these there lay the supreme creating reason. Science, in fact, requires theism for its very foundation; and if we are compelled to postulate a rational God in the interests of science, we are also compelled to postulate a moral God in the interests of morals. See then whither this leads Mr. Balfour. He "finds Nature's contrivances for protecting the species of ' some loathsome parasite' to be 'most cruel and disgusting'. We presume, therefore, as Mr. Balfour has beliefs as to the cruel and the loathsome, which can be easily traced back to sources having nothing cruel or disgusting about them, he is prepared to seek behind phenomenal sources for some ultimate ground with which *they* shall be congruous. We do not find him, however, attributing cruelty and loathliness to his deity."

Here, practically, Mr. Pearson's telling criticism ends. He has left few of the main positions of *The Foundations of Belief* untouched, and has shown that what Mr. Balfour describes as rationalism is a mere caricature, that the attack on science has failed, that the attempt to rehabilitate theology has equally failed, and that Mr. Balfour's arguments are merely superficial sophistry where they are not superficial ignorance. The critique ends with a timely warning to the religious Liberal press as to the dangerous political significance of such a book as *The Foundations of Belief*, coming, as it does, from the accredited leader of the Tory party in the House of Commons.

Here this volume might end. But a few words may not be out of place upon one of the most interesting, if not one of the most able, criticisms of *The Foundations of Belief*. In the *Fortnightly Review* for November, 1895, there appeared an article by Mr. Vamadeo Shastri, a Hindu gentleman, upon "Brahmanism and the Foundations of Belief," which is extremely exhilarating reading for the rationalist. Mr. Shastri does not throw much light either upon the foundations of belief or upon Brahmanism; and his article is for the most part a charmingly polite but uncritical eulogy of Mr. Balfour's attack upon naturalism and reason. But it is highly interesting as showing how a Western religion looks to the highly-cultured devotee of an Eastern religion; and incidentally it places some of Mr. Balfour's arguments in a very bad position indeed. Mr. Shastri begins by referring to a previous article of his, in which he had commented upon "the very moderate assistance obtainable from English sources by those who desire to exchange their old lamps for new ones, so far as this may enable them to adjust the traditional religion of India to its changing intellectual environments. I was then unwillingly forced to the conclusion that we had very little to learn from you in the matter of profound theology, and that the system of Christianity—a faith for which my practical understanding has the most sincere respect—could not satisfy the restless, inquisitive Hindu mind. Its moralising tendencies seemed to me to cloud and distract the true spiritual vision; and the narrow range of its conceptions regarding the soul and a future life appeared out of scale and incomplete."

Mr. Shastri, however, has had some of his troubles allayed by Mr. Balfour's book, which, in his opinion, has helped to throw up ramparts round Christianity that may be of service to it in its struggle with rationalism. We need not follow him too minutely in his gleeful excursions; suffice it to say that he quite agrees with Mr. Balfour that science ought to be told to keep its place and not allowed to intrude into the sacred halls of religion. Mr. Shastri's delicate soul rebels against this intrusion. "To a refined and cultivated temperament [*i.e.*, Mr. Shastri's temperament; for rationalists are of course never refined or cultivated] the theory that exquisite tastes and emotions could have been reared by that homely nurse Nature out of 'the complicated contrivances, many of them mean and disgusting, wrought into the organism by the shaping forces of selection and elimination,' must, I agree, be tolerably repulsive." This may serve to give the measure of Mr. Vamadeo Shastri's philosophic competence, and we may without any great loss let the remainder of his criticism of rationalism dissolve, to use one of his own exquisite expressions, into its fontal nothingness.

Mr. Shastri is only interesting when he comes to point out the superiority of Brahmanism to Christianity in the eternal conflict with science. Christianity has first of all to prove the existence of its Deity, and then to give historical evidence that certain events happened as they are alleged to have happened; and on neither of these grounds can it hope to be quite successful with science. Brahmanism is much more fortunate, in that it postulates no architectonic providence, and does not profess to be in any way historical. It is thus able to retire before the attack of science in an orderly retreat, while Christianity meets with something like utter rout. And with charming ingenuousness Mr. Shastri remarks that it is not altogether the interest of the Hindu to wish the Christian well out of his difficulties, " seeing that Christianity is one of the two religions which have taken up an active proselytising attitude against Hinduism. The attraction which any spiritual novelty presents to our people has induced me on rare occasions to listen with decorous curiosity to your Christian missionaries. I have found that they almost always employ against the Brahmanic teaching and tradition that very argument which in this book is termed rationalistic, touching the absurdity of our worships and beliefs, the incredibility of our miraculous narratives, the want of authenticity for our Scriptures, and so on, with appeals to reason, sense perception, and the new learning generally. Now, in these controversies . . . any confession that your own rationalistic orthodoxy is not unassailable would give us an effective rejoinder. . . . I make these remarks to prove that I am entirely disinterested in warning you English to take care what you are about."

Comment upon this is surely needless; it tells its own story, which all who run may read. Nor need I do more than compliment the ingenuous Brahman upon the security afforded to his religion by the fact that it has no canon of consistency and has never committed itself to any precise creed. These are advantages indeed, and advantages which Christianity—committed, alas! to certain very definite dogmas—would be delighted to acquire. The final interest of Mr. Shastri's article, however, lies in his closing passages, wherein he opines that Mr. Balfour and his fellows may possibly be on the road that leads to the divine wisdom as it is in Brahmanism. And most instructive of all are his final words, to the effect that Mr. Balfour's "needs" are not his needs, and Mr. Balfour's "satisfactions" are to him unsatisfactory. "I wish from my heart," he says, "that we Hindus could accept [Mr. Balfour's] method of satisfying our deepest needs; but if this is to be the speculative side of Mr. Balfour's theory, I fear it may not altogether withstand the utmost severity of critical analysis. At any rate the incurably subtle

Hindu intellect is absolutely incapable of contenting itself with a Deity whose very existence seems in a manner to depend on evanescent and mutable modes of human desire and consciousness."

Quite so; and thus is the rationalist justified and the theologian answered. It appears that Mr. Balfour's argument about men's "highest needs" and their satisfaction simply amounts to calling his own needs highest *because* they are his. Just as these needs have no meaning for the rationalist, so have they no meaning for the devotee of another religion, who has been brought up in a different psychological climate. It all confirms the rationalist's argument that early training and environment are the main factors in the production of religious belief; and that Mr. Balfour, had he been born a Hindu, would have employed in the cause of some Hindu religion precisely similar emotional arguments to those which he has used on behalf of Christianity. Thus also does Mr. Kidd's vulgar race-vanity go by the board; for it is evident that he sings the glories and virtues of Western civilisation merely because he is an occidental by birth and environment. And one only needs to read an article, such as this of Mr. Shastri,—in which one absurd religionist, while agreeing, as against the rationalist, that we must not be rational, uses reason against another absurd religionist,—to see how hopeless and inevitable is the confusion of those who endeavour to divide reason against itself. The consequences to philosophy of such an attempt have already been shown in the previous pages of this volume, and there is no need to pursue the subject any further here. I desire rather to close with the warning that its consequences are no less grave in the spheres of political and social life. Reason is the final arbiter to which every dispute must sooner or later be submitted, and from whose decision there can be no appeal.

And the nation that will not seek reason and ensue it, that will allow itself for long to be blinded by the sophistry of the modern irrationalist, will not be able ultimately to avoid the doom of those unfortunate animals which, as a most veracious record tells us, once ran down a steep place into the sea.

INDEX.

A.

Agnosticism, 287-290, 291-293
"Aggressive" unbelief, 30
"Aggressiveness" of Mr. Kidd, 31
Allen, Grant, 105
Altruism and evolution, 83, 147, 148, 157
— and progress, 117, 127, 148
— and reproduction, 111-114, 126, 149, 150
— physiological basis of, 114, 128
Ambrose, 6
Anglo-Saxon race and civilisation, 96, 97
Anselm, 248, 250
Antiquity of the irrationalist defence of religion, 3, 4, 6, 99
Authority of the Churches decaying, 4
Authority and belief, 218, 220, 221
— and reason (*see* Reason and authority)

B.

Balfour's (Mr.) *Foundations of Belief*, 1, 2, 5, 9, 11, 12, 179-304
— — reception of, 181, 182
— — Mr. Huxley on, 290-294
— — Mr. Karl Pearson on, 294-300
— — Mr. Shastri on, 300-303
— — Mr. Spencer on, 284-290
— chameleon ethics, 183, 189
— *Defence of Philosophic Doubt*, 180, 251
— "Fragment on Progress," 187-189
— general characteristics, 179, 180, 191, 251, 252
— inconsistencies, 205, 207, 210, 211, 222, 223, 271
— "Religion of Humanity," 182-187
Beliefs, formulas, and realities, 246-253
Bellamy, E., 90
Benn, A. W., 73, 181, 208
Berkeley, 293
Bible, Savonarola on the, 8
Biology, second-hand, 6
— and social science, 19
Bradlaugh, C., 30, 281, 296 *note*
Brahmanism and Christianity, 300-303
Browning, 5, 120
Büchner, 124, 148, 295, 296 *note*
Buckle, 79, 80
Buckley, Miss, 124, 148

C.

Calderwood, Prof., 120
"Central feature of human history," 24-26, 52-63
Christianity and altruism, 66, 68, 69, 79, 95
— and the ancient world, 64, 68, 78
— and caste, 67, 69
— and civilisation, 96
— and the equality of men, 67, 69, 72, 73
— and evolution, 67, 173
— and intellectual evil, 10
— and the masses, 67
— and progress, 66, 75, 80
— and rationalism, 183-187
— and the Roman State, 66
— and slavery, 67, 69, 70, 97
— Latin, 95, 96
Cicero, 72
Civilisation, ancient and modern, 64
Classes and masses, 49, 83
Comte, 37
Conditions of human progress, 18-20
— — No rational sanction for, 21-24, 44-51
Continuity of evolutionary laws, 20
Cosmic process and the ethical process, 115, 128

D.

Darwin, 18, 104, 125, 136
Darwinism and the Bible, 4
— and the future of religion, 18
— and Mr. Kidd, 16
— and the theologians, 107
Destructive and constructive ideas, 31
Diogenes the Cynic, 73
Drummond's (Mr.) *Ascent of Man*, 1-3, 5, 16, 103-175
— assumptions, 111, 112, 114, 123
— cast of mind, 104-106
— criticism of previous evolutionists, 104, 110, 147, 167
— euphemisms, 137
— fallacies, 103, 113, 114, 122, 123, 126, 134, 146, 147, 150, 155, 165
— false analogies, 108, 109, 123, 164
— general characteristics, 175
— Jesuitry, 135
— moral defects, 141, 142

Drummond's (Mr.) *Natural Law in the Spiritual World*, 103, 104, 170

E.

Early Christians, characters of, 69
Egoism and nutrition, 111-114, 126
Emotions and the intellect, 5, 61, 99
Epictetus, 73
Ethical systems and evolution, 28, 88
Evil, the problem of, 3, 5, 114, 115, 117, 119-121, 130, 136-144, 171, 262, 263
Evolution and environment, 162-171
— and hunger, 136, 137
— and love, 117, 128, 135, 147, 149, 172
— and mental development, 89-91
— and monogamy, 158
— and theism, 5, 115, 117, 119, 120, 131, 137-144, 171
— (human) not primarily intellectual, 88-93
Evolutionary theory, 4

F.

Faith and heresy, 7
— and reason, Savonarola on, 8
— and salvation, 7, 8
Farrer, J. A., 71
Feelings and ideas, 37
Fiske, John, 124, 148
Flint, Prof., 11
France and the population question, 92
French revolution (the) and slavery, 70
Froude, 63
Function of religious beliefs in social evolution, 18, 26-28, 34, 35, 52-63
Fundamental principle of social development, 23

G.

Galton, Francis, 89
Geddes and Thomson, 124, 148
General mind (the) and current science, 30
Gospels, criticism of the, 276-278
Greek ethics, 66, 68, 69
— scepticism, 208
Greeks, intellectual development of the, 89
Grotius, 248

H.

Hamilton, 291-293
Hegel, 234
History, perverted, 6
Humanitarianism in the ancient world, 68-74
Hume, 293
Huxley, 107, 115, 124, 127, 284, 290-294

I.

Immaculate conception (the), 36
Incarnation (the), 5, 9, 275-278

Individual and social interests, 21-24, 27, 44, 46, 48-50, 52, 53, 60, 65, 75, 84-86, 92
— (the) and the species, 127
Ingersoll, 30
Inspiration, 270-275
Intellect in evolution, 66
Irrationalism, 1-3
— ancient and modern, 3-6
— in the past, 2, 3

J.

Jesus according to the Gospels, 70, 174

K.

Kaftan, 11
Kant, 234, 238, 239, 240-243, 293
— and Mr. Kidd, 11
Kantian apriorism, 11
Kidd (Mr.) and Mr. Drummond, 103, 125
Kidd's (Mr.) *Social Evolution*, 1-7, 10-12, 15-99, 279, 303
— — fundamental fallacy of, 6
— — Mr. Robertson's summary of, 98
— confusion of thought, 15, 16, 30, 44, 48, 50 *note*, 55, 56, 84-86, 92-93
— estimate of his own work, 16, 45, 63
— ignorance of psychology, 37, 38, 54, 61, 62, 67, 99
— incompetence, 6, 17, 47, 97-99
— irrelevant distinctions, 15
— meaningless phrases, 15, 55, 60
— mental type, 16, 30, 31, 55
— reply to his critics, 97
— second-hand knowledge of history, 17, 62, 67, 68, 73, 78, 82, 94, 98, 99
— self-contradictions, 41, 43, 47, 50, 56-58, 77, 78, 83, 84, 94, 95, 99
— verbal fallacies, 15, 17, 30, 46, 61
Kingsley, 75
Knight, Prof., 120
Kropotkin, Prince, 124, 148

L.

Le Conte, 124, 148
Lecky, Mr., 17, 61, 62, 68-70, 74, 99
Leibnitz, 234
Lewes, G. H., 17, 66
Littré, 124, 148
Locke, 293
Love, God as, 5, 124
Luther, 12

M.

Mahaffy, Mr., 17, 68, 99
Man in conflict with his own reason, 25, 26, 36, 37
Mansel, 291
Maoris (the), 97
Marcus Aurelius, 72, 73
Martineau, Dr. J., 24

Masses (the) and the conditions of progress, 49
Materialism, 296 *note*
Mill, J. S., 4, 91
Miracles, 263-268
Moleschott, 295
"Moral purpose" in evolution, 118

N.

Natural and spiritual, 3
Natural selection and over-population, 20, 38, 49, 83
— and progress, 20, 21, 38, 40, 48, 83, 84
— and reason, 48
— and religion, 28
— and suffering, 5
Naturalism, 5, 109, 191, 203, 205, 210
— and æsthetic, 192-196
— and ethics, 197-201
— and reason, 257-261
— and religion, 215
— and scepticism, 206
— and science, 205, 207, 208, 210
Nature and man, 132, 133
"Needs" and beliefs, 231, 240
Newman, Cardinal, 11
Nutrition and reproduction, 111, 112

O.

Obscurantism (religious) and political reaction, 2, 304
Optimism, 5
Organism and environment, 40
Over-population and natural selection, 20, 38, 49, 83

P.

Pagan and Christian civilisation, 68-74
— — morality, 71-73
Pain and theism, 122, 124
Paine, 70, 71
Pascal, 9, 10
Pearson, Karl, 204 *note*, 207 *note*, 284, 294-300
Philosophy and religion in Savonarola, 7
Plato, 74
Plutarch, 72, 73
Pollock, Sir F., 182
Pope, 5
Practical judgment and theoretical reason, 11
"Problem of every progressive society," 65
Progress, 20, 21, 40, 41, 49
Pseudo-philosophy, 1, 3
Pseudo-science (modern) and primitive emotionalism, 4
"Purpose" in nature, 116, 117, 151, 152, 156, 159

R.

Rational and irrational beliefs, 37
— religion impossible, 27, 59

Rationalism and irrationalism, 2, 6, 7
— and religion, 5, 6
Reaction, 2, 294
Reading evolution backwards, 44, 122, 134, 151, 159
Reason and authority, 5, 212, 218-223, 236
— authority of, 3
— discrediting, 3, 6, 8, 9, 235
— and dogma, 6
— and evolution, 20, 22, 23, 25, 41, 46, 50, 51
— and the individual, 22-24, 46
— and instinct, 37, 53, 54, 62
— and progress, 22, 23, 42, 46, 50, 52, 91
— and religion, 18, 25, 26, 35, 36, 54, 214
— Savonarola on, 8
— and social freedom, 2
— and truth, 2
Religion as the prime factor in progress, 4, 27, 46, 54-63
— as a sanction for social conduct, 25
— and altruism, 87
— and evolution, 24, 27, 85
— in the future, 18, 25, 88
— natural and revealed, 213, 214
— and science (*see* Science and religion)
— and scepticism, 56-58
— and the social system, 59
Robespierre, 70
Robertson, J. M., 98, 170 *note*
Romanes, 120, 124, 148

S.

Sanctions, ethical, 18, 26-28, 62
— supernatural and ultra-rational, 25, 26, 62
Savonarola, 7-9
Scepticism in history, 34-36
Science and dogma, 7
— and religion, 1, 3, 4, 17-19, 30-35, 209, 223-235, 247
— and the philosophy of science, 205, 208
— and social evolution, 17
Seneca, 24, 71, 73, 74
Seth, Prof., 238, 240, 241, 243
Sex in evolution, 151-154
Sidgwick, Prof., 99
Social evolution, Mr. Kidd's theory of, 17-29
Social system, meaning of, 27, 59
Socialism, modern, 82-87
Socrates, 72, 74
Spencer, Herbert, 37, 124, 125, 127, 133, 148, 235, 256, 280, 284-290
Spinoza, 234
"Standard of value" in evolution, 40-42
Stoic and Epicurean views of happiness, 71
Stoicism and the equality of men, 71-74
Struggle for existence (the), 20, 21, 106, 110, 114, 116
— for life, 106, 110, 125, 127, 132, 136, 142, 143

Struggle for the life of others, 106, 110, 114, 116, 125, 127, 136
Supernatural and ultra-rational, Mr. Kidd's confusion of, 61
Survival of the fittest, meaning of, 122

T.

Teleology, 44, 45, 116
Theism and atheism, 254-256
— and evolution, 5, 120
— fundamental fallacy of, 121, 240
— and reason, 236-245
Thimble-rigging, theological, 9
Transcendentalism, 241-244
Trinity (the) and reason, 8

U.

Ultra-rational and supernatural, Mr. Kidd's confusion of, 61
Universality as a test of truth, 228-233.

V.

Villari, 7-9

W.

Weismann, 45, 152-154
Wilberforce (Bishop) and the evolutionary theory, 4, 107

Z.

Zeno, 73

www.ingramcontent.com/pod-product-compliance
Lightning Source LLC
Chambersburg PA
CBHW030741230426
43667CB00007B/804